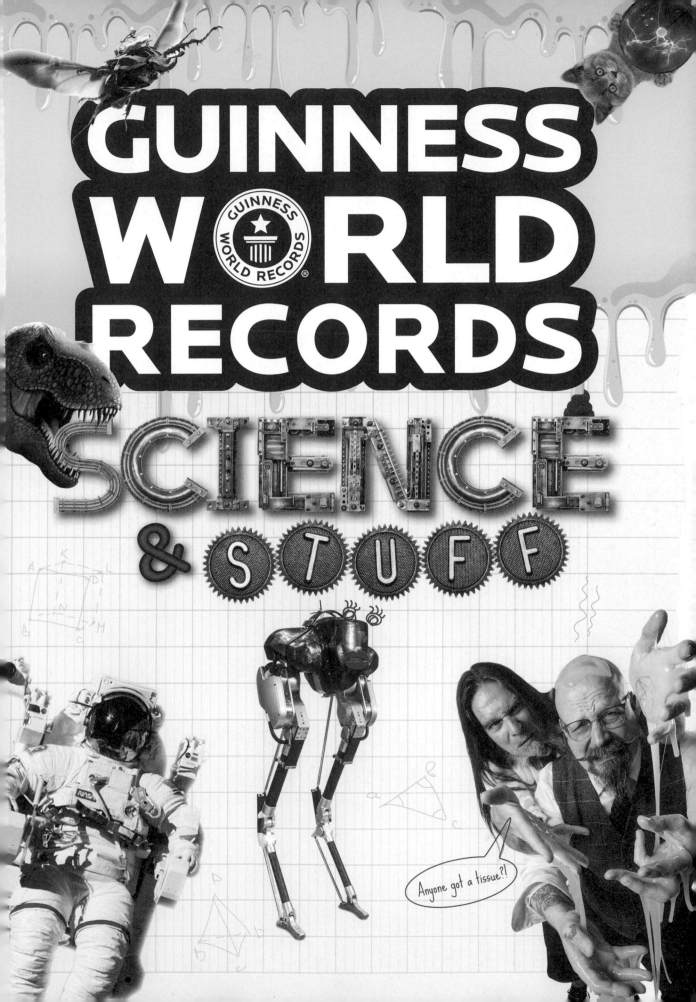

GUINNESS WORLD RECORDS

GUINNESS WORLD RECORDS®

SCIENCE & STUFF

Anyone got a tissue?!

ACKNOWLEDGEMENTS

Editor-in-Chief
Craig Glenday
Senior Managing Editor
Stephen Fall
Project Editor
Ben Hollingum
Senior Project Editor
Adam Millward
Gaming Editor
Stephen Daultrey
Information & Research Manager
Carim Valerio

VP Publishing
Jenny Heller
Head of Pictures & Design
Michael Whitty
Picture Editor
Fran Morales
Picture Researcher
Wilf Matos
Talent Researcher
Jenny Langridge
Designer
Billy Waqar
Assistant Designer
Andrew Sloan

Production Director
Patricia Magill
Publishing Manager
Jane Boatfield
Production Assistant
Thomas McCurdy
Production Consultants
Roger Hawkins,
Tobias Wrona
Reprographics
Res Kahraman at Born Group
Printing & Binding
MOHN Media Mohndruck GmbH,
Gütersloh, Germany

Indexer
Marie Lorimer
Proofreading
Matthew White
Consultants
Dr Mark Aston,
Sean Connolly,
David Hawksett
Original Photography
Paul Michael Hughes

British Library Cataloguing-in-publication data: a catalogue record for this book is available from the British Library

UK: 978-1-910561-63-8
US: 978-1-910561-64-5 (pb)
US: 978-1-912286-39-3 (hb)

Records are made to be broken – indeed, it is one of the key criteria for a record category – so if you find a record that you think you can beat, tell us about it by making a record claim. Always contact us before making a record attempt.

Check **www.guinnessworldrecords.com** regularly for record-breaking news, plus video footage of record attempts. You can also join and interact with the Guinness World Records online community.

Sustainability
The paper used for this edition is manufactured by UPM Plattling, Germany. The production site has forest certification and its operations have both ISO14001 environmental management system and EMAS certification to ensure sustainable production.

UPM Papers are true Biofore products, produced from renewable and recyclable materials.

Guinness World Records Limited has a very thorough accreditation system for records verification. However, while every effort is made to ensure accuracy, Guinness World Records Limited cannot be held responsible for any errors contained in this work. Feedback from our readers on any point of accuracy is always welcomed.

Guinness World Records Limited uses both metric and imperial measurements. The sole exceptions are for some scientific data where metric measurements only are universally accepted, and for some sports data. Where a specific date is given, the exchange rate is calculated according to the currency values that were in operation at the time. Where only a year date is given, the exchange rate is calculated from 31 Dec of that year. "One billion" is taken to mean one thousand million.

Appropriate advice should always be taken when attempting to break or set records. Participants undertake records entirely at their own risk. Guinness World Records Limited has complete discretion over whether or not to include any particular record attempts in any of its publications. Being a Guinness World Records record holder does not guarantee you a place in any Guinness World Records publication.

OFFICIALLY
AMAZING

THE J.M PATTISON GROUP

CORPORATE OFFICE
Global President: Alistair Richards

Professional Services
Chief Financial Officer: Alison Ozanne
Financial Controller: Andrew Wood
Accounts Receivable Manager: Lisa Gibbs
Management Accountants: Jess Blake, Jaimie-Lee Emrith, Moronike Akinyele
Assistant Accountants: Yusuf Gafar, Jonathan Hale
Accounts Payable Clerk: Tajkiya Sultana
Accounts Receivable Clerk: Jusna Begum
Trading Analysis Manager: Elizabeth Bishop

General Counsel: Raymond Marshall
Senior Legal Counsel: Terence Tsang
Legal Counsel: Kaori Minami
Legal Counsel: Paul Nightingale
Trainee Solicitor: Michelle Phua

Global HR Director: Farrella Ryan-Coker
HR Officer: Mehreen Saeed
Office Manager: Jackie Angus

Director of IT: Rob Howe
IT Manager: James Edwards
Developers: Cenk Selim, Lewis Ayers
Desktop Administrator: Alpha Serrant-Defoe
Analyst/Tester: Céline Bacon

Head of Category Management: Jacqueline Sherlock
Information & Research Manager: Carim Valerio
RMT Training Manager: Alexandra Popistan
Category Managers: Adam Brown, Victoria Tweedy
Category Executives: Danielle Kirby, Luke Wakeham, Shane Murphy

Global Brand Strategy
SVP Global Brand Strategy: Samantha Fay
Brand Manager: Juliet Dawson

Global Production
VP Creative: Paul O'Neill
Head of Global Production Delivery: Alan Pixsley

Global Product Marketing
VP Global Product Marketing: Katie Forde
Director of Global TV Content & Sales: Rob Molloy
Senior TV Content Executive & Production Co-ordinator: Jonathan Whitton
Head of Digital: Veronica Irons
Online Writer: Rachel Swatman
Social Media Manager: Dan Thorne
Digital Video Producer: Matt Musson
Junior Video Producer: Cécile Thai
Front-End Developer: Alex Waldu
Audience Development Manager: Sam Birch-Machin
Brand & Consumer Product Marketing Manager: Lucy Acfield
B2B Product Marketing Manager (Live Events): Louise Toms
B2B Product Marketing Manager (PR & Advertising): Emily Osborn
Product Marketing Executive: Victor Fenes
Designer: Rebecca Buchanan Smith
Junior Designer: Edward Dillon

EMEA & APAC
SVP EMEA APAC: Nadine Causey

Head of Publishing Sales: Joel Smith
Key Accounts Manager: Caroline Lake
Publishing Rights and Export Manager: Helene Navarre
Distribution Executive: Martino Borin

Head of Commercial Account Services Team & Licensing: Sam Prosser
Business Development Manager: Alan Southgate
Commercial Account Service Managers: Jessica Rae, Inga Rasmussen, Sadie Smith, Fay Edwards, Samantha Stennett-Patterson, William Hume-Humphreys
Country Representative – Business Development Manager, India: Nikhil Shukla
Commercial Executive, India: Rishi Nath

EMEA APAC Marketing Director: Chriscilla Philogene
Senior PR Manager: Doug Male
B2B PR Manager: Melanie DeFries
Senior Publicist: Amber-Georgina Gill
Publicist: Georgia Young
PR Assistant: Jessica Dawes
Senior Commercial Marketing Managers: Daniel Heath/Mawa Rodriguez, Saloni Khanna
Content Marketing Executive: Imelda Ekpo

Head of Records Management APAC: Ben Backhouse
Head of Records Management Europe: Shantha Chinniah
Records Managers: Mark McKinley, Christopher Lynch, Matilda Hagne, Daniel Kidane, Sheila Mella
Records Executive: Megan Double

Senior Production Manager: Fiona Gruchy-Craven

Country Manager, MENA: Talal Omar
Head of RMT, MENA: Samer Khallouf
Records Manager, MENA: Hoda Khachab
B2B Marketing Manager, MENA: Leila Issa
Commercial Account Managers, MENA: Khalid Yassine, Kamel Yassin, Gavin Dickson

VP Japan: Erika Ogawa
Office Manager: Fumiko Kitagawa
Director of RMT: Kaoru Ishikawa
Records Managers: Yoko Furuya, Lala Teranishi
Records Executive: Koma Satoh
Designer: Momoko Satou
Senior PR & Sales Promotion Manager: Kazami Kamioka
B2B Marketing Manager PR & Advertising: Asumi Funatsu
Project Manager Live Events: Aya McMillan
Digital & Publishing Content Manager: Takafumi Suzuki
Commercial Director: Vihag Kulshrestha
Senior Account Managers: Takuro Maruyama, Masamichi Yazaki
Senior Account Executive: Daisuke Katayama
Account Executive: Minami Ito

Official Adjudicators: Ahmed Gamal Gabr, Anna Orford, Brian Sobel, Glenn Pollard, Jack Brockbank, Kevin Southam, Lena Kuhlmann, Lorenzo Veltri, Lucia Sinigagliesi, Mariko Koike,

Paulina Sapinska, Pete Fairbairn, Pravin Patel, Richard Stenning, Şeyda Subaşı Gemici, Sofia Greenacre, Solvej Malouf, Swapnil Dangarikar, Justin Patterson, Mai McMillan, Rei Iwashita

AMERICAS
SVP Americas: Peter Harper
VP Marketing & Commercial Sales: Keith Green
VP Publishing Sales: Walter Weintz
Director of Latin America: Carlos Martinez
Head of Brand Development, West Coast: Kimberly Partrick
Head of Commercial Sales: Nicole Pando
Senior Account Managers: Ralph Hannah, Alex Angert
Account Managers: Giovanni Bruna, Mackenzie Berry, David Canela
Project Manager: Casey DeSantis
Head of PR: Kristen Ott
Assistant PR Manager: Elizabeth Montoya
PR Coordinator: Sofia Rocher
Digital Coordinator: Kristen Stephenson
Consumer Marketing Executive: Tavia Levy
Designer: Valentino Ivezaj

Head of RMT, North America: Hannah Ortman
Senior Records Manager, Latin America: Raquel Assis
Senior Records Manager, North America: Michael Furnari
Records Manager, North America: Kaitlin Vesper
Records Manager, Latin America: Sarah Casson
Records Executive, North America: Christine Fernandez
Junior Records Executive, North America: Callie Smith

HR & Office Manager: Kellie Ferrick
Office Assistant: Vincent Acevedo

Official Adjudicators, North America: Michael Empric, Philip Robertson, Christina Flounders Conlon, Jimmy Coggins, Andrew Glass, Mike Janela, Claire Stephens, Mike Marcotte
Official Adjudicators, Latin America: Natalia Ramirez Talero, Carlos Tapia Rojas

GREATER CHINA
President: Rowan Simons
Global SVP Records & General Manager, Greater China: Marco Frigatti
VP Commercial, Global & Greater China: Blythe Fitzwiliam
Senior Project Manager: Reggy Lu
Senior Account Managers: Catherine Gao, Jacky Yuan
Account Managers: Chloe Liu, Jing Ran
Head of RMT: Charles Wharton
Senior Records Manager: Fay Jiang
Records Manager: Alicia Zhao
Records Executive: Sophie Cao
Head of PR: Wendy Wang
PR Manager: Yvonne Zhang
Marketing Director: Karen Pan
B2B Marketing Manager: Iris Hou
Marketing Managers: Tracy Cui, Maggie Wang
Content Director: Angela Wu
HR & Office Manager: Tina Shi
Office Assistant: Crystal Xu
Official Adjudicators: Brittany Dunn, John Garland, Maggie Luo, Dong Cheng, Peter Yang, Louis Jelinek, Wen Xiong

WELCOME FROM SCIENCE BOB

Welcome to the all-new *Guinness World Records: Science & Stuff* book!

I love sharing science with millions of people on television and YouTube, and if there's one thing I know, it's that science is EVERYWHERE. This book will show you some of the noisiest, weirdest, smelliest and yuckiest extremes in the world of science like you've never seen them before. It's packed with amazing facts, figures and, of course, world records, covering everything from robots to reptiles.

You'll also find exclusive Q&As highlighting some men and women who have some really cool jobs in science – yours truly included!

Oh, one other thing; we don't just want you to *read* about science, we want you to *DO* it. I've always encouraged people to try "Random Acts of Science", and so we've included 10 experiments for you to try at home – who knows, maybe you'll even set a Guinness World Records title in the process!

Well, what are you waiting for? It's time to explore and experiment!

Science Bob

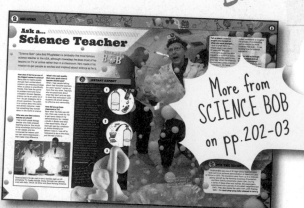

More from SCIENCE BOB on pp.202-03

3

CONTENTS

WEIRD WORLD

SPACE

ROBOTS

This book's on fire! No, I mean it's ACTUALLY on fire!

Make & Break

AWESOME INVENTIONS

IT'S ALIVE!

MAD SCIENCE

PLUS

THE SCIENCE OF GWR

You think you've got it bad, my <u>mouth</u> is on fire!

Blow me up! I'm on p.118

Make me! I'm on p.120

TIL
TODAY I LEARNED

Dotted throughout the book are these **Today I Learned** panels, which will hopefully expand your brain (not literally, that would be dangerous) with nuggets of information, weird extra details or unbelievable world records.

Welcome to the first ever edition of ***Guinness World Records: Science & Stuff***, in which we sneak up to the pizza of knowledge and pick off the crispy bits for you to enjoy.

We've always kept an eye on the world of science here at GWR Towers. Many great technological breakthroughs have brought a string of new records in their wake, and lots of scientists are as interested as we are in the extremes of the physical world.

To demonstrate that *everything* is science when you get down to it, we've taken the time to delve into the science of a few landmark records. We explore how, for example, the **tallest man** got so tall and the **most venomous spider** so very venomous.

It's not just about the world records, however (although records are our first love).

Science & Stuff also aims to answer the big questions that keep people up at night: How do you poop in space? What does woolly mammoth taste like? Why do we yawn? Is the answer to this question no? *Science & Stuff* will give you the answers to all of these questions (with the possible exception of that last one), plus many other bits of life-changing information (here's one to get you started: Moon dust smells like fireworks). You'll find chapters that cover outer space and how to get there; how the planet is trying to kill you; our future robot overlords; the squishy and strange world of living things; the wondrous creations of the world's engineers and inventors; and fantastic new developments from the cutting edge.

Make & Break!
Having someone tell you the answers isn't very scientific, though. It's more fun to figure them out yourself, so we've included a whole chapter of chaotic challenges and experiments to try at home. Build a soda-spraying rocket car and let it loose! Drop eggs off buildings! Mix strange chemicals and smear them everywhere! You'll probably make a mess, hopefully learn something, and maybe even break a record in the process.

Science isn't just a class you have to take at school; it's a way of looking at the world. With this book, we hope to show you the weird and wonderful things you can find by just scratching the surface.

For the Record boxes highlight world records related to each subject

STINKY & GROSS

I DIDN'T KNOW THAT!

The **Make & Break** chapter includes 10 individual challenges, each with their own record, presented by our very own mad scientist Prof Orbax and his trusty lab assistant Sweet Pepper Klopek

In **The Science of Guinness World Records,** we explain how our landmark records are broken

Super Slime

Official GWR rules

LOUDEST BUUUUURP!!

Step-by-step instructions

SHOPPING LIST

Attempt experiments using stuff you'll find lying around the home

The science behind the mess

TOP TIP!
FROM PROFESSOR ORBAX

Professor Orbax offers his sage advice

The **Big Question** answers the questions you've always wondered about

Ask a... pages offer exclusive Q&As with people from the worlds of science and technology

Hot Shot pages showcase a single amazing image

HOT SHOT

7 CRAZY CONTRAPTIONS

Profile boxes reveal the men and women behind the science

Instant Expert boxes tell you everything you need to know about a subject

Each chapter's **I Didn't Know That!** offers a random assortment of wondrous facts

These yellow circles are really helpful for discussing things that don't fit anywhere else. They're also good for explaining what's going on in the pictures when we need more space...

Other times we just scribble stuff in

Poop! See p.26, p.128 and p.194

HOW DO I BECOME A RECORD HOLDER?

THE BIG QUESTION **?**

Suppose you want to build a nuclear reactor in your shed and you're wondering if it's worthy of a Guinness World Records title – what do you need to do?

1. Apply online
The first thing you need to do is tell our Records Managers as much as you can about your record-breaking idea: are you going to use pressurized water or a liquid sodium coolant? How are you going to handle neutron moderation? Do your parents know about this crazy idea?

The best way to do this is at **www.guinnessworldrecords.com**. Give us as much information as you can: what the record is, how you plan to measure it (we're scientists here, we need numbers!), plus where and when you plan to make the attempt.

2. Get the guidelines
If you want to attempt an existing record, we'll email you the guidelines that everyone must follow. If it's a new idea, our Records Managers will decide if it's a valid Guinness World Records challenge. If approved, we'll write guidelines for you.

3. Attempt your record
Once you have your guidelines, you're ready to attempt the record. Be prepared to gather the evidence to prove your claims. Typically, we'll ask for independent witness statements, photographs, video footage, Geiger counter readings and GPS data.

How big?!

4. Submit your evidence
Package up your evidence and send it in. If there are any queries, your assigned Records Manager will be in touch to request more information. Good luck!

I'm a naked mole rat! Find me on p.151

★ FOR THE RECORD

You don't have to wear a white coat to be a scientist; you can get your science while wearing whatever you want. It might get ruined pretty fast, though – especially if you're making slime. This is why lab coats are a thing, and safety goggles as well – everything's better with safety goggles. The **largest gathering of people dressed as scientists** (or rather, people *dressed for science*) is 489, set by the staff and students of Stivichall Primary School in Coventry, UK, on 9 Jul 2016. This event was held to celebrate the school's successes in science, technology, engineering and maths (STEM) education.

SPACE

ALL WALKS OF LIFE

Keeping the *International Space Station* (*ISS*) in working order is a big job. Most of the maintenance can be done from inside, but every few months someone has to suit up and go outside. There have been a record-breaking 202 spacewalks from the *ISS* since its first components were launched in 1998 – the **most spacewalks from a spacecraft**.

Spacewalks are a complicated and dangerous business. Every decision – such as which hand-holds to use, which bolt to undo first – has to be planned in advance. But even the busiest astronaut can find time to take a photo or two! This amazing picture was taken on Christmas Eve 2013 by astronaut Rick Mastracchio of fellow spacewalker Mike Hopkins. (You can see Rick in the reflection.) They were fixing a worn-out cooling pump, which took 5 hr 28 min to repair.

Find out more about the life of an astronaut – and how to become one! – on pp.24–25.

REUSABLE ROCKETS

In 2015, US rocket company SpaceX achieved the **first successful landing of an orbital-class rocket**. For 2017, they planned to take one of their landed rockets and send it into space for a second time...

40 m (about the same height as an eight-storey office block)

Going into space is really expensive. A single rocket costs between five and 20 times more than a jumbo jet. Until recently, most of these orbital-class rockets were used just once then plunged into the sea. Surely there was a better way?

There and back again
Falcon 9 core B1021 is a 40-m (131-ft) tower of fuel tanks balanced on a cluster of car-sized rocket engines. It first flew on 8 Apr 2016 (see right) and, after inspection, was chosen to be the first Falcon 9 to fly again.

On 30 Mar 2017, B1021 was back on the launchpad. At 18:27 EDT it made its second trip into space before re-entering the atmosphere and landing just a few hundred metres from where it started. This was the **first reuse of an orbital-class rocket**, a major milestone in the development of cheaper space travel.

FOR THE RECORD

On 8 Apr 2016, after sending the CRS-8 mission's cargo delivery ship to the *International Space Station*, Falcon 9 core B1021 became the **first orbital-class rocket to land at sea**. The scale of this achievement is apparent when you see how huge these boosters are. The inset picture (above right) shows SpaceX technicians (who are actual, normal-sized people!) standing under the landing legs after the barge got back to port.

IF AT FIRST YOU DON'T SUCCEED...

URRR!

EEEH!

AAAGH!

Landing a rocket is insanely difficult, but landing a rocket on a barge in the middle of the ocean is *even more* difficult than that. It took a few attempts before SpaceX got it right. The first time, the rocket smashed into the barge at high speed and exploded. The second time it landed OK, but then one of the legs failed and it fell over and exploded (pictured above). "At least the pieces were bigger this time!" was Elon Musk's response.

ELON MUSK

South-African-born engineer and businessman Elon Musk is the founder and CEO of SpaceX. He studied physics at university, but made his millions by creating (and then later selling) a series of tech firms – most notably the online payment service PayPal.

In 2002, Musk became interested in space travel and went shopping for rockets (as you do). After visiting many of the big names in the industry, he decided they were all inefficient and too expensive. It would be better, he felt, to build his own.

While building up SpaceX into what it is today, Musk has also found time to run electric-car maker Tesla Motors, solar-energy firm SolarCity and high-speed mass-transit developer Hyperloop. He even decided to start his own tunnelling firm – The Boring Company – after getting annoyed with Los Angeles traffic jams!

Filled with secret things

SPACE

INSTANT EXPERT

LANDING A ROCKET... It's a tricky business. By the time the Falcon 9's first stage has finished its portion of the trip to orbit, it's travelling at around six times the speed of sound and about 100 km (62 mi) above Earth's surface.

The first thing the rocket has to do is lose some of that speed. It does this by flipping its whole body around and blasting its engines in the opposite direction. It then glides for a while, letting air resistance and its steering fins slow it down further, before firing the engines again.

When ready to return to Earth, the rocket performs a manoeuvre known as the "boostback burn" so that it's once again facing "up". The engines are then fired up one last time to bring the rocket gently down on the landing pad.

We've said "the rocket" because this is all handled by the rocket's onboard computer. The process happens too fast and requires too much precision for human input to be any help.

FOR THE RECORD

SpaceX aren't the only ones experimenting with reusable spacecraft. First launched in Apr 2010, the Boeing X-37B OTV (Orbital Test Vehicle) is a small, unmanned space plane – like the Space Shuttle, but only about the size of a truck. It was developed for the US Air Force to do, er, secret things. (Nobody is sure what, and the USAF isn't telling!)

This spacecraft is launched on top of a rocket, does whatever it does in orbit, then glides back to Earth and lands like a plane. On 20 May 2015, it was launched into space and didn't come back down until 7 May 2017. This 717-day mission (just short of two full years) set a new record for **longest orbital flight by a reusable spacecraft**.

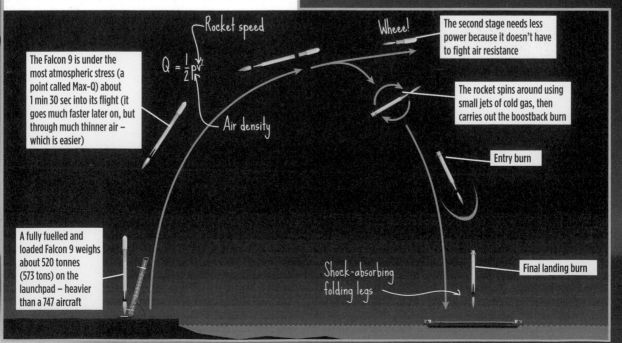

Rocket speed

$$Q = \frac{1}{2}\rho v^2$$

Air density

Wheee!

The Falcon 9 is under the most atmospheric stress (a point called Max-Q) about 1 min 30 sec into its flight (it goes much faster later on, but through much thinner air – which is easier)

The second stage needs less power because it doesn't have to fight air resistance

The rocket spins around using small jets of cold gas, then carries out the boostback burn

Entry burn

A fully fuelled and loaded Falcon 9 weighs about 520 tonnes (573 tons) on the launchpad – heavier than a 747 aircraft

Shock-absorbing folding legs

Final landing burn

MAGNETIC STORMS

Occurring some 400 km (250 mi) above Earth's surface, aurorae (also known as the northern and southern lights) are the **highest atmospheric phenomena**. These beautiful patterns of light are created by powerful charged particles from the Sun. This "solar wind" hits Earth's natural magnetic field, resulting in a dazzling light show. Astronaut Scott Kelly posted this photo of an aurora from the *International Space Station* to Twitter on 15 Aug 2015, with the caption: "Another pass through #Aurora. The Sun is very active today, apparently."

Ask a... Spaceplane Engineer

Scott Ostrem has one of the coolest job titles in the world. He's the Director of Spaceship Design Engineering for the manufacturing arm of Virgin Galactic. We find out what it's like to work on the **first commercial passenger space aircraft**.

How does a spaceplane like SpaceShipTwo differ from a normal aeroplane?

Fewer than 560 people have travelled to space. Virgin Galactic's *SpaceShipTwo* is our reusable space vehicle built to realize Virgin Galactic's vision to open access to space.

Built and tested by the Spaceship Company, *SpaceShipTwo* is designed to be air-launched from its mothership, *WhiteKnightTwo* [both pictured above right], giving it more initial altitude and speed than if it were launched from the ground.

SpaceShipTwo has no jet engines to fly on its own because it's flown by its mothership to altitude, at which point it's released and then fires a rocket motor to reach space. There, our passengers experience weightlessness and enjoy views of Earth against the blackness of space.

From the point of mothership separation to landing, the spaceship uses pressurized air stored in composite tanks for breathing, reaction-control system thrust, as well as pressure to power numerous actuators.

To re-enter the atmosphere, *SpaceShipTwo* relies on a unique "feathering" system that slows the vehicle as it transitions from space to the lower atmosphere. At this point, the vehicle "de-feathers" and glides back to the spaceport. The spaceship has no auxiliary engines, so from the point the rocket motor shuts down to landing, it acts purely as a glider.

Likewise, how does a spaceplane differ from a more traditional rocket/shuttle?

A traditional rocket launches from the ground. *SpaceShipTwo* is released from its mothership at around 50,000 ft [15,240 m].

Also, *SpaceShipTwo* goes through this feathering process – no other rocket or plane does that. Feathering allows *SpaceShipTwo* to re-enter the atmosphere in a controlled and slower manner. Traditional rockets may have small fins to keep them going in a straight path. *SpaceShipTwo* has a big wing and dual tail system that keeps us going straight, and the wing generates lift.

What lessons were learned from SpaceShipOne that went into SpaceShipTwo?

Burt Rutan designed *WhiteKnightOne* and *SpaceShipOne*, which won the $10-m Ansari X Prize in 2004 for being the first privately funded aircraft to fly to 100 km [62 mi] twice within two weeks and capable of carrying three people.

Launching the spaceship from a mothership worked well, so that's the same approach used by *SpaceShipTwo* and *WhiteKnightTwo*.

SpaceShipTwo uses feathering and has a large open cabin with 19 windows: *SpaceShipOne* proved the feathering approach and big open cabin for passengers to float around in a microgravity environment. *SpaceShipTwo* uses a hybrid rocket motor similar to the rocket motor used on *SpaceShipOne*.

What materials are these aircraft made of?

Carbon composite materials are used extensively on both vehicles. "Composite" is a general term that means combining more than one material to make something unique. Most of our spaceship is made of carbon and epoxy.

Carbon is a filament that is super-strong, lightweight and allows us to create a spaceship with a unique

3. At the flight's apogee (highest altitude), passengers will experience micro-gravity and be able to see Earth's surface approximately 500 mi (800 km) in every direction

2. The rockets burn for 60 sec, pushing *SpaceShipTwo* to a maximum velocity of Mach 3.5 (2,685 mph; 4,321 km/h)

1. *WhiteKnightTwo* releases the plane at roughly 50,000 ft (15,240 m)

4. The tail booms move into the "feather" position

5. *SpaceShipTwo* experiences up to 6 g as it re-enters Earth's atmosphere

6. After slowing down, the plane "de-feathers" and glides to the ground

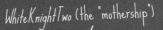

WhiteKnightTwo (the "mothership")

N348MS

VIRGIN GALACTIC

SpaceShipTwo (the bit that goes to space)

In its "feathered" position, *SpaceShipTwo* looks like something out of a *Star Wars* movie!

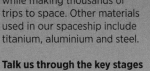

exhaust goes in one direction, and *SpaceShipTwo* is propelled in the opposite direction – thanks to Newton's Third Law! The process is controlled by our pilots, who can shut down the rocket motor at any time and glide the spaceship home.

What data is being gathered on the flight tests that VSS *Unity* is currently undergoing?
Our flight tests give us a lot of information about how the spaceship flies at different altitudes, speeds, attitudes – that's the inclination of the three principal axes of an aeroplane in flight – and *g* levels. The hundreds of gigabytes of data are then analysed by our team.

The spaceship has about 200 different sensors to measure the composite material's stresses and strains, temperatures, vibration levels and accelerations.

For every point in the sky, we collect parameters of speed, Mach number, attitude and acceleration, and compare this data to what we anticipated for the flight.

Any tips to budding rocket scientists/engineers?
Take advantage of every aeroplane, rocket-building and robotics activity your school or community offers. The best rocket engineers have a strong hands-on skill-set. Be creative and build and launch your own rockets, with adult supervision!

Besides mechanical and aerospace engineering classes, be sure to take chemistry. To understand rockets, it's important to understand how the mechanical systems behave when you add the chemical rocket.

shape. Epoxy is the glue used to bind the carbon. The way we use carbon and epoxy resin is similar to making a cake. Engineers define exactly how the composite layers are stacked, and then the resulting product is "cured".

The composite materials we use ensure that our spaceship

won't degrade or corrode while making thousands of trips to space. Other materials used in our spaceship include titanium, aluminium and steel.

Talk us through the key stages of building *SpaceShipTwo*...
We start *SpaceShipTwo*'s cabin by first building the outside

skin. We put the outside skin into a tool and then layer honeycomb material, concluding with an inside skin. We build the cabin in two halves and then install the big contents before bonding the halves together.

We add in systems such as electrical wiring, flight-control cables and air ducting. Then we combine the cabin with the wing and the two booms that make up the feathering system. After that, we route the final wires and install pneumatic plumbing.

Once the main structure is complete, we test the various systems, making sure, for example, that each wire is hooked up to where it needs to go and is doing what it's supposed to be doing.

Can you tell us about the *SpaceShipTwo*'s engines?
The hybrid rocket motor works by combining a solid fuel, liquid oxidizer and ignition source. The fuel and oxidizer are kept separate until the last minute, when they're combined in a combustion event that generates tremendous thrust. Hot

SPACE

Virgin Galactic's base of operations is Spaceport America, located across 28 sq mi (72 km²) of New Mexico desert (below is the main hangar, known as the "Gateway to Space"). The other major feature of the site is a 12,000-ft (3,657-m) runway, designed to suit the take-off and landing needs of *SpaceShipTwo*. This is generally considered the first spaceport built from scratch with commercial space travel in mind.

VIRGINGALACTIC   N348MS

I DIDN'T KNOW THAT!

You can learn a lot by smashing rocks open with a hammer. Project A119 aimed to scale this up with a massive rock and a really big "hammer"!

You can pull these two zips together to make it easier to sit down. Normally, pressurized spacesuits are constantly trying to pull you into a standing position.

Following the Soviet Union's successful launch of *Sputnik 1*, the **first artificial satellite**, on 4 Oct 1957, the US government felt it needed to do something to reassure the American people that they weren't losing the space race. Searching around for a project that would boost public spirits, the US Air Force came up with an inspiring plan to, er, nuke the Moon. The initiative was called Project A119, and it progressed a surprisingly long way before someone pointed out that it was: **(1)** a terrible idea and **(2)** not reassuring *at all*.

LOST IN SPACE

One of the big problems with zero-g is that you can't put anything down. There *is* no "down". Let go of something, just for a moment, and it will drift away. If you're wearing a bulky spacesuit and tethered to the outside of a spacecraft, the object can be out of arm's reach within seconds, never to return.

Things astronauts have lost in space include a spatula, a pair of pliers, a camera, and, largest of all, an entire toolbag (below), which drifted away from Heide Stefanyshyn-Piper in 2008 while she was repairing a solar panel on the *International Space Station*.

Going... Going... Gone...

It burned up in th[...]phere about [...] later

Q&A DO SPACESUITS HAVE TO BE WHITE?

It depends on the spacesuit. The ones astronauts wear on spacewalks need to be white to reflect the Sun's rays, but the protective suits astronauts wear inside their spacecraft during launch and landing can be any colour.

The Project Mercury suits were silver and shiny, while the Space Shuttle suits were bright orange. More recently, Boeing revealed this fetching blue number (above) as part of their Starliner programme. It features Reebok-designed boots and a hoodie-like soft helmet.

It may not hold the title of "coolest spacesuit" for long, however: rival rocketeers SpaceX have reportedly hired the designer of the superhero suits from the movie *Batman vs Superman* to put the finishing touches to their own design.

Take me to your leader!

The standard-issue greeting of aliens in science-fiction movies – "I come in peace. Take me to your leader." – was inspired by a short speech prepared by NASA's first orbital astronaut, John Glenn. He was worried that his capsule might come down in the middle of nowhere, and so wrote a simple speech to get word out that he was alive. The full text, which he had translated into many languages, read, "I am a stranger. I come in peace. Take me to your leader and there will be a great reward for you in eternity."

The spatula was for pasting over heat-shield cracks, in case you were wondering

ASTROSOCKS! Every visitor to the *International Space Station* (*ISS*) goes around in socks, but no shoes. They don't wear shoes because, well, why would you? It's not like your feet are going to get tired. Plus, you need your toes to grab on to rails and handles while moving around.

The reason for the socks is a bit less obvious, and a lot more gross. Without any pressure pushing down on them, feet start to lose the thick skin on the soles. This skin then starts to flake off like dandruff. To avoid everyone having to float through clouds of foot-flakes every day, astronauts all have to wear socks... and have to be very careful when taking them off to avoid spraying dead skin everywhere!

In 2016, the US Army managed to make a pizza that can be kept at room temperature for up to three years!

SPACE FIRSTS #1: PIZZA

Only one person has ever eaten pizza in space – cosmonaut Yuri Usachov. He was sent a specially designed pizza by the American restaurant chain Pizza Hut in 2001 as part of a multi-million-dollar publicity stunt. Pizza is not on the menu in space because it can't be kept at room temperature without going mouldy (the *ISS* has no fridges for food). It's possible that advances in military pizza technology might overcome this problem, but there's still the issue of crumbs.

SPACE FIRSTS #2: DINOSAURS IN SPACE

As far as we know, dinosaurs never mastered space flight, but some have gone to space. The **first dinosaur fossil in space** was a bone and eggshell fragment from a *Maiasaura* nest in Montana, USA, which went to space in the personal bags of astronaut Loren Acton during the *Spacelab 2* mission in Jul 1985. There wasn't really a scientific reason for this – he just thought it was neat.

Dinosaurs didn't return to space until 1998, when the skull of a *Coelophysis* (right) visited the *Mir* space station.

The closest thing to a living dinosaur to go to space were two Horsfield's tortoises that were part of a mini "astro Noah's Ark" launched by the USSR in 1968. Along with worms, flies and other organisms aboard the *Zond 5* probe, they were among the **first animals to circle the Moon**.

They get everywhere in zero-g

There seems to be no sign of intelligent life anywhere...

Buzz Lightyear comes from the (fictional, obviously) planet Morph.

SPACE FIRSTS #3: BUZZ LIGHTYEAR

On 31 May 2008, Buzz Lightyear – space ranger and star of the *Toy Story* films – flew into orbit on board the Space Shuttle *Discovery*. He was photographed eating dinner with the astronauts and gazing out of the windows before being installed as part of the crew on the *International Space Station*. Buzz remained on the station for 463 days before returning on the *Discovery* on 8 Sep 2009. His flight was part of an education programme called "Toys in Space" that NASA has been running since 1985. Other toys to go to the *ISS* include a yo-yo and a LEGO model of the *ISS* itself.

BIG SPACE ROCKS
AND HOW TO AVOID THEM

Earth is constantly under attack by meteors, ranging from those as small as grains of sand to house-sized boulders. They've inspired many a doomsday movie, but how scared should we be?

Some things don't bear thinking about... The millions of rocks hurtling around the inner Solar System with the potential to smash into our planet at any time is definitely one of them.

Meteors, asteroids and comets – collectively known as space rocks – have been plaguing Earth since it formed. (Ask the dinosaurs if you don't believe us.) It's not all doom and gloom, though. These apocalyptic collisions have actually been credited by some as the catalyst for all life – so, swings and roundabouts...

Fortunately, smart scientists and even smarter computers are continually scouring the skies for potential impactors. Gathering the latest data, they plot out space-rock trajectories for years to come. Should Earth be deemed at risk, we have a number of sci-fi-esque contingencies up our sleeve...

Let's take a look at the space rocks that smashed records as well as Earth. Plus, it's time to find out once and for all what sets a "meteorite" apart from a "meteor" and a "meteoroid".

INSTANT EXPERT

METEORITE MAKE-UP... All rocks are heavy (duh), but space rocks are even heavier because many of them contain a high density of iron. Meteorites come in three types: stoney, iron and (the much rarer) stoney-iron. To put the Chelyabinsk Meteor (opposite page) into context, it had an estimated mass of 12,000 tonnes (13,227 US tons) – that's almost a third heavier than the metal structure of the Eiffel Tower!

TIL
TODAY I LEARNED

If a similar-sized meteorite to the one that created the Barringer Crater were to strike Manhattan, the damage would be far more extensive than the crater shown below. The explosive energy resulting from such an impact would be akin to 2.5 megatons of TNT, or 166 Hiroshima bombs.

MORE *STUFF!*

With a diameter of 4,150 ft (1,265 m), the **first identified meteor crater** – and the largest in the Americas – is Arizona's Barringer Crater. It's the result of a collision that occurred approximately 2 billion years ago, long before humans evolved. For an idea of scale, this is roughly the area the crater would occupy if placed in Manhattan.

It was also the first meteorite impact caught on film

FOR THE RECORD

Our most dramatic recent encounter with a space rock was the Chelyabinsk Meteor, which broke up about 50 km (31 mi) above the Russian city of Chelyabinsk on 15 Feb 2013. The meteor was about 17 m (55 ft) across, making it the **largest measured impact on Earth**. Below is a hole created by just one fragment of the meteor after it plunged into Lake Chebarkul.

ANN HODGES

"There has never been a scientifically confirmed report of someone being killed by a meteorite impact." So said NASA's Planetary Defense Officer Lindley Johnson in 2016. The closest anyone has come is Ann Hodges (right). She was hit by a baseball-sized rock that crashed into her home in Alabama, USA, on 30 Nov 1954. Amazingly, she walked away with just bruises, becoming the **first person injured by a meteorite**.

INSTANT EXPERT

HOW TO STOP SPACE ROCKS... A worldwide network of telescopes and observatories is tasked with monitoring the movements of asteroids and comets – especially NEOs (near-Earth objects) that might pose a threat to our planet.

This data is fed into impact-monitoring systems, such as NASA's "Sentry", which extrapolate a rock's course for up to a century ahead. If it's bound for Earth, we (hopefully!) have enough time to figure out a way to avoid it.

There's been much debate about the best way to do this, along with a number of conceptual "asteroid-buster" designs. The most dramatic approach is to fire nuclear bombs at it. Rather than aiming to obliterate the space rock, the idea is that the force of the explosion *should* alter its course.

A similar solution could be achieved by using a laser (example below) or a giant mirror to shear off chunks. Alternatively, we could attach some form of net or solar sail to alter the amount of sunlight absorbed/reflected.

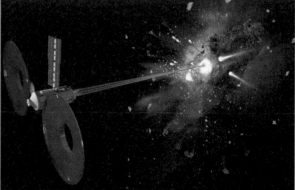

SPACE

METEORITE: Any fragment of space rock that doesn't get burned up in the atmosphere and goes on to hit the surface.

BOLIDE (aka FIREBALL): Particularly bright space rock that explodes in the atmosphere. The Chelyabinsk Meteor was a superbolide.

METEOR (aka SHOOTING STAR): Streak of light as a result of debris burning up in Earth's upper atmosphere.

METEOROID: Chunk of interplanetary matter ranging in size from dust to a metre wide' observed in space before reaching the atmosphere.

ASTEROID: Large chunk of rock that orbits the Sun, mainly comprised of minerals. Bigger ones are known as "planetoids".

COMET: Mass of ice and dust – averaging 5 km (3.1 mi) wide – that begins to "sublime" (when a solid turns to gas) as it approaches the Sun, creating the characteristic tail.

➕ MORE *STUFF!*

Space rocks aren't all made the same. They vary in size, composition and behaviour. Some even change their name depending on their proximity to Earth.

TALLEST PERSON EVER

When Robert Wadlow started growing up, he just kept growing – and growing! Discover the unique biology that enabled him to claim this iconic record.

Robert Pershing Wadlow (USA) was a record-breaker throughout his life. The reason? He never stopped growing. In his tragically short lifetime, he clocked up records for the **tallest teenager**, the **largest hands** and the **largest feet**, and – by the age of 21 – the ultimate title: **tallest person ever.**

Wadlow was always outgrowing things: shoes, clothes, beds and even the family car. Despite a lot of teasing, he was known for his placid nature, and was frequently referred to as the "Gentle Giant".

One month before his untimely death aged 22 in Jul 1940, he was measured at 272 cm (8 ft 11.1 in) tall, a record that has stood to this day.

Although he died from an infection – rather than anything directly linked to his height – the odds were always against Wadlow reaching a great age. As with most extremely tall people, his heart would have struggled to supply his body with blood. His nervous system would also have been less effective at his body's extremes, which might explain why he didn't notice the fatal blister on his ankle.

But just *why* was Wadlow so tall? To answer this, we need to take a look inside his head...

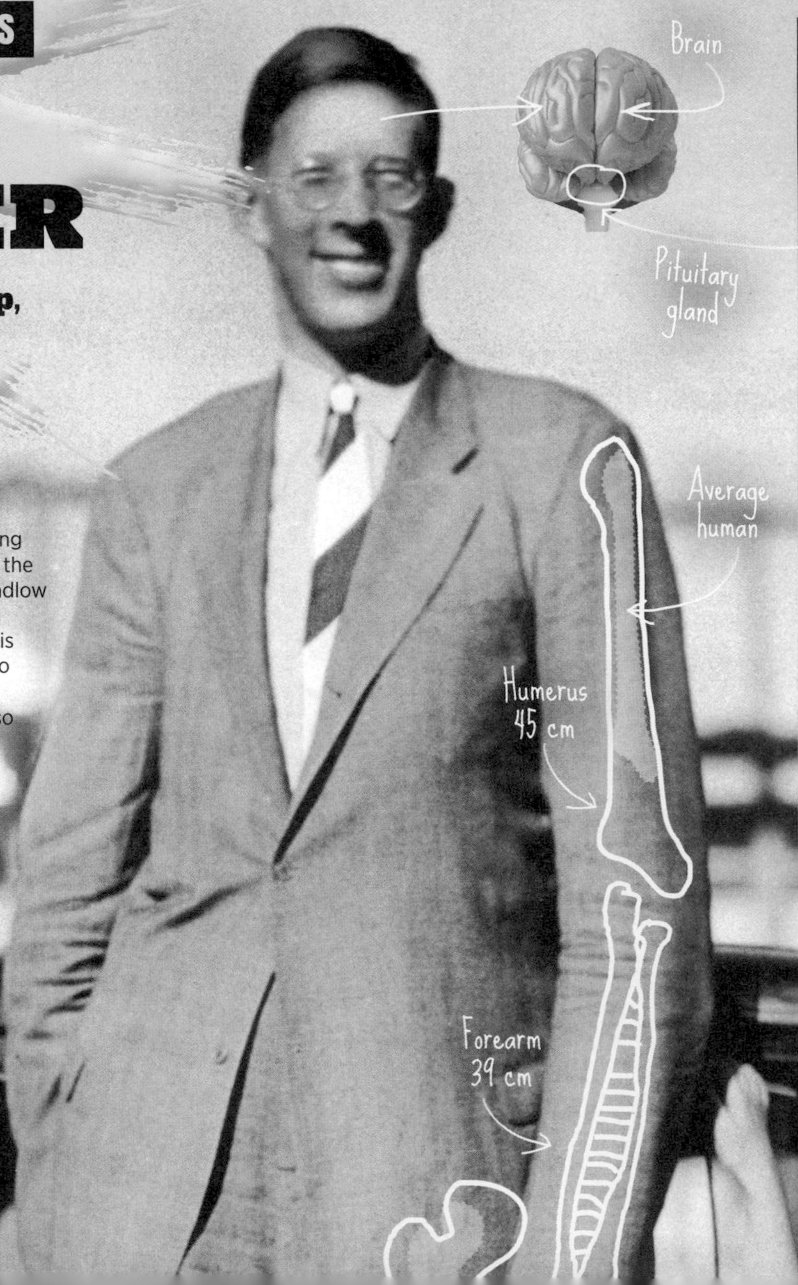

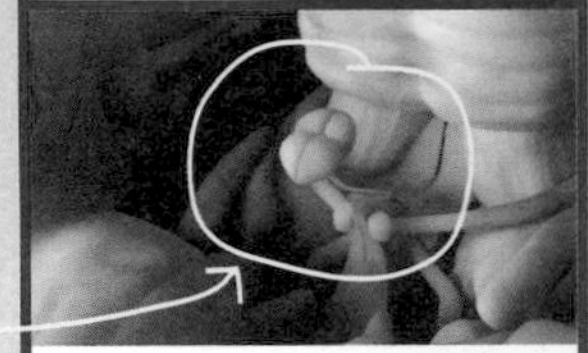

THE PITUITARY GLAND...
This pea-sized organ in the brain regulates the production of hormones. These are chemical messengers that control most body functions, including growth.

In your late teens, the pituitary gland usually sends a signal to stop the production of growth hormones. Wadlow had a condition known as pituitary hyperplasia, which meant that his gland was enlarged. This resulted in him receiving far more growth hormone than the average person during his developmental years, explaining his stature.

Brain

Pituitary gland

Average human

Humerus 45 cm

Forearm 39 cm

LEAST YOU NEED TO KNOW

Name: Robert Pershing Wadlow
Nationality: USA
Born: 22 Feb 1918 in Alton, Illinois, USA
Died: 15 Jul 1940 in Manistee, Michigan, USA
Height: 272 cm (8 ft 11.1 in)
Weight: 222.2 kg (490 lb) – more than three times the average weight of an adult man
Ring finger: Size 25 (4.2 cm; 1.6 in) – that's bigger than the diameter of a golf ball
Hand size (wrist to fingertip): 32.3 cm (12.75 in)
Arm-span: 288 cm (9 ft 5.38 in) – roughly the same as the wing-span of an Andean condor, the **largest living bird of prey**
Shoe size: 37AA shoes or UK 36 (47 cm/1 ft 6.5 in)
Cost of made-to-order shoes: $100 (or about $1,700/£1,300 in today's money)
Typical breakfast: Eight eggs, 12 slices of toast, several glasses of orange juice, five cups of coffee

Femur 60 cm

Foot 47 cm

Image colourized

WADLOW'S RISE TO FAME

Weighing 3.8 kg (8 lb 6 oz) at birth, Wadlow was on the heavy side, but still within the "commonly occurring" weight range. However, by the age of six months, he was already tipping the scales at 13.6 kg (30 lb) – setting the stage for a lifetime of superlative stature records.

By the time he was five years old, Wadlow was the same height as the average 14-year-old boy – and by 12, he was taller than Michael Jordan!

While everyone undergoes a growth spurt during puberty, Wadlow took it to a whole new level. He was measured to be 245 cm (8 ft 0.5 in) at the age of 17, easily making him the **tallest teen ever.**

If he hadn't fallen victim to an infection in his early 20s, who knows how tall Wadlow could have grown?

Estimated – no data available

HEIGHT IN METRES

HEIGHT IN FEET

AGE IN YEARS

— Wadlow   WHO average

TIL
TODAY I LEARNED

The tallest people don't always have the biggest feet to match. The current owner of the largest feet – Jeison Orlando Rodríguez Hernández (VEN) – has a 40.1-cm-long (1-ft 3.7-in) right foot and 39.6-cm (1-ft 3.5-in) left foot. At 7 ft 2.6 in (220 cm) tall, Jeison is about a foot shorter than the tallest living man (left).

FOR THE RECORD

The **tallest living person** is Sultan Kösen (TUR). At 251 cm (8 ft 2.8 in) as of 2011, he is 21 cm (8.2 in) shy of Wadlow.

Sultan's huge height is also the result of an over-active pituitary gland, although his was caused by the presence of a tumour. Since the tumour was operated on in 2010, tests have seen Sultan's hormone levels return to normal, so he's unlikely to grow any taller.

Sultan also currently boasts the **largest hands,** at 28.5 cm (11.2 in) from wrist to fingertip. So you might want to think twice about giving him a high five...

"Mr Average"

5 REASONS NOT TO VISIT VENUS

Looking for the hottest new holiday destination? Somewhere not too far away? For a vacation with an unforgettable atmosphere and striking scenery, you could do worse (but not much worse) than take a day trip to our closest planetary neighbour, Venus...

VENUS

SEE YOU AT THE CLOUD 9 OBSERVATORY.
WORLD'S *finest* PLACE IN THE SOLAR SYSTEM TO WATCH THE MERCURY TRANSIT

NASA has suggested building floating Zeppelin-style research stations in the Venusian sky

Venus

Earth

At its closest point of orbit, Venus is a mere 40 million km (25 million mi) from Earth – a relatively short hop in the grand scheme of things. You'll need to put aside about four months to get there, but at least when you arrive one Venusian day lasts just over 116 Earth days – so it's great value for money!

1 THE PRESSURE

Looking to lose a little weight? Not only will you weigh less (about 9% lighter), but there's no risk here of an expanding waistline in the Venus spa! Atmospheric pressure on the surface of Venus is about 92 times greater than that of Earth, equivalent to the pressure about 910 m (2,986 ft) beneath the surface of the ocean. This means that if you dropped a nuclear submarine through Venus's atmosphere, it would start to crumple long before it even hit the ground. Only the sturdiest deep-sea submersibles would remain intact on the surface.

2 THE HEAT

If you like it hot, then Venus is the perfect place for you. Temperatures on the planet's surface average 480°C (896°F), making it the **hottest planet in the Solar System**. This is easily hot enough to melt lead or cook a pizza in the open air – perfect for those *al fresco* picnics!

LOCAL TIP: Be sure to avoid those polyester and nylon spacesuits (like those used by NASA) – they would melt instantly! The oxygen leaking out of your ruptured suit would then spontaneously catch fire. So yes, dress appropriately...

3 THE AIR

If extreme sports are more your thing, you'll certainly feel the adrenaline flowing on Venus! The pressure and heat of the Venusian atmosphere transforms the "air" (mostly carbon dioxide with some other really nasty stuff, such as hydrogen fluoride, thrown in for good measure) into a supercritical fluid. This is a sort of halfway point between liquid and gas, with a density of 65 kg/m³ (Earth's air is 1.2 kg/m³ at sea level). Walking through this would feel a bit like walking underwater, or pushing your way through a snowdrift. Also, because the atmosphere is so dense, a wind gust of just 3 km/h (1.8 mph) would exert about the same force as a 32-km/h (20-mph) wind on Earth, pushing you (and your imploding, flaming spacesuit) over. Woo, selfie time!

4 THE WEATHER

It's always wise to check the weather before any trip, but the good news is that you won't need an umbrella on Venus! We can't see the surface of the planet because it's shrouded by clouds. Light, fluffy clouds... of sulphuric acid. Just like on Earth, these clouds are part of a cycle of evaporation and condensation – which means it rains sulphuric acid on Venus! So why should you leave your brolly at home? Well, the fatally high temperatures of the lower atmosphere mean that the raindrops boil away back up to the clouds long before they can hit the ground (er, good?). But do take care to avoid the near-constant thunderstorms raging around the planet. You don't want a powerful lightning strike to zap you (and your toppling, imploding, flaming spacesuit).

5 THE GIANT VOLCANOES

If you enjoy dramatic landscapes and out-of-this-world views, then you're in for a treat! Venus has more volcanoes than any planet or moon in our Solar System. You'll also be glad to hear that Venusian volcanoes only seem to erupt every few million years, so nothing to fear! When Venus's volcanoes *do* erupt, they really go for it – flooding the broad, flat plains that cover most of the planet with seas of scorching-hot lava. So rather than make a dignified descent from your lander – well, as dignified as you can while being crushed – you'd have to scramble out of the melting wreckage, then catch fire, implode, and so on...

★ FOR THE RECORD

For Venusian landers, life is nasty, brutish and short. The record for **longest survival on Venus**, set by the Soviet Union's *Venera 13* lander on 1 Mar 1982, is just 127 min. That's less time than it takes to play a game of baseball or watch *Avatar*. And it's not as though this was a delicate little rover like *Opportunity* – the Venera series landers (*Venera 11*, right) resembled deep-sea submersibles – big, armoured cannonballs filled with scientific instruments.

INSTANT EXPERT

Ssshhh

Here (apparently!)

LIFE ON VENUS... In 2012, Russian space scientist Leonid Ksanfomaliti published claims that the pictures sent back by *Venera 13* showed living creatures, specifically a crab-like thing referred to as "the scorpion".

Ksanfomaliti's claims have largely been dismissed by the scientific community. The engineers who worked on the Venera programme are pretty sure that the mysterious object is a bit of a camera lens cap. However, it's not beyond the realms of possibility that we might find life on Venus.

So-called "extremophiles" – sturdy microorganisms and fungi – have been found in incredibly harsh environments on Earth. These include inside the nuclear reactor at Chernobyl in Ukraine, in the toxic-waste-filled water of the Berkeley Pit in Montana, USA, and even inside deep-sea hydrothermal vents where the pressure and temperature are comparable with the surface of Venus. Some of these tiny creatures – such as tardigrades (below) – can even survive being frozen for thousands of years.

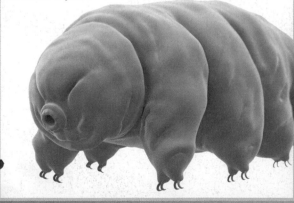

Ask an... ///////////////////////////////
Astronaut

NASA's Dr Peggy Whitson (USA) became the **oldest female astronaut** in 2016, when she headed to space aged 56 years 282 days. She has since achieved the **most spacewalks by a female** (10) and **longest accumulated time on spacewalks by a female** (60 hr 21 min). Dr Whitson spoke to us from space (!) on her latest mission...

You've been in space since Nov 2016 – it's now Jul 2017. What are you doing up there?
We've been doing a lot of interesting research. We've also done a few spacewalks – I've done four so far. We do routine maintenance to keep the station up and running – it's a huge vehicle and it's been up here for 17 years and we're trying to develop new systems, so things have to be worked on and upgraded all the time.

You've been interested in being an astronaut since the fourth grade. Who inspired you?
When I was nine, I saw the astronauts walk on the Moon and thought, "Wow, cool job!" But I think when you're nine, you want to be lots of things. It wasn't until the time I graduated from high school and they selected the first female astronauts that it went from being a dream to becoming a goal.

Throughout the years, I've had the pleasure and the privilege to have wonderful mentors and leaders, who've shown me that it's possible to become an astronaut and a female scientist. I was lucky enough to have many advisors, who happened to be female. I was inspired by their motivation, their energy and their drive. They made me feel like I could do the things that I wanted to do.

Now you're a role model, what do you hope to inspire in people?
I hope to inspire folks to dream big. To go after your dreams even if they seem impossible, because you never know... I think the most important piece of advice is to try to do something more than you think you're capable of – because you'll surprise yourself.

So, as we speak to you, you're floating in zero-gravity. Is that still fun, or is it just "another day in the office" now?
Actually, it's still amazing. To be able to float and move around and pretty much effortlessly do whatever you want with your body is still amazing. It does have some disadvantages, though. When you're working with small items, it's easy to lose them. It requires some extra planning: make sure you have Velcro or tape sticky side up so you can put things down.

Is training to be an astronaut as hard as it seems?
I found it extremely challenging. Everyone has got their strengths and weaknesses. A lot of hard work really paid off for me, so I feel like it can pay off for others as well. Going in as a biochemist, one of the hardest things I had to learn was orbital mechanics. But the very hardest thing was learning the Russian language.

So you're fluent in Russian?
I'd say I'm "Soyuz fluent". I flew in the Soyuz [spacecraft], so I can talk a lot about pumps, pressures and temperatures – very mechanical things. But

She's floating – she's actually floating!!!

DR PEGGY WHITSON

GUINNESS WORLD RECORDS RECORD HOLDER

This interview marked a milestone for Guinness World Records. It was the first live Q&A we've ever conducted with someone in space! Broadcast on our Facebook Live channel, it was very surreal watching Dr Whitson answer our questions while she floated in zero-g (left). Watch the video for yourself at **www.guinnessworldrecords.com/science**. Who knows, perhaps one day we'll be interviewing the **first person on Mars**…

talking to someone in a conversation, my vocabulary is not very deep.

Describe a typical day on board the *ISS*.
We get up at 6 a.m. Greenwich Mean Time [GMT] and talk to control centres all around the world. Any one day could be made up of different kinds of experiments. It could be robotics investigations for capturing a vehicle, it could be practising skills that we hope we never have to use like medical training or emergency [procedures]. Occasionally, we get to do spacewalks.

Is there any research you get particularly excited about?
Interestingly, most of the time, we don't have a lot of details on investigations before we come to launch. We're trained generically to do lots of different things. Some of my favourite ones on this mission have involved cell cultures. We're growing bone tissue, stem cells and, most recently,

lung-cancer cells. We were adding a drug conjugated to an antibody that recognized those specific lung-cancer cells to see if it could be a more targeted chemotherapy treatment.

What's the benefit of doing cancer research in space?
It's not just cancer research, but a lot of physical properties. We're looking at combustion, protein crystallization and other types of crystallization. All those things happen differently in a zero-g environment. They can teach us lessons about how things work on the ground. That's what this laboratory up here, moving at 17,150 mph [27,600 km/h], is giving us.

How have things changed over your career?
Definitely the complexity of the research now is at a much higher level. In part, that's because when I first flew in space we were still assembling the space station – so the majority of our time was spent on that. I did do some research – I grew superconductor crystals and soy beans on my first flight.

What do you do if you get a toothache or cold up there?
We're trained as crew medical officers and we always have the ground to help us out. We receive some emergency medical training, getting exposure to different things that might happen in orbit.

In terms of illness, because we live in a pretty isolated environment, we don't really get sick for the most part. We quarantine our crews for one or two weeks before launch to try to prevent us bringing up germs or other illnesses. It seems to work well!

Are there any rituals you do for luck before take-off?
I don't really have any good-luck routines. It's interesting to see the traditions that develop in different countries and what's important to people. For me, I'm just focused on the mission and always worried about trying not to screw up – that's the big thing on my mind prior to flight! Once you get here, you relax a bit more.

Is there anything you would still like to discover/achieve?
I'd love to step foot on another planet – lunar or [otherwise]. But I'm afraid that I might be getting a tad old for that! I'm hoping the future will provide folks an opportunity to live and work on Mars and explore space even beyond.

SPACE

FOR THE RECORD

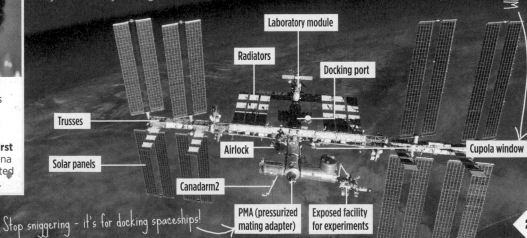

On 23 May 2017, Dr Whitson (left) once more donned a spacesuit to go on her 10th extravehicular activity (EVA) – the **most spacewalks by a female**. Along with a colleague, she was fixing a faulty data relay box. Made up of several interlocking modules and covering an area the size of a soccer field, the *ISS* (below) is the **largest space station**.

Where Peggy is sitting in the picture opposite

Sally Ride (USA, above) was one of Dr Whitson's role models. In 1983, she became the first US woman in space. It was two decades after the **first female in space**: Valentina Tereshkova (USSR) orbited Earth on 16–19 Jun 1963.

Laboratory module

Radiators

Docking port

Trusses

Airlock

Cupola window

Solar panels

Canadarm2

PMA (pressurized mating adapter)

Exposed facility for experiments

Stop sniggering – it's for docking spaceships!

SPACE POOP CHALLENGE

On 15 Feb 2017, NASA announced the winners of its Space Poop Challenge, a contest that offered a big cash prize to whoever could come up with a not-disgusting way of pooping in space. So, why is space poop such a sticky problem?

Space isn't all about riding awesome rockets and taking beautiful pictures. It also has an unglamorous side. A *really* unglamorous side.

Liquids tend to escape and float away in zero-g, and that has nasty implications for the bathroom. Bad handling of human waste is a major health risk, so – gross though it is – engineers have to spend a lot of time thinking about poop.

The big problem is the fact that astronauts have to spend long periods in spacesuits during rocket launches and re-entry. They can't take them off to use the toilet, so they have to just wear diapers.

And as any screaming baby would tell you (if it could speak), sitting in a used nappy for hours isn't very pleasant.

To try to tackle the spacesuit issue, NASA laid down the Space Poop Challenge in 2016, asking members of the public to submit designs for a better in-spacesuit toilet system.

The winning entry was developed by US Air Force doctor Thatcher Cardon (pictured above right). He used techniques developed for keyhole surgery to pass all sorts of things – including inflatable bedpans and diapers - through a 5-cm-diameter (1.9-in) airlock in the crotch of the suit (right).

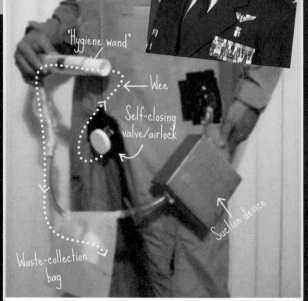

This picture shows Thatcher Cardon modelling the prototype version of his MACES Perineal Access & Toileting System (M-PATS). To deal with poos, the suction-powered "hygiene wand" is applied at the, erm, other end.

Rumble, rumble...

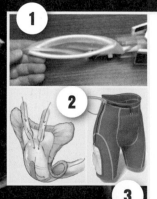

NASA picked three winners from the 5,000 submitted solutions, each of which received a portion of the $30,000 (£23,996) prize pot. Picture 1 shows an example of the ingenious folding attachments for Thatcher Cardon's system (a urine collector for female astronauts). Picture 2 shows the Air-powered Spacesuit Waste Disposal System, developed by an American team called the Space Poop Unification of Doctors (SPUDs). Picture 3 shows the SWIMSuit, an advanced diaper-like system invented by British designer Hugo Shelley.

INSTANT EXPERT

MOON TOILETS... Unpleasant as modern space toilets can be, they're an improvement on the systems used in the past. During the Apollo Moon missions, NASA's astronauts had to use what was called the Fecal Containment System (FCS) – a grand-sounding name for what was actually just a plastic bag that you had to tape to your butt.

Once astronauts had done their business, they had to help the poop "disconnect" from their bodies (using their fingers!). They then had to unstick the bag from their butt and close it up. This was very hard to do without *things* escaping.

The grossness didn't end there, however; the astronauts still had to inject an anti-microbial gel into the bag and knead the mixture into the poop before they stored it away for later analysis. Oh, and did we mention? The bags (below) were clear plastic, so nothing was left to the imagination.

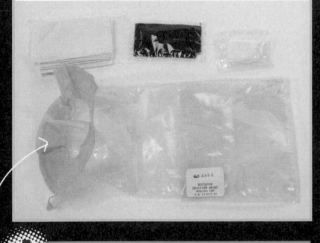

FOR THE RECORD

The **most expensive toilet ever** was the Space Shuttle's Waste Collection System (WCS). By the time the final revision of the design flew in Jan 1993, the cost had risen to $23.4 m (£15.8 m) per unit. The WCS was about the size of a telephone booth and had more than 4,000 individual parts. It was so complicated that it had a set of gear-shifter-style control switches that worked a system of fans, pumps and airlocks. It required hours of training to operate correctly.

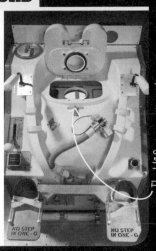

NO STEP IN ONE - G   NO STEP IN ONE - G

The WCS occasionally broke and exposed people's bums to space... which no one wants!

INSTANT EXPERT

SPACE STATION TOILETS... Compared with previous generations of spacecraft, the *International Space Station* has positively luxurious bathroom facilities, but they're still pretty weird compared with those on Earth.

The toilets (there are two: one in *Zvezda* and one in *Tranquility*) are identical Russian designs. Each one has a urine-collection hose hooked up to a suction pump, and a solid-waste receptacle that works in a similar way to the vacuum-of-space design used on the Shuttle. There's also a back-up toilet on the *Soyuz* "lifeboat" (pictured right), but it's a bit grim.

In addition to the suction features required to make everything work in zero-g, these toilets have a few other odd features. For example, all the air from the urine hose and the poop receptacle gets pumped out, filtered and fed back into the ventilation system. Also, the urine is collected in bags and run through a filtration system to produce drinking water (eeww!). What's left is vented into space and burns up in the upper atmosphere.

Er...

flusssh

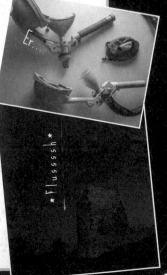

MORE *STUFF!*

Problems with NASA's early toilet arrangements led to the infamous "floating turd incident" during the Apollo 10 mission in 1969. Declassified transcripts (extract below) have revealed astronauts Tom Stafford, Gene Cernan and John Young (below) joking about a poop that somehow got loose in the cockpit; they all deny it was theirs! They managed to get the unwanted "visitor" under control with a napkin.

05 13 29 44	CDR	Oh - Who did it?
05 13 29 46	CMP	Who did what?
05 13 29 47	LMP	What?
05 13 29 49	CDR	Who did it? (Laughter)
05 13 29 51	LMP	Where did that come from?
05 13 29 52	CDR	Give me a napkin quick. There's a turd floating through the air.

~~CONFIDENTIAL~~

A 1975 NASA report noted, "The collection process required a great deal of skill to preclude escape of faeces from the collection bag and consequent soiling of the crew, their clothing, and cabin surfaces." Gross!

MARS: THE NEXT FRONTIER

Is there life on Mars? The Red Planet is too far away for us to go and check ourselves (at least at the moment), but our robot explorers are hard at work checking rocks and craters for little green men.

Of the 15 landers that have been sent to Mars, only seven landed safely. The most recent casualty of what scientists refer to as "the curse of Mars" was the European Space Agency's *Schiaparelli* lander, which struck the Martian surface at 300 km/h (186 mph) on 19 Oct 2016 after its landing computers became confused.

Landing on Mars is difficult – even for rocket scientists. Mars has an atmosphere thick enough to generate friction during entry (hence why landers need a heat shield). But it's *not* thick enough to slow down a lander for a soft landing. It's also too thin for parachutes to work.

To get things down intact, engineers have tried everything from a gentle rocket-assisted landing to bouncing the lander in giant airbags. As landers get bigger, the methods used to bring them down have to keep innovating (see below).

Take that, you stupid rock!

Curiosity has a top speed of 2.5 cm/sec (0.09 km/h). This means its operators have a lot of time to look at the scenery. As they often spend weeks staring at the same area, they name everything they see. This rock, for example, is called Jake Matijevic.

WHY GO TO MARS?

THE BIG QUESTION ?

At a glance, Mars' surface doesn't look like much. It's more appealing than the Moon, certainly, but not somewhere that many people would want to live. So why *are* we so interested in Mars?

The reason is that Mars wasn't always like this. We know that it once had abundant surface water, with large lakes and even seas. It's quite possible that life once evolved on Mars, but died out as conditions on the planet worsened. If we can find evidence of this past life – probably only in the form of fossilized single-cell organisms – then we stand to learn a lot about how life might have evolved on Earth, or on other planets.

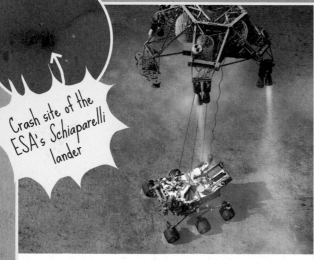

Crash site of the ESA's Schiaparelli lander

To land the 899-kg (1,982-lb) *Curiosity* rover, NASA designed this Sky Crane system. The lander descended most of the way under a parachute before switching to rockets for the last 1,600 m (5,250 ft). Once it was down to within 20 m (66 ft) of the surface, the descent module stopped and lowered the lander to the ground on cables.

TIL
TODAY I LEARNED

In 1993, videogame designer Richard Garriott bought the *Lunokhod 2* rover at auction for $68,500. Unfortunately, it's still on the Moon. Although he has managed to go into space since then, he still hasn't been able to collect his purchase.

The lunar speed record

RACE OF THE ROVERS

Here's a list of vehicle speeds on the Moon and Mars. For reference, the **land-speed record** on Earth is 1,227.98 km/h (763 mph). If you put that in centimetres per second – the unit used for rover speeds – you get a figure of 34,110 cm/sec.

500 cm /sec

Lunar Rover (USA, 1972)

55 cm /sec

Lunokhod 1 & 2 (USSR, 1970/1973)

OPPORTUNITY

On 25 Jan 2004, NASA's *Opportunity* touched down on Mars. It was planned to be a 90-day mission, taking in some 600 m (1,960 ft) of Martian scenery before powering down. Ninety days came and went, but *Opportunity* kept going. It's been 13 years now, and this lander from before the age of smartphones is still healthy.

Opportunity has left the plain where it landed and moved up to the edge of the Endeavour Crater – a distance of 43.5 km (27 mi). In doing so, it has broken the record for **farthest distance travelled on another world**, set by the USSR's *Lunokhod 2* Moon rover (below) in 1973.

SPACE

⭐ FOR THE RECORD

In 2004, NASA's Jet Propulsion Laboratory started work on a super-rover, which had all the tools needed to detect water and possibly even life on Mars. The final design for what would become *Curiosity* weighed 899 kg (1,982 lb), making it the **largest planetary rover** ever. By comparison, *Opportunity* weighs only 185 kg (408 lb).

NASA's upcoming *Mars 2020* rover is set to be even bigger, at around 950 kg (2,094 lb). It will look like *Curiosity*, but it will have a different scientific instruments and chunkier wheels (the ones on *Curiosity* are falling apart). It might also have a tiny helicopter to explore further, which would be the first drone to fly on another planet.

Robotic arm/ "selfie stick"

ChemCam laser

Cameras

Damaged wheels

The Martian land-speed record

5.8 cm /sec

Yutu, aka "Jade Rabbit" (CHN, 2013)

5 cm /sec

Spirit & Opportunity (USA, 2004)

2.5 cm /sec

Curiosity (USA, 2012)

1 cm /sec

Sojourner (USA, 1997)

29

HIGHEST SKYDIVE WITHOUT A PARACHUTE

On 30 Jul 2016, veteran skydiver Luke Aikins jumped out of a plane 25,000 ft (7,620 m) over the Californian desert with no parachute... and didn't die!

1 THE FALL

Maintaining control in freefall is tricky. You need to spread yourself out to maximize your air resistance (and so keep your speed down), but doing so can make you drift off target.

When he made his record-breaking jump, Luke steered by making tiny movements of his arms and legs. This shifted the flow of air around his body to pull him in one direction or another.

During the first part of Luke's fall, the air was too thin and cold (-34°C/-29°F) to breathe, so he had a hand-held oxygen canister hooked up to a face mask. Once he passed 15,000 ft (4,572 m), however, he gave this stuff to another skydiver who jumped with him (it would be bad if the mask landed on someone's head!).

Stretch out a sheet of paper and drop it – it won't fall straight down!

LEAST YOU NEED TO KNOW

25,000 ft (7,620 m): Luke jumps from the plane with three other skydivers

23,500 ft (7,162 m): Luke reaches terminal velocity, which is something like 250 km/h (155 mph) at this point

15,000 ft (4,572 m): Oxygen mask discarded

10,000 ft (3,048 m): By this point, the thicker air has slowed Luke to about 190 km/h (120 mph)

5,000 ft (1,524 m): Luke's companions release their parachutes

370 ft (112 m): Luke flips on to his back for a safe landing

200 ft (60 m): Luke hits a suspended net, which stretches to absorb his fall

TERMINAL VELOCITY... It sounds awesome, doesn't it? The term refers to the speed at which the air resistance pushing up on a falling object equals the force of gravity pulling down on it. It doesn't mean that the object stops falling, just that it can't fall any faster.

For a person falling in a horizontal position, terminal velocity is about 195 km/h (122 mph) near the surface (where air is thicker) and about 250 km/h (155 mph) at the height of Luke's jump. If there wasn't any air, Luke would have kept accelerating until he hit the ground... at about 1,391 km/h, or 864 mph, and you'd need a *really* big net for that landing!

Gravity

Air resistance

Air resistance ↙

$$F = \frac{\rho C_d A v^2}{2}$$

Air density — Drag coefficient — Surface area — Speed

Target

Net pylons

Nervous spectators

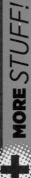

2 THE LANDING

In the last few seconds of Luke's dive, he flipped over so that he was falling backwards towards the net. Scary though it was to do the crucial last part of his fall while looking the wrong way, it would have been worse if he had hit the net face-first – people's spines don't like to bend sharply backwards!

Even though Luke is an expert skydiver and had trained for more than a year, this record attempt still came very close to going horribly wrong: Luke barely made it to the net, hitting it a long way off centre, less than 5 m (16 ft) from the edge.

KINETIC ENERGY

$$E = \frac{1}{2}mv^2$$

$$0.5 \times 70 \text{ kg} \times 53 \text{ m/s}^2$$

$$= 98,315 \text{ joules}$$

This means that Luke hit the net with as much force as a family car moving at 30 mph (48 km/h)

Backup net

The net was attached to compressed air pistons that absorbed the impact

Luke's plans were nearly thwarted when an organization involved in the TV broadcast of his stunt insisted he wear a parachute for safety in case something went wrong. He continued last-minute negotiations with them – even after the plane had taken off. He insisted that the parachute would actually make the jump *more* dangerous because it would mess with his aerodynamic shape during the crucial last-second flip.

★ FOR THE RECORD

Of all the activities we've seen here at Guinness World Records, few are crazier than "banzai skydiving". This is the sport of throwing a parachute out of a plane, then jumping out after it.

This is a thing that people actually do on purpose (that picture, right, is real). The **longest banzai skydive** was by Yasuhiro Kubo of Japan, who managed a nerve-wracking 50-sec freefall before finally catching, putting on and opening his parachute.

Why am I doing this?

Certain death

✚ MORE STUFF!

Luke was not the first person to jump from a plane with nothing and live to tell the tale...

- The **highest fall survived without a parachute** was set by air stewardess Vesna Vulović in 1972. She fell 10,160 m (33,333 ft) in the wreckage of her plane after it exploded mid-air. Her fall was broken by deep snow.

- Another famous freefall survivor was 17-year-old Juliane Koepcke, who fell 3,000 m (9,842 ft) after her plane was struck by lightning over Peru. Her fall was broken by the thick rainforest canopy, and luckily she'd been given jungle survival training as a child!

- The **first skydive without a parachute** was carried out on 23 May 2012 by stuntman Gary Connery (above). He used a wingsuit to control his descent, before landing on a giant pile of cardboard boxes.

OTHER EARTHS

Astronomers recently discovered seven Earth-like planets in the Trappist solar system, hundreds of trillions of miles from our own. Three of the planets are in the star's "habitable zone". Does this make them contenders for a new home for us humans?

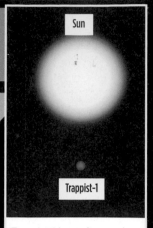

Sun

Trappist-1

People have always wondered if there might be life out there in the darkness of space. For a long time, we pinned our hopes on the planets of our Solar System, but the last 60 years of exploration have failed to find any signs of life.

Space is unimaginably huge, however. There are trillions of stars out there, many like our own, each potentially with planets around them. Can we

really be alone in the universe? Surely there are other Earths – other inhabitable (or even inhabited) planets?

It wasn't until 1992 that the **first confirmed discovery of an extrasolar planet** took place (they were named Draugr and Poltergeist). For a while, extrasolar planets were curiosities – indistinct shadows that could be only guessed at from a star's light.

In the last 15 years or so, however, astronomers have greatly improved the art of planet-spotting, and now find new ones every week.

The recent detection of the star Trappist-1, and its seven planets, is one of the most exciting discoveries we've made in a while. The planets are Earth-like, relatively close (in astronomical terms) and potentially habitable...

Trappist-1 is an ultra-cool dwarf star with a temperature of about 2,280°C (4,130°F). Our Sun, by comparison, burns at 5,505°C (9,941°F). It has about one-tenth of the mass of our Sun, and isn't much larger than Jupiter. Trappist-1 is in the constellation Aquarius, but is so dim that we can't see it without a huge telescope.

The Trappist-1 system is interesting because planets "e", "f" and "g" all sit within what's called the "Goldilocks zone" (or habitable zone) around their parent star. This is a band of space that is far enough away to not be uninhabitably hot, but not so far away as to be too cold – it is "just right".

A planet's habitability depends on many more factors than just temperature, though. A lot of it depends on the quality of the atmosphere, which is affected by things such as solar wind and a planet's gravity. It's impossible to be sure about any of these things from where we are.

One big snag for any future colonists is that Trappist-1's planets are all tidally locked. This means that one side is always facing the Sun while the other is in the shade. This would make the weather pretty wild.

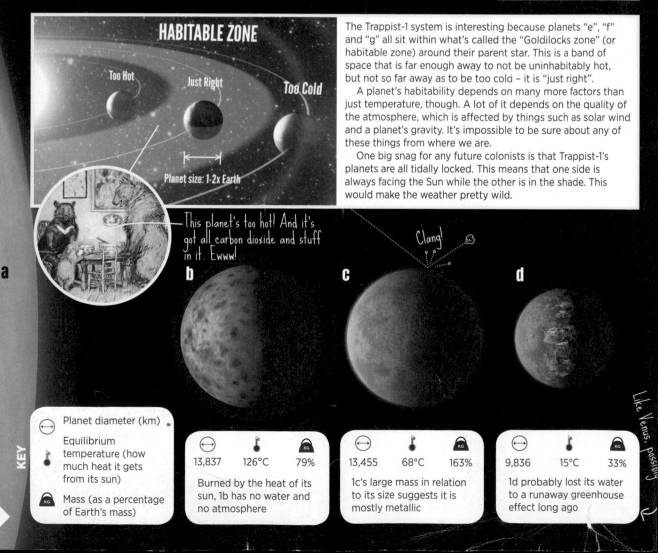

HABITABLE ZONE

Too Hot

Just Right

Too Cold

Planet size: 1-2x Earth

This planet's too hot! And it's got all carbon dioxide and stuff in it. Ewww!

Clang!

a

b

c

d

Like Venus, possibly

KEY

⟷ Planet diameter (km)

🌡 Equilibrium temperature (how much heat it gets from its sun)

⚖ Mass (as a percentage of Earth's mass)

⟷	🌡	⚖
13,837	126°C	79%

Burned by the heat of its sun, 1b has no water and no atmosphere

⟷	🌡	⚖
13,455	68°C	163%

1c's large mass in relation to its size suggests it is mostly metallic

⟷	🌡	⚖
9,836	15°C	33%

1d probably lost its water to a runaway greenhouse effect long ago

The name is a reference to a kind of Belgian beer

THE TRAPPIST PROJECT

This star system was spotted by a project called the Transiting Planets and Planetesimals Small Telescope (TRAPPIST), run by Belgium's University of Liège from the La Silla Observatory in Chile (left).

The astronomers identified the planets (which are much too far away to see directly) by looking for tiny variations in the light output of their parent star; this is caused by the planets passing (aka "transiting") between the star and us.

They were also able to get some information from subtle shifts in the wavelength of the star's light. These were caused by the star wobbling slightly as the planets swung around it.

Their own telescope was enough to confirm there were planets around the star, but couldn't say much about them (there just wasn't enough detail). Once they'd made the initial discovery, however, the researchers were able to call in the big guns – NASA's Spitzer Space Telescope (right) and the Very Large Telescope in Paranal, Chile. These two telescopes were able to provide the exciting details about this star system.

Not a real thing, sadly. NASA made it up!

The Exoplanet Travel Bureau made this poster to mark Trappist-1's discovery. Some of the planets are as close as the Earth and its Moon.

INSTANT EXPERT

VISITING TRAPPIST-1... There's always hope, but unless we discover something that completely changes our understanding of physics and the universe, humans are not likely to ever see Trappist-1's planets up close.

Trappist-1 is roughly 39.5 light years away (that's about 373,000,000,000,000 km). The **fastest man-made object**, NASA's *Helios 2* satellite, travels at 246,960 km/h (153,453 mph) in its looping elliptical orbit around the Sun. At this speed it would take 155,914 years to get there. It would take *Voyager 1* (left) – the **most distant man-made object** – even longer: c. 790,000 years.

We might be able to do a bit better than that with current technology, but a quick journey would require us to somehow break the fundamental laws of the universe.

It's too much to explain properly here, but what you need to know is that accelerating something with mass to the speed of light requires infinite energy (which is impossible). Even accelerating to *near* the speed of light would require more energy than is contained in all the matter in our Solar System.

It involves special relativity, something called the Lorentz factor, and algebra with a lot of Greek letters in it

Brrrrr!

e

↔	🌡	KG
11,697	−21.8°C	62%

This most-Earth-like planet is a strong candidate for liquid water and life

f

↔	🌡	KG
13,315	−54°C	68%

With an atmosphere like Earth's, 1f could be an iceberg-filled ocean planet

g

↔	🌡	KG
14,360	−75°C	56%

Its distance from its sun means 1g is the most likely to have a thick atmosphere

h

↔	🌡	KG
9,110	−104°C	86%

1h might have a liquid ocean hidden under a thick layer of ice

BLUE "LAVA"

At a hydrothermal site in Ethiopia's Danakil Depression – the **hottest place on Earth**, based on annual mean temperatures – lava sometimes appears blue/violet at night. However, looks can be deceptive. What we're actually seeing here is a layer of burning sulphuric gas that has seeped out of cracks in the ground. When these vapours come into contact with air, they are set alight by the super-hot molten rock below. Some of the gas also condenses into liquid sulphur, which trickles across the surface – further adding to the illusion that it is blue lava.

WEIRD WORLD

WHERE ON EARTH...?!

Chances are, you live in (or near) a city and that your city lies on a river, and that the river runs through a fairly flat, grassy plain. Whether it's Paris or São Paolo, Cleveland or Beijing, humans tend to settle in the same sort of places.

This arrangement is practical – people need farmland to grow food and water to drink – but it's a bit dull. No one travels halfway across the world to marvel at the landscape of suburban New Jersey.

What if people chose to settle down using the same criteria as movie villains? Here are some ideal locations for mountaintop castles, fortresses of solitude and secret hermit hideaways.

② The Colorado Plateau, in southwestern USA, has the **highest concentration of slot canyons** – up to 10,000. These formations include wild, alien-looking places such as Antelope Canyon (pictured), formed by the action of grit-carrying winds, which wore down and smoothed the rocks like sandpaper.

① This plume of steam and near-boiling water is the **tallest active geyser** known to science: the Steamboat Geyser in Yellowstone National Park, USA. The roughly twice-monthly eruptions reach heights of 60–115 m (197–377 ft), with water temperatures of 71°C (160°F).

Taller than the Tower of Pisa (57 m)!

③ This cavern in Chihuahua, Mexico – unsurprisingly known as the Cave of Crystals – holds gypsum crystals that measure as much as 11 m (36 ft) long and weigh more than 55 tonnes (121,254 lb). They are the **largest gypsum crystals** in the world.

Secret Bond-villain lair here...

④ If you're wondering what you're looking at here, it might help to know that the white stuff is the cloud layer, not sea foam. This is Monte Roraima, which at 2,810 m (9,220 ft) is the **highest mountain tabletop** (aka "tepui"). It's the largest of a chain of similar outcrops along the Venezuela–Brazil border, many of which are so remote that no one has ever been to the top.

⑦ This terrifying chasm is the Miao Keng Cave in China, which features the **deepest unbroken vertical shaft in a cave** – it's 501 m (1,643 ft) straight down. The cave is part of a system that includes cathedral-sized caverns and underground rivers.

⑤ Lake Retba, near Dakar in Senegal, looks like a gigantic strawberry milkshake. You really wouldn't want to drink it, though; it gets its colour from an extremely hardy bacteria that has colonized the hyper-salty waters. This is the world's **largest pink lake**.

Ah, Mr Bond... We've been expecting you...

WEIRD WORLD

⑥ Monte Stromboli, located on a small island off the coast of southern Italy, is the **longest continuously active volcano**. The earliest references to its hourly micro-eruptions come from the Ancient Greeks in around 700 BCE.

Wish you were here?

On this side, yes.

LIGHTNING:
BOLTS FROM THE BLUE

How long is a lightning bolt? And what exactly is lightning anyway? Perhaps the most important question you should be asking, though, is how do you avoid being struck?!

The **most common type of lightning** is intracloud (aka sheet) lightning, which takes place inside a storm cloud, making it flicker and glow

Just after 6 a.m. on 20 Jun 2007, a powerful negative electrical charge built up in thunderstorm clouds over Tulsa, Oklahoma, USA. A massive spark (technically a channel of negatively charged plasma) burst out from the bottom of the cloud, arcing across the sky as it sought an area to "ground" its energy.

Usually sparks like this – called "stepped leaders" – reach the ground or an area of positively charged air within a tiny fraction of a second. They discharge the static charge from the cloud in a massive blast of electrical energy and this is what we call lightning.

On this occasion, however, the combination of the incredibly powerful static charge and some unusual atmospheric conditions kept this bolt of lightning going horizontally across the sky for more than five seconds.

It passed over Oklahoma City, occasionally sending down secondary leaders to the earth, before continuing west. It finally petered out somewhere near the Texas border, east of the city of Amarillo – an astonishing 321 km (199.5 mi) from where it started.

This lightning flash, which was picked up on weather radar, was officially recognized by the World Meteorological Organization in Jun 2017 as the **longest lightning flash**.

The record-holding lightning flash travelled 321 km (199.5 mi) – the distance from London to Paris or New York to Washington, DC – in 5.7 sec. This means that the leader was moving at about 202,734 km/h (125,973 mph).

At points in the air where two routes offer an equally viable chance of reaching the ground, a stepped leader will split, or branch

⭐ FOR THE RECORD

1. Lake Maracaibo
(233 flashes per km²)

4. Cáceres, Colombia
(172 flashes per km²)

5. Daggar, Pakistan
(142 flashes per km²)

2. Kabaré, DRC
(205 flashes per km²)

3. Kampene, DRC
(176 flashes per km²)

Around 95% of strikes are "negative lightning", where negative charge transfers from the cloud base to the positively charged ground

In Nov 2016, lightning researcher Dr Rachel Albrecht (USA) and her collaborators published the first definitive ranking of the world's lightning hot spots. They used data collected by NASA weather satellites between 1998 and 2013 to assess the frequency of cloud-to-ground and cloud-to-cloud lightning all over the world. They confirmed Venezuela's Lake Maracaibo as the place with the world's **highest concentration of lightning strikes**, with 233 flashes per km² every year. They also highlighted several largely unknown hot spots in the Democratic Republic of the Congo, in Central Africa.

Aaah!

● ROY C SULLIVAN

In Apr 1942, Roy C Sullivan, a park ranger at Shenandoah National Park in Virginia, USA, was struck by lightning while fleeing his watchtower (which had been set on fire by another lightning strike). He suffered burns and lost the nail on a toe, but survived.

For most people this would be a crazy once-in-a-lifetime experience, but Roy was not so lucky. He was, in fact, quite amazingly unlucky. Over the next 35 years, he was on the receiving end of another *six* lightning strikes – earning him the unenviable record for the **most lightning strikes survived**.

Along with various lightning-related injuries acquired while walking the trails in Shenandoah National Park, he had his eyebrows burned off while driving, his hair set on fire in a guardhouse and his shoulder burned while mowing the lawn.

In a storm cloud, a differential of charge builds up, with the top becoming largely positive and the base mostly negative

"Stepped leaders" move in short jumps of about 50 m (160 ft), pooling their charged particles before making another leap

Ouch!

✚ MORE *STUFF!*

- Around 310 people are struck by lightning in the USA every year (only around 10% of these unlucky people die as a result).
- Lightning strikes leave unique patterns on people's skin called Lichtenberg figures (left). They're created by the electrical charge moving through skin and fade after a few days.

WEIRD WORLD

HOW DO I AVOID BEING STRUCK BY LIGHTNING?

THE BIG QUESTION

The best way to avoid being struck by lightning is to be inside. If you will insist on venturing into the great outdoors, however, there are a few things you can do to avoid becoming the next Roy C Sullivan.

If you think a lightning strike is imminent (your hair might stand on end shortly beforehand), you should get away from any nearby trees. The lightning might strike the tree instead of you, but if you're near it, the charge will come up through your feet as it dissipates through the ground.

The next thing you should do is make yourself as small as possible – crouch down low with the balls of your feet on the ground and your heels together. This position lowers your profile while also minimizing the surface area you have in contact with the ground (lying down is a very bad idea). Putting your heels together makes it easier for the current to pass through you without going through your squishy, delicate innards. Finally, put your hands over your ears, because it's going to be *really* loud.

The downward-moving, negatively charged leader induces a positive current in the ground, which sends up a positively charged "streamer"

When the leader and streamer meet, they complete the path between the charged clouds and the ground, allowing the electricity to flow

Positively charged ground/sea + + + +

More than 120 dB – that's enough to perforate your eardrum

GREATEST OCTOPUS MIMIC

The mimic octopus is a master of disguise. Using its colour-changing skin and flexible body, it can imitate anything from a sea snake to a rock. Let's take a closer look at this incredible creature... if we can find it!

Thaumoctopus mimicus, better known as the mimic octopus, is a 60-cm-long (2-ft) camouflage specialist found in coastal waters of Australia and Southeast Asia. It can change colour and shape at will, and is so good at evading unwanted attention that scientists didn't even notice it existed until 1998!

Several species of octopus can disguise themselves as scary or inedible creatures, but none have the range of the mimic octopus. Marine biologists have recorded this shape-shifter impersonating 16 very different animals including sea snakes, stingrays and hermit crabs, making it the **greatest octopus mimic**.

So, to make sure you're "well armed" with all the facts, we present the science behind this eight-limbed wonder...

+ MORE *STUFF!*

- If an octopus is attacked by a predator, it can detach one of its limbs to make a quick getaway.
- The blue-ringed octopus is the **most venomous mollusc**. A bite can kill or paralyse an adult man in just a few minutes.
- Octopuses have arms/legs, not tentacles. Tentacles only have suckers at the end, while arms have suckers along their whole length.
- Octopus arms have taste receptors in the suckers and on the skin, so

they can decide if they want to eat something just by touching it.
- Octopuses have three hearts: two to pump blood to the gills, and one to circulate it around the body.
- The **largest octopus** is the Pacific giant octopus. Its arms span up to 9.6 m (31 ft 5 in) – as long as a London double-decker bus!
- The **smallest octopus** is *Octopus arborescens* from Sri Lanka – it has an arm-span of just 5.1 cm (2 in).

PARTY-TRICK IMPRESSIONS

The body of an octopus is a strange thing. They're invertebrates, so there's no skeleton under there, nor is there any sort of shell on the outside. With the exception of their beak, which is hard and, well, beak-like, an octopus is essentially a web of muscles with no particular shape. Imagine if your arms and legs were made like your tongue and you're halfway there.

This means that in addition to changing colour, the mimic octopus can radically change its shape – stretching here, puffing out there – to imitate other animals. Below, we've made a gallery of the mimic octopus' impressions, along with the animals being imitated. Can you tell which is which? The answers are on the opposite page.

BANDED SOLE   BLENNY   BRITTLE STAR   SEA SNAKE

TIL
TODAY I LEARNED

Only about a third of an octopus' brain cells are actually in its brain – the rest are dispersed throughout its body, particularly in its arms. This means that their arms can act on their own initiative, and even learn how to do things without the central brain's help.

NO TANKS!

For scientists and zookeepers, octopus intelligence can be both amazing and annoying. Put an octopus in a tank and it will do amazing things, but after a while it can become bored and start causing trouble.

In Feb 2009, for example, an octopus at the Santa Monica Pier Aquarium in Los Angeles, USA, dismantled the water recycling pipes feeding into her tank. She then redirected the flow of water to the room outside, flooding the aquarium!

Another octopus, this time at the University of Otago in New Zealand, learned to short-circuit the building's electricity by squirting jets of water into the light fittings above its tank. This was so costly to fix that the researchers eventually had to release it back into the ocean.

Most famously, in Apr 2016, an octopus called Inky at the National Aquarium of New Zealand managed a proper jailbreak, like Hank from the movie *Finding Dory* (above). When someone left the lid of his tank ajar, he squeezed through the gap, climbed down the side of the tank, crossed the floor and dropped down a drain that led directly to the sea!

Octopuses have 6 arms & 2 legs!

INSTANT EXPERT

HOW OCTOPUSES CHANGE COLOUR... The skin of the octopus is covered with special pigment cells called chromatophores. Octopuses can make these cells more or less prominent by pushing them flat against the surface of their skin (the effect is a bit like pressing a water balloon against a window). Different chromatophores contain different coloured pigments, allowing the octopus to conjure up a wide range of patterns by pushing different cells to the surface.

There is one part of this process that we still don't entirely understand: how do octopuses know what colours they need to be? While octopuses have very good vision, they're also completely colour-blind. The leading theory at the moment is that they simply see colour in a different way to other animals: a way that we don't understand.

Another, weirder possibility – raised by the presence of light-sensitive cells in the skin – is that their whole body acts like a sort of eye, sensing the colours and patterns around it.

CLOSE-UP OF COLOUR-CHANGING SKIN

CHROMATOPHORE CELL

Pigment grains

Muscle-like cell walls that can shrink or stretch the cell

An octopus' throat goes through the middle of its doughnut-shaped brain

Beak

Secondary clusters of neurons that control the arms

Banded sole: bottom, octopus: top; blenny: bottom, octopus: top; brittle star: top, octopus: bottom; sea snake: bottom, octopus: top

41

ANTARCTICA: ON THIN ICE

> Some time between 10 and 12 Jul 2017, a massive iceberg – which scientists are calling A-68 – broke off from the Larsen C Ice Shelf in Antarctica. This huge new "mega-berg" is one of the largest icebergs ever recorded by science.

Forget any images you might have of a craggy block of ice bobbing around in the ocean – Iceberg A-68 is more like a major landmass. This monster ice-island covers an area of 5,800 km² (2,239 sq mi), making it larger than 31 of the world's sovereign nations and close to the size of the US state of Delaware. It's also about 800,000 times the size of the iceberg that sank the RMS *Titanic* in 1912.

It's not just big in terms of area; ice shelves aren't like floating sea ice, they're hundreds of metres thick and anchored to glaciers on dry land. When bits break off, they make for very big icebergs. A-68 has an estimated mass of around 1 trillion tonnes.

What does this mean?
Well, first of all, it means that sailors travelling in the south Atlantic are going to need to keep their eyes open – ocean currents are going to break this mega-berg into hundreds of stadium-sized icebergs, which may drift as far north as the Falkland Islands.

In the longer term, it might threaten the stability of the whole Larsen C Ice Shelf, which covers around 50,000 km² (19,300 sq mi). This has the potential to raise sea levels worldwide, if the shelf were to break off and melt.

No one is directly monitoring this ice shelf, so we can only check on the area when a satellite/aircraft makes a pass overhead

"Calving" is the process of an iceberg detaching from a glacier into water

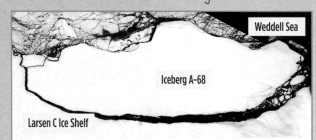

Weddell Sea

Iceberg A-68

Larsen C Ice Shelf

This NASA photograph is a "panchromatic" image taken by a weather satellite on 12 Jul 2017. It confirmed that the trillion-tonne berg had separated from the ice shelf.

⭐ FOR THE RECORD

The **largest iceberg ever** was estimated to be 31,000 km² (12,000 sq mi) in area – larger than Belgium! It was 335 km (208 mi) long and 97 km (60 mi) wide and was sighted off Scott Island in the Southern Ocean by the USS *Glacier* on 12 Nov 1956. The largest iceberg reliably assessed by satellite is B-15 (pictured), which broke off the Ross Ice Shelf in Antarctica in 2000. At around 11,000 km² (4,250 sq mi), it was slightly larger than Jamaica.

Before the shelf separated, the crack was wide enough to accommodate a football pitch!

TIL
TODAY I LEARNED

This picture was taken from an aircraft in Jan 2017. In the time between us starting these pages and finishing them, the crack finally reached the sea and the iceberg "calved" off. This was both alarming and annoying, because it meant we had to rewrite everything!

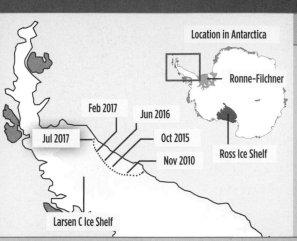

Location in Antarctica

Ronne-Filchner

Feb 2017
Jun 2016
Jul 2017
Oct 2015
Nov 2010
Ross Ice Shelf

Larsen C Ice Shelf

INSTANT EXPERT

LARSEN C ICE SHELF... It's not clear when the crack first appeared in the ice – it may have been there for decades, just not doing much. Scientists started monitoring it in 2010 after it broke through an area of flexible ice that usually stops faults spreading. By late 2016, it was clear that the crack was not going to close up on its own.

There is some controversy over whether or not this event can be attributed to climate change. The UK-based team monitoring the fault for the last few years (Swansea University's Project MIDAS) believe that it's a normal "calving" event, but others see it as part of a pattern of climate-change-related erosion.

Because the ice was already floating (and displacing water) it won't change sea levels when it melts, but if the shelf collapses, there is a risk that more ice will melt into the sea from dry land.

For the same reason that melting ice cubes don't make your glass of soda overflow

31 Jan | 17 Feb | 23 Feb | 5 Mar

Some scientists are worried that Larsen C might follow the example of its little brother, Larsen B (formerly located just up the coast), which disintegrated between Jan and Mar 2002.

The images above show the progression of Larsen B's final collapse. In the first picture you can see the ice shelf as it usually looked at the end of the Antarctic summer. The second and third images show the aftermath of several icebergs breaking away, shrinking the shelf by 800 km² (308 sq mi) and weakening what remained. The last one shows the ice shelf after it collapsed, with the shelf replaced by a sea of broken icebergs and thin sea ice.

MORE STUFF!

- No one is entirely sure how the Antarctic is being affected by climate change. Unlike in the north, where there's a straightforward, if depressing, trend towards melting ice, the Antarctic's ice levels have been fluctuating wildly from one extreme to another.
- The illustration below shows what London, UK, could look like in 2100 if sea levels rise at the rate predicted in a recent scientific paper. The authors believe that a sea-level rise of as much as 10 m (32 ft) could result from an increase in global temperatures of just 4°C (7.2°F).

The red bits will be under water if the sea level rises by 10 m

This image was created by ClimateCentral.org using data published on 12 Oct 2015 in the Proceedings of the National Academy of Sciences of the USA.

Ask a... Hurricane Hunter

Dr James McFadden is an oceanographer with the National Oceanic and Atmospheric Administration (NOAA), the US agency that monitors hurricanes and other weather phenomena. He has flown into 57 hurricanes, and is still flying in his 80s.

What drew you to a career that involves throwing yourself into something that most of us do everything we can to run away from?

I'd already done some research involving weather-monitoring aircraft by the time I finished graduate school in 1965. When I was offered the opportunity to join the Research Flight Facility, I jumped at the chance. Their aircraft were engaged in fascinating atmospheric and oceanographic research activities – including hurricane hunting – all around the globe.

Can you remember how you felt on your very first flight?

My first hurricane penetration took place in Oct 1966. I was on a research aircraft flying in the vicinity of Hurricane Inez, which had just entered the Gulf of Mexico.

We only performed one pass. It was a relatively weak storm, so I was a bit underwhelmed by the lack of turbulence. This, of course, was to change in future years!

What does a typical hurricane mission involve?

The transit to the storm is comfortable but a bit noisy because of our aircraft's turbo-prop engines. Each crew member and scientist has a seat in front of an array of instruments and controls.

Once we get to what's called the initial point, or "IP" – our starting point on the edge of the storm – everyone's attention turns to their particular roles. This is a very busy time, especially for the flight crew – the two pilots, flight engineer, navigator and flight meteorologist. They have to guide the aircraft safely, through turbulence and high winds, into the eye of the storm.

What's that like?

Entering the eyewall is the moment of truth. It may take only a minute or two to get through the wall, but it is a time when the adrenalin flows. The plane is buffeted by a combination of updrafts and downdrafts that alternately press you deep into your chair then pull you tight against your harness.

Occasionally this severe turbulence is accompanied by lightning, which serves only to heighten the fear. Flying into a hurricane at night is especially nerve-wracking as you can see nothing outside the aircraft unless it's illuminated by lightning strikes.

Once you're through the turbulent eyewall, the ride becomes very smooth as the winds die down to zero. The eye of a well-developed storm is truly breathtaking – you see a clear, blue sky over a giant ring of twisting clouds. It's like being in a massive circular football stadium. It's well worth the rocky road through the eyewall to see.

Once you're in the storm, what does the aircraft do?

Each flight pattern consists of a series of penetrations of the hurricane. We fly through the eyewall into the eye, then back out the other side. The crew then flies around the hurricane and performs another pass at a roughly 90° angle to the first. Drawn on a map, these legs resemble a figure "4".

Once this is done, we typically fly a little farther and repeat the figure-4 pattern at a 45° angle to the first two passes. Usually by the end of this second pattern it's time to climb up above the storm clouds and return to base.

What sort of instruments do you have on board?

NOAA's hurricane-hunting aircraft carry a whole host of instruments that can collect data on every aspect of the environment in a storm. This includes everything from conditions under the ocean surface to wind speeds in the highest clouds.

The most distinctive tool we've got on our aircraft is the

🤯 INSTANT EXPERT

THE PERFECT STORM... Hurricanes form over warm tropical waters when the winds whip water droplets into a rising column of hot air. The rising air creates an area of low pressure at sea level, which sucks more air in. This vortex, called a "tropical depression", starts to spin as it grows, creating a whirling mass of storm clouds. When the wind speeds inside the depression pass 63 km/h (39 mph) the storm is classified as a "tropical storm", and when they get past 119 km/h (74 mph) it becomes a "tropical cyclone" – also called a hurricane (when it forms over the Atlantic) or a typhoon (when it forms over the Pacific).

The NOAA's two Orions are called Miss Piggy and Kermit the Frog

Dr McFadden is involved in planning for the future of hurricane prediction. This includes helping to train the next generation of hurricane hunters and develop the technology they will use.

For most of his career, Dr McFadden has flown in a specialized hurricane-hunting aircraft called the WP-3D Orion. The NOAA has two of these rugged planes, which are loaded with weather radars and meteorological equipment. The blue line in the inset picture below shows the flight path for a typical mission, outlining the curving approach and the straight-line dive through the centre of the storm.

huge C-band radar mounted in a fairing under the fuselage. This allows us to map the wind field in the storm from sea level to the cloud-tops.

Each aircraft has lots of other sensors as well. These include cloud-particle sampling devices and "dropsondes" – these are small buoys that are dropped through the storm to measure the temperature and pressure layers in the storm, or in the currents in the ocean below.

All the information from these sensors is then relayed by a satellite communications system to weather centres on the ground.

How has the technology evolved since you started?
In the 50-plus years I've been flying into hurricanes, the technology has improved tremendously. It's hard to believe now, but there were no computers on board when I started! All calculations had to be done using graphs or slide rules.

The instrumentation and communications gear used glowing-hot vacuum tubes and could only relay a few important bits of information; most of the rest of the data could only be studied once we got back to base.

How is the data that hurricane hunters collect used?
The data we gather is distributed to forecast centres or assimilated into models with the intent of improving the forecasts. Every hurricane we fly through gives the research community more to work with in its continuing efforts to better understand the dynamics of storms – what makes them tick – and to improve the models to achieve more accurate forecasts.

What's the worst thing that has gone wrong during a flight for you?
Our first flight into Hurricane Hugo on 15 Sep 1989 was pretty bad. We were expecting a Category 2 storm [from

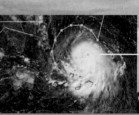

The rotating clouds of the eyewall

The relatively calm clouds of the eye

The data-gathering pass through the storm starts here

satellite observations], but what we encountered was a far stronger hurricane than expected: a Category 5.

We encountered extreme turbulence in the eyewall and wind speeds that exceeded 180 knots [333 km/h; 207 mph]. The plane was subjected to forces of around 5.6 g – more

than twice its design limit! In addition to the turbulence, in the middle of the eyewall one of the engines suffered a catastrophic failure and had to be shut down. On three engines, the plane had a tough time climbing in the eye to find a safe way out of the storm, but we finally made it.

WEIRD WORLD

This weather probe is called a "barber's pole sampler", on account of its red and white stripes

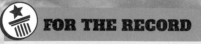

FOR THE RECORD

The 2005 hurricane season was a doozy. The NOAA recorded 28 tropical storms, 12 of which turned into hurricanes – the **most hurricanes in a single season**.

The most damaging of these was Hurricane Katrina (inset), which made landfall over New Orleans on 20 Aug (after smashing its way across Florida). Katrina's storm surge over-topped New Orleans' flood

defences, inundating the city (flood damage, right). In total, the storm killed 1,245 people and did $108 bn (£58 bn) of damage, making it the **costliest tropical cyclone**.

New Orleans

Florida

Cuba

I DIDN'T KNOW THAT!

Stinkfruit

The durian is an odd-looking fruit native to Southeast Asia. Its flavour is an acquired taste – many find it overpowering – but it pales in comparison to its smell. Raw durian has been described as smelling like a mixture of sewage, rotting onions and sweat. The fruits smell so bad that bringing them on public transport is illegal in many countries!

Alien island

Cut off from the rest of the world, life on remote islands can get really strange. These bizarre trees are the result of a few million years of adaptation to the harsh climate of Socotra, an island off the coast of Yemen. The trees pictured on the left and right have bulbous trunks that store water, while the central tree (the wonderfully named dragon's blood tree) has a dense canopy that acts as a sunshade.

Q: CAN I SLEEP IN MY TREEHOUSE?

A: Well, you can if it looks like this one! This 97-ft-tall (29.5-m) mansion – the world's **tallest treehouse** – was built from mostly recycled wood around a group of oak trees by landscaper-turned-minister Horace Burgess. The amazing – if somewhat rickety-looking – building stands in an area of woodland near Crossville, Tennessee, USA.

Horace built the 10-storey, 80-room treehouse over the course of about 20 years, with no particular plan in mind. It started after he claimed he'd had a vision telling him God wanted it done, so he just built as his feelings moved him.

Sailing stones

This isn't an optical illusion, or a trick of wind erosion; these rocks, located on Racetrack Playa in California, USA, really do move! Various theories have been put forward over the years to explain how, including pranksters, mini-tornadoes and flooding. The mystery was finally solved in 2014, when researchers set up cameras around the remote lake and fitted some rocks with GPS sensors. It turns out that the dry lake floods with a few centimetres of water during the winter, and that thin layers of ice form on top. These sheets of ice are blown around by the wind, building up against the rocks and pushing them along. The **longest sailing stone trail** on record was 880 m (2,887 ft), created by a rock nicknamed "Diane". Of course...

At up to 1,000 km (620 mi) long and 1 km (0.6 mi) high, these are the largest roll clouds

IT'S RAINING FISH!

They sound like the stuff of legend, but rains of fish, frogs or shrimp are well-documented phenomena. They're not entirely understood, but the most likely explanation is that waterspouts – which form during storms and are similar to the tornado pictured below – suck up the creatures while travelling over seas or lakes, then drop them over land.

WHAT'S THE STORY [WITH] MORNING GLORY?

If you head to the Gulf of Carpentaria in Northern Australia, there's a good chance you'll see some very strange clouds. These things, known as Morning Glory, are a variant of a formation called an arcus cloud, each created by a single powerful pressure wave moving through the air. These massive waves, like big waves in the sea, attract their own surfers: glider pilots flock to the area to ride the wild winds that wrap around the clouds as they move along. Their formation is a bit mysterious, but it seems to be associated with the collision of two different pressure systems.

To... I've a feeling we're not in Kansas any more

Woof woof Texas)

THE TORNADO CAPITAL OF THE WORLD

The USA records more tornadoes every year than any other nation on Earth, with the largest share of them touching down in the state of Texas. Since 1950, Texas has had more than 8,500 tornadoes, including 48 rated EF-4 (with winds of 165 mph/265 km/h) and five rated EF-5 (winds of 200 mph/322 km/h and above).

THE TECHNOSPHERE

Over the centuries, humans have built up a crust of concrete, metal and plastic on the surface of the Earth. It's not a particularly significant layer in geological terms, but at an estimated 30 trillion tonnes (33 trillion tons) it's big enough to warrant its own name: the Technosphere. According to geologists – who work with unimaginably long time-scales (hundreds of millions of years) – everything humanity has built will one day form a layer of "technofossils" beneath the Earth's surface.

HOLLYWOOD

BEWARE THE ARKSTORM! There's a lot to be said for the theory that California is a trap; it lures people in with sunshine and natural beauty, then hits them with earthquakes, wildfires and supervolcanoes. Recently another potential natural disaster was added to the list of things for Californians to worry about: the ARkStorm. This is an extreme version of a Californian weather pattern called an atmospheric river, which creates a conveyor belt of storms, bringing heavy rain to the state. The ARkStorm is an atmospheric river big enough to turn California's central valley into an inland sea up to 20 ft (6 m) deep. Something similar happened in the 1860s, back when California was mostly uninhabited.

A CAVE OF ICE AND FIRE

This picture was taken from one of the many ice caves that dot the surface of the Vatnajökull glacier in Iceland. These caves are melted out of the ice by the heat from volcanic vents and hot springs. In 1996, the Vatnajökull glacier's location over a geothermally active area earned it the title of **fastest-melting glacier**. The Grímsvötn volcano erupted under the ice sheet, creating an effect like lighting a fire in a freezer, producing some 45,000 m³ (1.58 million cu ft) – or about 18 Olympic-sized swimming pools – of meltwater every second!

HEAVIEST HUMANS

Being obese (very overweight) is bad for you. We all know this. So why do our bodies often seem to want to pack on the pounds, and what is fat anyway?

On 18 Dec 2016, 32-year-old Juan Pedro Franco Salas (MEX, right) weighed an astonishing 594.8 kg (1,311 lb 4.9 oz), making him the **heaviest man living**. For context, 594 kg is almost 10 times the weight of the average adult male, and would even be a little on the heavy side for a grizzly bear.

Juan Pedro is an extreme case, obviously, but obesity – the term for when a person has accumulated enough excess body fat that it has a negative effect on their health – is becoming more of a problem every year. It's estimated that about 12% of the world's population is now obese.

For Juan Pedro, who is now being treated – he'd lost 170 kg (374 lb) as of May 2017 – health problems may be avoidable, but others aren't so lucky. The **heaviest man ever** – American Jon Brower Minnoch (who weighed 1,400 lb/635 kg) – died when he was just 41.

INSTANT EXPERT

UNDER THE SKIN... Our bodies create fat when we take in more energy (from food) than we currently need. We take that energy and transform it into fat, which is then stored in special cells – called adipocytes – distributed throughout our bodies.

This mechanism was vital for early humans, whose food came from unreliable sources such as hunting. Our fat stores meant that we could survive a few days of failed hunts, running on the energy we'd stored as fat during easier times.

Today, most of us have access to reliable supplies of energy-dense foods, and don't do nearly as much exercise as our bodies are set up for. This means that unless we're careful, this useful safety feature starts working against us, storing more fat than we need and putting strain on our organs.

Hair
Sweat pores
Skin
Epidermis
Sweat gland
Dermis
Hypodermis
Blood vessels
Fat cells (adipocytes)
Hair follicle
Sensory receptors

PAULINE POTTER

The **heaviest woman living** is Pauline Potter (USA), who weighed 643 lb (293.6 kg) when she was measured in Jul 2012. Pauline attributes her weight to the trauma of a period during her childhood when she regularly had to go hungry.

Large though she is, Pauline would be dwarfed by the **heaviest woman ever**, Rosalie Bradford (USA), who weighed some 1,200 lb (544 kg) at her heaviest in Jan 1987.

FOR THE RECORD

The **heaviest person to complete a marathon** is Charles Bungert (USA), who ran the 2013 Los Angeles Marathon in 8 hr 23 min 40 sec. This isn't a great time – for context, the current record for **fastest marathon carrying a household appliance** (a tumble dryer) is 5 hr 58 min 37 sec – but it *is* impressive for someone who weighs 427 lb 9 oz (193.9 kg). Charles' training included drinking peanut-butter smoothies so that he'd weigh more than the previous record holder, sumo wrestler Kelly Gneiting (USA).

TIL
TODAY I LEARNED

Humans are the only primates with subcutaneous fat – a feature more commonly seen in marine mammals. The lack of subcutaneous fat is why chimps and gorillas have such wrinkly skin on their faces and hands – ours would be too if we weren't all padded underneath.

+ MORE *STUFF!*

- Despite what you might have been told, exercising a specific area of your body does not burn fat in that area. The energy burned by lifting weights with your arms, for example, comes from fat cells all over your body.
- Some people put on weight more easily and quickly than others, but it's not clear why this is. Scientists have identified a few genes that seem to go along with weight gain, but they're not sure how those genes are involved.
- Men and women put on weight in different ways. Men tend to accumulate most of their fat in their abdominal cavity, while in women it goes to the subcutaneous tissue.

INSTANT EXPERT

BODY FAT... It's healthy for your body to have a certain amount of fat stored up, but there are different types of fat. Brown fat, derived from muscle cells, is used to burn calories and keep us warm, while white fat is "padding" just under the skin (subcutaneous fat) and around our internal organs (visceral fat). Subcutaneous fat serves as an energy store, thermal insulation and gives us our smooth skin (see TIL, left). Visceral fat is worse for us due to the toxins it stores, flowing directly from the surrounding organs into the liver. It's also difficult to surgically remove, owing to its proximity to major organs. Both types of white fat can be seen in the cross-sections of an obese and healthy person below.

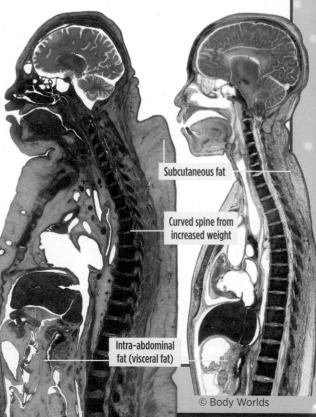

Subcutaneous fat

Curved spine from increased weight

Intra-abdominal fat (visceral fat)

© Body Worlds

That's a person

So is that

TREE-MENDOUS

There are around 3 trillion trees on Earth today, ranging from tiny saplings to Hyperion, the **tallest living tree**, which is the same height as a 30-storey building and has been growing since the Middle Ages.

The title of **tallest living tree** changes hands (well, branches) surprisingly often, considering how long it takes for anything to grow that big. A big tree might weaken with age and fall down in the wind, while a smaller tree might undergo a growth spurt. It's even possible that another previously unknown giant might be found by an intrepid explorer.

The golden age of colossal trees has probably passed (it ended around the time we started chopping them down), but there's still enough wilderness out there for these majestic giants to reach awe-inspiring proportions.

How do you measure the world's **tallest tree**? The answer is surprisingly low-tech: you climb to the top and then you drop a tape measure to the ground. That's exactly what botanist Steve Sillett (pictured) and his research team did back in 2006.

🜨 HYPERION

The sapling that would one day become the **tallest living tree** put down roots near Redwood Creek, in what is now northern California, USA, around 600 years ago. Hyperion is a coastal redwood, typically taller and thinner than inland redwoods (giant sequoias) such as General Sherman (see below).

Hyperion was one of the millions of trees in the old-growth forests that once covered northern California. It survived the intensive logging of the 19th and early 20th centuries by being very hard to get to, and since 1978 has been protected by the rangers of the US National Park Service.

The tree was discovered in 2006 by two tall-tree experts, Chris Atkins and Michael Taylor, and found to be 115.5 m (379 ft) tall when it was measured later that year (see above).

Hyperion has more than 500 million leaves. Based on its current growth rate of 1.5 in (3.9 cm) per year, it will hold on to its record until the 2030s, when it will be overtaken by a smaller but faster-growing redwood named Paradox.

HOW DO TREES GET SO BIG?

The trees of California grow into giants because the conditions there are perfect.

Firstly, there's a lot of rain – as much as 350 cm (140 in) every year. And the temperature is just right – typically 7-16°C (45-61°F) year-round. The soil is also extremely rich.

Redwood trees also benefit from a unique adaptation to their environment. Their upper leaves are able to absorb water from mist and fog, reducing the amount of liquid that has to be sucked up from the ground (which uses a lot of energy).

FOR THE RECORD

It's technically a shrub

DANGER
Fruit from the Manchineel Tree is poisonous. Handling leaves and bark may irritate skin and eyes

Trees are nice and peaceful, right? Well, not always. The manchineel tree of Central America, Florida and the Caribbean oozes a sap so toxic that just standing under it in a rainstorm can give you chemical burns! When coupled with its deadly fruits (which look like apples but taste like burning), this sap has earned the tree the title of **most dangerous tree.**

It's not the only killer tree, however. The New Zealand tree nettle has the **most dangerous stinger** in the plant world. Its hair-like stingers contain a powerful neurotoxin that has been known to kill dogs, horses and, on at least one occasion, a person.

FOR THE RECORD

GENERAL SHER

Hyperion may be the **tallest tree,** but it's not the **largest.** That title goes to General Sherman, located near Trinidad in California. The General is 82.6 m (271 ft) tall and 8.2 m (26 ft 10 in) wide at its base. The trunk contains some 1,530 m³ (54,000 cu ft) of timber – enough for about 5 billion matches, if you were mean enough to cut it down.

The **largest tree ever** was the Lindsay Creek tree, which had a volume of 2,550 m³ (90,000 cu ft) when it blew down in a storm in 1905.

+ MORE *STUFF!*

- There is only one known example of the ancient tree species *Encephalartos woodii*: it's male, and as there are no known females, it may be the last of its kind.
- Guinness World Records monitors many giant tree categories, a few of which we've illustrated below.

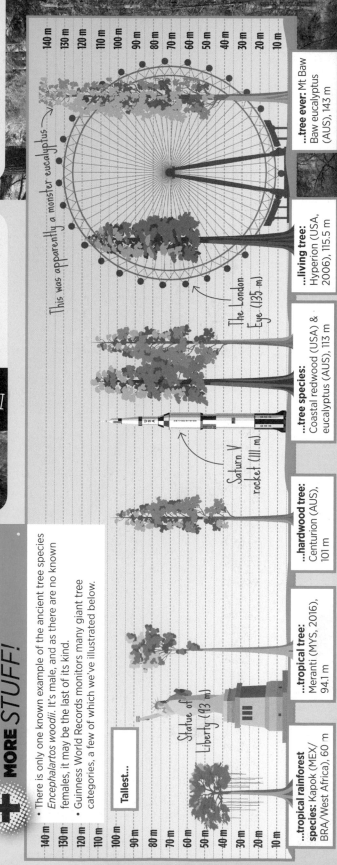

This was apparently a monster eucalyptus

The London Eye (135 m)

Saturn V rocket (111 m)

Statue of Liberty (93 m)

Tallest...

...tree ever: Mt Baw Baw eucalyptus (AUS), 143 m

...living tree: Hyperion (USA, 2006), 115.5 m

...tree species: Coastal redwood (USA) & eucalyptus (AUS), 113 m

...hardwood tree: Centurion (AUS), 101 m

...tropical tree: Meranti (MYS, 2016), 94.1 m

...tropical rainforest species: Kapok (MEX/ BRA/West Africa), 60 m

140 m
130 m
120 m
110 m
100 m
90 m
80 m
70 m
60 m
50 m
40 m
30 m
20 m
10 m

MONSTER WAVES

In 2016, meteorologists confirmed the height of the tallest wave ever measured by instruments: an impressive 19 m (62 ft). But some waves are just too big to measure, which means even this record-breaker was just a ripple by comparison...

For thousands of years, sailors have been returning to port with stories of ship-eating sea monsters, mile-wide whirlpools and beautiful mermaids. Most of their stories were clearly rubbish – half-woman, half-fish?! – but no one knew enough about what happened at sea to prove them wrong.

Today, in the age of aircraft, satellites and smartphones, we like to think we've conquered the mysteries of the oceans: mermaids aren't real, nor are giant maelstroms (the **most**

powerful natural whirlpool – the Moskstraumen in Norway – is "only" 50 m wide, or 164 ft). And while there's no shortage of sea monsters (see pp.130–31), we're pretty sure none of them can eat ships.

There is one question that still remains unanswered, though – how big can waves get? Sailors have long told tales of skyscraper waves that could swamp even the biggest vessels, or ship-smashing "rogue" waves that come out of nowhere. The more we learn

about the oceans, the more plausible these stories seem.

The record announced in 2016 by the World Meteorological Organization doesn't sound devastating – it wouldn't even have reached the toes of the Statue of Liberty (see #2 below) – but it was only the tallest wave to be officially *measured*. When it comes to *estimated* wave heights, such as the record-breakers listed here, we're looking at much more extreme phenomena. Surf's up!

In certain parts of the world, occasional extreme tides create a phenomenon called "tidal bores" – large waves that flow *up* a river.

The **largest tidal bore** occurs on the Qiantang River in China. Tiny tidal bores occur with every high tide, but occasional strong tides (called spring tides) create waves as high as 9 m (30 ft) that travel upstream at 40 km/h (25 mph). Tourists come to watch these waves, but sometimes get more than they bargained for – as happened in 2011 (above).

2

On 4 Feb 2013, sustained wind speeds of 80 km/h (50 mph) whipped an area of the North Atlantic into a series of 19-m (62-ft 4-in) waves. The only witness to this storm was Automatic Weather Station K5 (above). In Dec 2016, after a long review process, the World Meteorological Organization confirmed this as the **greatest significant wave height**.

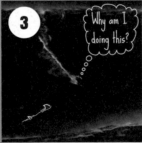

3

Why am I doing this?

As they approach the shore, waves get pushed up and amplified by the rising sea-floor. This effect creates the massive cresting waves that surfers love. The **tallest wave surfed** was this 23.77-m (78-ft) giant, which professional surfer Garrett McNamara (USA) tackled (after being towed in by a jet-ski) off the coast of Praia do Norte in Nazaré, Portugal, on 1 Nov 2011.

4

On 1 Jan 1995, a 25.6-m (83-ft 11-in) wave smashed into the Draupner oil rig in the North Sea. The wave appeared out of nowhere, and was more than twice the height of the waves that came before and after. This was the **first proven "rogue wave"**, finally confirming the existence of a terrifying phenomenon that sailors had been reporting for centuries.

5

The **highest wave** credibly reported is a 34-m (112-ft) monster seen by Lt Frederic Margraff of the USS *Ramapo* on 6–7 Feb 1933. This wave was encountered as the ship passed through a typhoon (example pictured) with winds of 126 km/h (78 mph) while travelling from the Philippines to the USA.

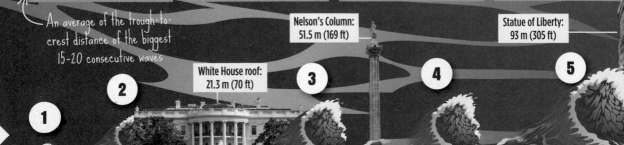

↖ An average of the trough-to-crest distance of the biggest 15–20 consecutive waves

Nelson's Column: 51.5 m (169 ft)

Statue of Liberty: 93 m (305 ft)

White House roof: 21.3 m (70 ft)

1 **2** **3** **4** **5**

6

CN Tower: 553 m (1,814 ft)

6

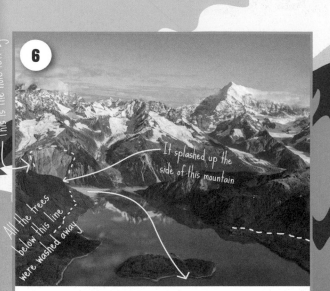

This is the hole left by the landslide

It splashed up the side of this mountain

All the trees below this line were washed away

The **highest tsunami wash** occurred in Lituya Bay, Alaska, USA, on the evening of 9 Jul 1958. A massive landslide at the far end of the bay sent a skyscraper-sized mass of rock and earth crashing into the water. In the enclosed space of the bay, this had an effect like dropping a car in a backyard pool – the water surged up the side of the mountain on the opposite side, reaching a height of 524 m (1,719 ft) before it subsided.

The shockwave also sent a 150-ft-high (45-m) tsunami wave along the bay. This wave picked up two small fishing boats, snapping their anchor chains like string and carrying them out to sea. The captain of one boat reported looking down on treetops as his boat surfed the giant wave!

WEIRD WORLD

INSTANT EXPERT

MEASURING WAVES... We measure wave heights by taking the distance from the bottom of a wave's trough to the top of its crest. However, getting wave heights correct is surprisingly difficult. This is because there's no baseline to measure the waves against (sea level changes with air pressure). Even the best instruments often get confused when they're being thrown around by a storm.

The World Meteorological Organization prefers to measure an average of wave heights over a given period, because it's impossible to say where individual wave measurements are real or just instrument errors.

Crest

Wave length

Wave height

Still water level

Trough

Seabed

FOR THE RECORD

Regular waves build up slowly as the wind pushes the water around, whereas tsunamis happen suddenly when something shoves a large volume of water out of the way. This can be a landslide (as happened at Lituya Bay – see #6) or an earthquake raising the seabed. The fact that they appear without warning makes them particularly dangerous. On 26 Dec 2004, an earthquake under the sea near Indonesia caused a tsunami (pictured below) that killed at least 228,000 people – the **highest death toll from a tsunami**.

Ask a...
Deep-Sea Explorer

In 1960, Don Walsh (USA) was one of the two-man crew who plunged 10,911 m (35,797 ft) as part of the **deepest manned descent**. The intrepid voyage took them to one of the last unexplored places on Earth.

Captain Don Walsh is Honorary President of The Explorers Club – an organization dedicated to the pursuit of exploration of land, sea, air and space.

How did you get involved with this groundbreaking project?
The US Navy purchased *Trieste* from the Piccards in 1958. It was brought to the Naval Electronics Laboratory [NEL] in San Diego, California, USA, later that year. NEL was chosen over other waterfront Navy laboratories as there was access to deep water just offshore. Jacques Piccard – son of the bathyscaphe's inventor – was hired to teach the US Navy how to operate and maintain the submersible.

At the time, I was a serving submarine officer in San Diego. We got a radio message asking for volunteers for the *Trieste* project. I volunteered and was accepted, along with another submarine lieutenant.

What training did you do?
Since there were only two bathyscaphes in the world at that time (the French Navy had the other one), my training was more of an apprenticeship under the direction of Jacques. That said, as a qualified submarine officer, I had a good general knowledge of undersea systems.

What pressure did the vessel have to withstand?
As purchased from the Piccards, *Trieste* was capable of diving to about 20,000 ft [6,000 m]. But because the Navy's plan was to take it to the deepest place in the ocean [~11,000 m; ~36,000 ft], we had to significantly modify it.

This included getting a new sphere [cabin] to cope with the greater pressure. In addition, the "float" [balloon] had to be enlarged to give us more buoyancy. The sub needed to withstand a pressure of about 16 tons per square inch [or 2,180 atmospheres].

After all our operational and mission equipment was installed, the interior of the sphere was quite small. Our two-person crew had about the same space as a large household refrigerator – and the temperature inside was about the same as a fridge too!

Tell us about the descent.
The dive took nine hours: about five hours going down,

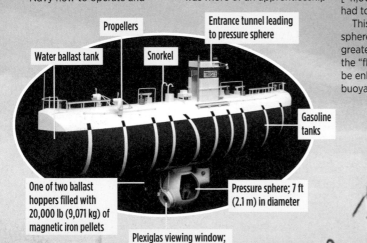

Propellers

Entrance tunnel leading to pressure sphere

Water ballast tank

Snorkel

Gasoline tanks

One of two ballast hoppers filled with 20,000 lb (9,071 kg) of magnetic iron pellets

Pressure sphere; 7 ft (2.1 m) in diameter

Plexiglas viewing window; 5.9 in (14.9 cm) thick

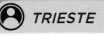

⊖ *TRIESTE*

Built by Jacques' father, Auguste Piccard, *Trieste* was launched in 1953, then sold to the US Navy five years later. A bathyscaphe is a deep-sea sub with a pressure sphere positioned under a "float" filled with gasoline. It works a bit like an underwater Zeppelin balloon, except that it uses tanks of water and metal pellets to control buoyancy, rather then gas.

FOR THE RECORD

After a series of progressively deeper test dives in the Pacific Ocean to check the *Trieste*'s instruments, Don Walsh and Jacques Piccard (CHE) took the ultimate plunge on 23 Jan 1960. After a five-hour journey, they finally neared the bottom of the Challenger Deep (see Instant Expert). At 10,911 m (35,797 ft) below the surface, their dive remains the **deepest manned descent** to this day.

More than 50 years after Walsh and Piccard's milestone dive, movie director and adventurer James Cameron (CAN) followed in their wake. On board the *Deepsea Challenger*, he took two hours to plunge 10,898 m (35,755 ft) into the Challenger Deep – the **deepest solo manned descent**. Walsh (above right) was part of the 2012 expedition, sharing his invaluable first-hand expertise with Cameron and his team.

20 minutes on the bottom and the rest returning to the surface. Going down, the speed was much slower in case we encountered an unknown geographic obstruction.

How did it feel to reach the deepest part of the ocean where no human had been?
I think the first "feeling" was that our small team [14 people] had done what we set out to. So as the Navy representative of *Trieste*, I was proud of my team.

Of course, Jacques was proud that a manned submersible he and his father had built had reached the deepest point in the ocean, with a Piccard on board.

Just before we landed, we did see what appeared to be a fish just below us. That has been a matter of controversy ever since. Some biologists don't think a high-order marine vertebrate would be found at such depths.

They may be right. Neither Jacques nor I were marine scientists. We were engineer "test pilots" to ensure the submersible was reliable and safe for use by scientists.

After touching down, our visibility was completely obscured by bottom sediment stirred up by our landing. It was so fine that even after

20 minutes we couldn't see to take pictures, so we decided to return to the surface.

You didn't have the advantage of modern technology – what instruments did you have?
It was all pretty primitive back then. We had various gauges to monitor systems such as life support and battery usage, etc. Communications were via voice-modulated sonar – similar to those used between a submarine and a ship. We had no hard-wire connection to the surface.

As we learned the *Trieste*'s capabilities, we developed various sensors, imagers and samplers. Since there were only two manned bathyscaphes at that time,

there weren't catalogues of equipment or even companies making it. We had to design and build what we needed.

How was the return and seeing your team at the surface?
A great relief after a year of hard work to prepare *Trieste* for the ultimate dive and then to actually do it. At Guam, our team put in seven-day weeks and 10–12 hours each day. But it was all worth it.

What's the legacy of your record-setting dive?
There was the general

excitement of conquering one of the last geographic frontiers in the world. It's impossible to measure how what we did may have encouraged young people to become explorers, scientists or engineers.

More specifically, our "fingerprints" can be found in most undersea vehicles – manned and unmanned – today. It's great to be at a trade show seeing equipment on a new submersible and thinking, "Yeah, we made the first one of those 50-plus years ago."

INSTANT EXPERT

THE CHALLENGER DEEP... Part of the much larger Mariana Trench in the western Pacific, the Challenger Deep is a gently sloped depression in the sea floor. At almost 11 km (7 mi) down, it is the **deepest point in the ocean**. If Mount Everest were dropped inside the Challenger Deep, its summit would still sit 2.1 km (1.3 mi) beneath the surface!

Everest is the world's **highest mountain**, standing 8,848 m (29,029 ft) above sea level

The Mariana Trench is a 2,550-km-long (1,584-mi) marine canyon. It forms the border between two tectonic plates

Everest and the Mariana Trench don't really sit next to each other – they're more than 6,000 km apart – but this helps to illustrate Earth's highest and lowest points

9 km
8 km
7 km
6 km
5 km
4 km
3 km
2 km
1 km
0
1 km
2 km
3 km
4 km
5 km
6 km
7 km
8 km
9 km
10 km
11 km

Located at the bottom of the Mariana Trench, the Challenger Deep lies 10,994 m (36,070 ft) below the surface (according to the latest data)

CORPSE FLOWER:
THE STINKIEST PLANT

Roses are red, violets are blue, and the corpse flower stinks of dead bodies and poo... This giant bloom, as tall as a phone box, attracts insects by smelling of decomposing flesh. Find out why the **smelliest plants** evolved their record-breaking reek!

The spadix (flower-bearing spike) is a dull yellow-green and hollow in the middle

The corpse flower – aka *Amorphophallus titanum* or *titan arum* – is not the kind of flower you should give to your mum...

For one thing, they're massive, measuring some 3 m (9 ft 10 in) tall. They're also not the kind of blooms you can pick up at your local florist. In the wild, they are only found in the dense rainforest on the Indonesian island of Sumatra.

But there's another more potent reason you shouldn't give a corpse flower to a loved one: they stink of rotting flesh. The whiff is so rank that it can be detected 0.5 mi (0.8 km) away!

While *eau de corpse* may not appeal to us, it's *very* attractive to flies and dung beetles, who are fooled into thinking these flowers are a great place to lay their eggs. Little do the bugs know that they are actually ensuring the next generation of *titan arum* by pollinating their flowers.

The interior of the spathe is deep red and textured to look like flesh (yum...)

Once insects have pollinated the flowers, fleshy fruits develop; these will be eaten by birds, with the seeds dispersed in their poo!

The spathe is a modified leaf that protects the spadix, like a natural cloak

The orange berries of *titan arum* are poisonous to humans, though some scientists believe they could hold the cure to "sleeping sickness" – a disease that claims thousands of lives in Africa every year (see p.146).

At the base of the spadix, there are female flowers (red) and pollen-producing male flowers (yellow)

Nature stinks!

TIL
TODAY I LEARNED

What we call the "flower" of this plant is technically an "unbranched inflorescence", or flowering structure. This comprises tiny blooms as well as the stem that bears them. The key parts are the "spadix" (the spike) and a "spathe" (the petal-like leaf that surrounds the spike).

Amorphophallus titanum
Titan arum, corpse flower
Sumatra

INSTANT EXPERT

CORPSE FLOWER LIFE CYCLE... As you'd expect, producing a flower as big and as stinky as this takes a *lot* of energy. That's why *titan arum* only blooms once every four to five years.

The cycle begins with a "corm", which is something of a cross between a bulb and a tuber that lives underground. These normally weigh about 50 kg (110 lb) – though the largest ever weighed 117 kg (257 lb 15 oz) – and the corpse flower has the **largest corms** of all.

Most years, the plant sends up a single leaf (with many "leaflets") that stands as tall as a small tree. Over several years, via photosynthesis, the corpse flower builds up a store of energy in its corm.

When a flower finally unfurls, it only has one to two days to attract pollinators before it starts to die.

...R THE RECORD

Another funky-smelling bloom known as a "corpse flower" is *Rafflesia arnoldii*. This plant from south-east Asia grows as a parasite on jungle vines, from which the rancid flower buds burst out. With a petal span of some 91 cm (2 ft 11 in) and a weight of 11 kg (24 lb 4 oz), these fleshy blooms are the **largest single flowers** on any plant.

Leaf can reach 6 m (19 ft 8 in) tall

After 12–18 months, the leaf dies back. It will repeat this cycle for several years

The corm produces its first flower bud after 7–10 years

The "bracts" (purple leaves) peel back and the spathe loosens

Flower starts to wither after just 24–36 hr

Berries form on the base of the spadix, where they will be picked off by birds; they, in turn, spread the seeds in their droppings

Corm produces a spike

The leaf divides into leaflets to absorb sunlight. Glucose produced is stored in the corm

Corm enters a period of dormancy

The bloom grows a few inches per day

Flower unfurls, letting in bugs for pollination

The spathe and upper spadix die back

INSTANT EXPERT

RECIPE OF THE REEK... A number of scientists have tried to pin down the exact combination of chemicals responsible for the corpse flower's superlative stench. The Huntington Botanical Gardens in California, USA, helpfully likened the chemicals to everyday smelly objects we can identify with:

Gone-off beer (isovaleric acid)

Sweaty feet (isovaleric acid)

Limburger cheese (dimethyl trisulphide)

Rotting fish (trimethylamine)

Cooked onions (dimethyl trisulphide)

Garlic (dimethyl disulphide)

MORE *STUFF!*

- Italian botanist Odoardo Beccari was the first European to discover this unusual plant, during a tour of Asia in 1878.
- In 2016, the Eden Project gardens in Cornwall, UK, developed a new male perfume called "Eau de Titan", derived from the world's **smelliest plant**.
- The sporadic nature of the plant's flowering patterns means that it always receives a lot of attention in botanical collections. In 1926, the UK's Kew Gardens had to call in the police to control the crowds!
- The original Latin name for this plant is *Amorphophallus titanum*, which translates as... well, let's just say something that naturalist Sir David Attenborough (right) preferred not to say on TV in the 1990s! For this reason, he coined a new, less embarrassing name: *titan arum*.

It means giant misshapen penis!

GIANT MUTANT VEGETABLES

Farmers and green-fingered gardeners have been creating freakish (and wonderful) mutants for centuries – without any genetic modification. But how do you take produce to the next level?

It may sound like the title of a horror movie, but giant mutant vegetables are very much real – and they're a *very* serious business. Mastering the art of growing super-veg can take years, but there are a few tricks to get you started.

It all begins with selecting varieties with "bigness" coded into their genes. Even this can take years of trial and error, so a shortcut is to get your hands on the seeds of proven record-breaking produce.

Like any monsters, giant vegetables have monstrous appetites. Enrich the soil with nutrients using compost or manure (record-breaking can be dirty work). Water regularly and be sure to use the right fertilizer (e.g., pumpkins are partial to potassium).

You want the plant to put all its energy into just two or three fruit, so pick off any others early. Don't forget to look out for pests – even monsters need looking after when they're growing up.

The new record pumpkin weighed roughly the same as a small family car!

⬤ FOR THE RECORD

On 9 Oct 2016, Belgian farmer Mathias Willemijns (right) set a new giant veg record with his 1,190-kg (2,624-lb) pumpkin. This super-squash surpassed the previous **heaviest pumpkin** by more than 100 kg (220 lb). The record was verified by the Great Pumpkin Commonwealth in Ludwigsburg, Germany.

This pumpkin was the result of seeds created by cross-breeding several generations of prize-winning specimens. It was then grown in a climate-controlled greenhouse with daily checks on moisture levels and soil nutrients.

Ian beet all the competition...

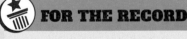

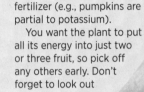

MORE STUFF!

According to the Chinese Academy of Sciences, one way to super-size your veg is to fly the seeds to space. In 2006, China sent 2,000 seeds to orbit in the *Shijian-8* satellite, where they spent two weeks circling Earth. Back home, the healthiest germinated seeds were grown out. The out-of-this-world plants all bore mega-fruit (like the pumpkin below). Why is unknown, but it may be due to micro-gravity and cosmic radiation...

WEIRD WORLD

INSTANT EXPERT

LOCATION, LOCATION, LOCATION... Britain has traditionally dominated the monster vegetable world: around two-thirds of GWR's gargantuan gardening records have been set in the UK. In recent years, however, an unlikely new powerhouse has emerged in the big

veg world: the frigid US state of Alaska. Despite experiencing 24-hr darkness in winter, and temperatures that stay well below freezing from November to March, the Alaska State Fair has become one of the most hotly contested events in the giant veg calendar.

Alaskan growers such as Scott Robb (above, third from left), who holds five

Guinness World Records titles, including **heaviest cabbage** (above and below opposite), have turned the state's harsh climate to their advantage. They start their plants under grow lamps in the winter, move them to heated greenhouses in the spring, and finally to outdoor poly-tunnels, where they grow to monstrous sizes under the 24-hr summer sun.

SCI-FI SCIENCE

In sci-fi blockbuster *The Martian* (2015), a stranded astronaut survives on Mars by growing potatoes in a mixture of Martian soil and his own poop. Is this possible? Well, perhaps... Thanks to robo-explorers (see pp.28–29), we know quite a lot about the make-up of Mars's surface. In 2014, a team from Wageningen University in the Netherlands found that hardy plant species are perfectly happy in simulated Martian soil.

I'll call them... poo-tatoes!

HEAVIEST...

1 Beetroot
23.4 kg (51 lb 9.4 oz)
Ian Neale (UK)

2 Green cabbage
62.71 kg (138 lb 4 oz)
Scott Robb (USA)

3 Apple
1.84 kg (4 lb 1 oz)
Chisato Iwasaki (JPN)

4 Watermelon
159 kg (350 lb 8 oz)
Chris Kent (USA)

5 Leek
10.6 kg (23 lb 5.9 oz)
Paul Rochester (UK)

6 Cantaloupe melon
29.4 kg (64 lb 13 oz)
Scott & Mardie Robb (USA)

7 Cauliflower
27.48 kg (60 lb 9.3 oz)
Peter Glazebrook (UK)

8 Avocado
2.19 kg (4 lb 13.2 oz)
Gabriel Ramirez Nahim (VEN)

5

6

7

8

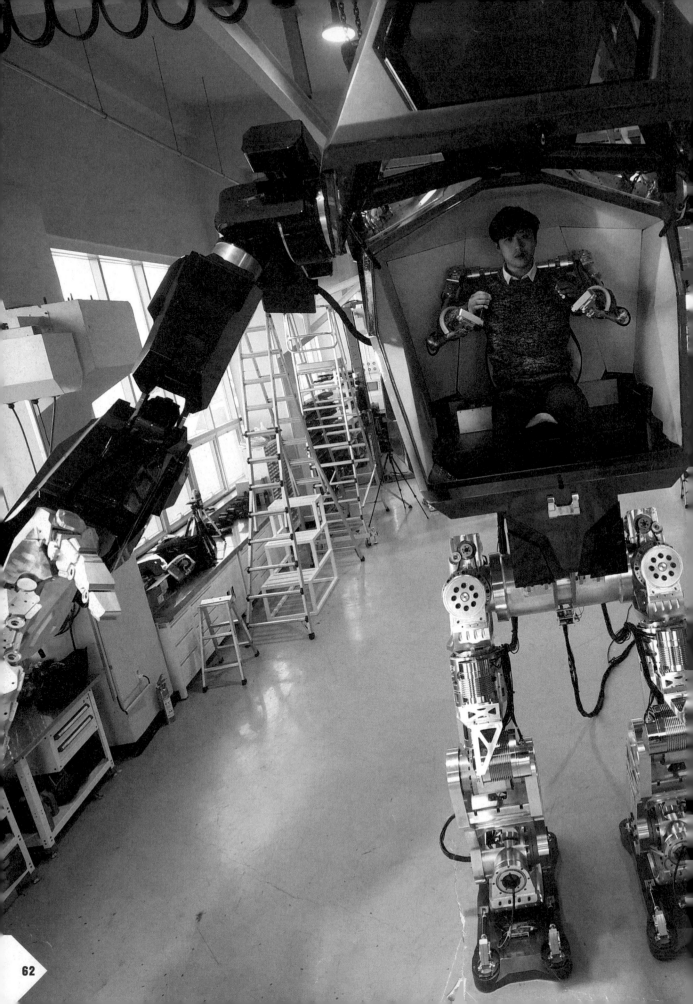

SUPER MECHA

This amazing-looking construction is the *Method-2* robotic exosuit. The suit, which stands at 4 m (13 ft 1 in) tall and weighs 1,500 kg (3,306 lb), was built by South Korean technology firm Hankook Mirae in partnership with Hollywood special-effects artist Vitaly Bulgarov. In Mar 2017, American internet billionaire and space entrepreneur Jeff Bezos borrowed the prototype so that he could stomp around on stage at Amazon's annual tech conference, striking fear into investors and making the world feel just a little bit more like a sci-fi dystopia.

ROBOTS

WALK LIKE A ROBOT

Want a robot of your own? You'll need a lot of cash; even the SoftBank Robotics Nao (right), which is only 58 cm (23 in) tall, costs about £5,300 ($6,880).

In the 1950s, science-fiction writers all assumed we'd be surrounded by helpful robots by now. Despite all the technological progress we've made, however, this hasn't happened. Why not?

It turns out that humanoid robots are tricky. Walking is hard and running is even harder. Just standing still is a challenge because we don't have enough legs. We're not aware of it, but our bodies constantly make tiny adjustments to keep us from falling over, dropping things or poking ourselves in the eye.

For years, the king of the humanoid robots has been Honda's Asimo, but now a new generation of robots is stepping up. Many of these, including Boston Dynamics' Atlas and NASA's Valkyrie, were developed for an event called the DARPA Robotics Challenge, which was organized to spur new research into search-and-rescue robots.

So, they might be able to walk the walk but can these humanoid helpers talk the talk? Let's find out...

THE BIG QUESTION

WHY MIMIC HUMANS?

We make humanoid robots because being human-sized and shaped is useful in a world of buildings and devices designed for use by things (people) that are human-sized and shaped. We also do it because we're not very imaginative (which is also why sci-fi aliens usually look more or less like people).

Making humanoid robots is hard, though; our wobbly two-legs-and-tiny-feet arrangement makes balancing very difficult. Some robot makers have been playing with this shape in an attempt to make something more robot-friendly – keeping the two legs part (because of stairs) but changing things up a bit. Agility Robotics' Cassie (**1**) puts all its weight at waist level, Boston Dynamics' Handle (**2**) has wheels for feet, and Schaft's bipedal robots (**3**) have their bodies at knee height (although technically speaking they don't have knees).

ATLAS

In 2013, American robotics lab Boston Dynamics unveiled the first version of Atlas, an agile humanoid robot. Atlas caught the internet's attention because, unlike earlier robots – which walked in shuffling steps and fell over at the slightest obstacle – Atlas could stride confidently over rough ground, balance on one leg, and keep its balance even when people shoved it.

This last part is particularly useful because (if the videos they've released are anything to go by) there's a lot of workplace robot bullying at Boston Dynamics' headquarters, most of it done by Atlas' nemesis, a mysterious figure known to the internet as "beard guy" (below).

Meanie

1 Cassie walks like a robot chicken

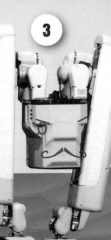

2 Handle can do totally sick stunts (see p. 72)

This robot doesn't have a name yet. We think it looks like a Greg, or possibly a Sharon. What do you think?

3

BATTLE OF THE BOTS

Can we be friends?

To infinity, and beyond!

Asimo vs Valkyrie... the old master versus the new kid on the block. Despite his youthful looks, Asimo is getting on a bit (the latest model is six years old, which is ancient for a robot), but with age comes wisdom (well, bug-free software, which is sort of like wisdom). Valkyrie, on the other hand, is state of the art, with the latest version being finalized in 2016. She (most researchers working on the programme agree it's a she) is powerful and smart, but still has a lot to learn.

ASIMO BY HONDA

VS

VALKYRIE BY NASA

HEIGHT At only 4 ft 2 in (130 cm), Asimo is never going to be playing for the NBA: he's not even tall enough to get on the cool rides at theme parks. He's not far to fall, though, which is good for a robot.

WEIGHT Asimo weighs about 110 lb (50 kg), which is about as heavy as a small human or a large dog. It's also about the weight of a porcelain toilet. He's not the strongest robot around.

TOP SPEED Asimo doesn't have the bouncy, animal-like legs of a Boston Dynamics robot, but he's got a surprising turn of speed. His normal walking pace is about 1 mph (1.6 km/h), but he can run at speeds of 4.3 mph (7 km/h).

DEGREES OF FREEDOM Asimo has 57. This is the total number of ways a robot's joints can move. A knee joint has two (forward, back) and back), while a wrist joint has six (forward, back, left, right, and clockwise/counter-clockwise twist).

HEIGHT Valkyrie is 6 ft 2 in (188 cm), so she would tower over Asimo and most of her operators. Despite her size, researchers working with the robot say Valkyrie is much less scary than Boston Dynamics' Atlas robot.

WEIGHT Valkyrie weighs in at a hefty 286 lb (130 kg). Luckily, her body is modular, and can be taken apart for transport. You can even attach her right arm to her left shoulder (and vice versa) and she will still work.

TOP SPEED Although Valkyrie's body is state of the art, the systems that control her movement are still in a very early stage of development. Her legs might be capable of running, but all she can do now is shuffle along at 0.67 mph (1.08 km/h).

DEGREES OF FREEDOM Valkyrie has fewer degrees of freedom than Asimo (only 44), but most of the difference is in her hands. Asimo's hands are designed to look and move like our hands, whereas Valkyrie's hands have to lift things.

CONCLUSION
Asimo wouldn't win a robot fist fight, but if it's a charm offensive you're after, then he's your robot. He's also small and nimble and got years of experience behind him. He'd know better than to get into a fight...

CONCLUSION
NASA's latest humanoid robot is certainly intimidating, but she'll need a lot of help before she's ready to step into the ring. She might be chunky but she's no fighter – not with those delicate, lady-like hands...

Result? "NO CONTEST!"

65

CYBORG OLYMPICS

On 8 Oct 2016, the **first competition for bionic athletes** was held near Zurich in Switzerland. Teams came from all over the world to test their latest technologies against each other.

The Paralympics, and other events like it, are tests of strength and endurance. They're all about the athletes themselves, with the assistive technologies they use relegated to a very minor role. Prosthetic (artificial) limbs have to be driven by muscle power alone, with designs that are highly specialized for the demands of an individual event.

The Cybathlon is very different. The contestants are teams that include both engineers and disabled athletes – "pilots", as they're called – who work together to combine human and machine. There are no limits when it comes to technology, and everything from the simplest mechanical arms to computer-controlled carbon-fibre exoskeletons are on display.

The events are also quite unlike anything you'd see at the Paralympics. The Cybathlon's creator, Swiss academic Robert Riener, realized that purely athletic tests weren't kickstarting much useful development – you can move really fast in a racing wheelchair, but you can't fit through doors, let alone go up stairs.

The Cybathlon ditches the usual track-and-field events in favour of more boring – but in many ways much more difficult – tasks. Rather than throw a javelin, for example, prosthetic arm pilots must open a jam jar and change a light bulb against the clock; prosthetic leg pilots must walk up and down a flight of stairs without spilling their tea; wheelchair pilots must cross lumpy and uneven ground.

Featured here are the six categories planned for the 2020 Cybathlon...

SUPER-WHEELCHAIRS

For the Powered Wheelchair Race, pretty much anything goes: pilots ride on wheelchairs with unusual features such as tank tracks and gyroscope stabilizers, controlling them with everything from eye trackers to Xbox controllers. Speed isn't the only requirement; they also have to scale stairs and ramps, pass through doorways and slalom between poles.

ROBOT ARMS

The Powered Arm Prosthesis Race challenges pilots to negotiate a series of fiddly hand- and arm-mobility tests. They have to pick up and move things with awkwardly shaped handles, complete a wire loop game (pictured), change a light bulb, and carry a tray of plates and cutlery over a series of obstacles without dropping anything.

The winner of the 2016 arm race, Bob Radocy (USA) of Team DIPO Power, navigates the ring and wire game

MIND CONTROL

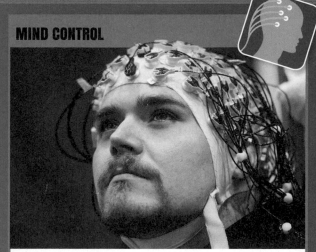

The Brain-Computer Interface Race challenges pilots to complete a videogame-like test using only their thoughts. The teams design the brain-mapping hardware (pictured) and the software that interprets the signals. This technology could one day be used to control prosthetic limbs as naturally as real ones. It could even be used to allow people to "inhabit" robot avatars or control machinery as if it was part of their bodies.

ELECTRO-POWERED CYCLING

The Functional Electrical Stimulation (FES) Bike Race is open to pilots with spinal cord injuries that have immobilized their legs. Teams use sticky computer-controlled electrodes to pass a current to the muscles in their pilot's legs, carefully co-ordinating the pulses to work the pedals of the bike. The pilot controls the intensity of the pulses, allowing them to control their speed and pace themselves around the course.

ROBOT LEGS

The Powered Leg Prosthesis Race is for pilots with one leg that has been amputated. The prostheses used in this race have motors to control the movement of the knee and ankle joints. Pilots must navigate ramps, steps and low hurdles, pick up a plate of jelly, and then go back the way they came without spilling anything.

EXOSUITS

The Powered Exoskeleton Race is the star event at the Cybathlon. Pilots are strapped into powered motorized supports (or "orthoses", to use their proper name), which act like a set of robotic legs, guiding the movement of their own, paralysed legs. Pilots have to navigate their way across an obstacle course of everyday objects, including flights of stairs, slopes and uneven ground. The pilots are allowed to use crutches to steady themselves, but the legs must bear their weight.

FASTEST MAN

Jamaican sprinter Usain Bolt is the fastest man on Earth. He can cover 100 m in less than the time it takes some people to yawn. How *does* he do it?

In the mid-2000s, the 100 m sprint had become a bit, well... slow. The world's finest had managed to knock only 0.16 sec off the record between 1983 and 2006, and people were starting to wonder if we'd run as fast as we ever could.

Then Usain Bolt appeared. In the summer of 2008, he beat the world record three times, improving the time by 0.16 sec – the same margin that had taken everyone else 23 years to chip away!

Today, Bolt holds the records for the **fastest 100 m** (9.58 sec) and the **fastest 200 m** (19.19 sec). Plus, he helped set the team record for the **fastest 4 x 100 m relay** (36.84 sec).

Usain Bolt is the **first athlete to achieve the "triple-double"** – winning the 100 m and 200 m at three consecutive Olympic Games.

The unbeatable 100 m sprint?
There will come a point in the future when humans won't be able to beat the 100 m record – there *has* to be an upper limit. Here we identify the ideal conditions and requirements for this unbeatable 100 m time:
Head: shaved, with aerodynamic sunglasses
Height: 1.87 m (6 ft 2 in)
Reaction time: 100 milliseconds
Muscles: ideal balance of muscle fibres: 55–65% fast-twitch; 35–45% slow-twitch; 30.4-cm-wide (12-in) thighs
Running suit: skin-tight material so air flows smoothly around you
Top speed: 47.3 km/h (29.4 mph)
Weight: 87 kg (192 lb) – 4% fat
Leg length: 1 m (40 in)
Shoes: lightweight 87-g (3-oz) spiked shoe

(And for the perfect venue...)
Altitude: 1,000 m (3,280 ft)
Tailwind: 2 m/s (4.4 mph)
Climate: air pressure of 986.78 millibars (29.14 in), 11% humidity, temperature of 27.7°C (82°F)

How does he do it?
Sports scientists have studied every detail of Usain Bolt's record-setting runs to work out how he goes so fast. Here's a breakdown of what happens during those sub-10-sec sprints.

Out of the blocks
Usain Bolt's enormous frame – he's 196 cm (6 ft 5 in) tall and weighs 95 kg (210 lb) – means that he's not as quick to accelerate as his competitors. Runners can only accelerate when their feet are pressing against the ground (obviously) and Usain Bolt's long stride – around 1.78 m (5 ft 10 in) at its shortest during the first 20 m (65 ft) of the race – means that he has less foot-on-floor time than shorter runners.

Force against blocks

HOW FAST CAN A HUMAN RUN...? This is a question that researchers and writers have pondered for decades. Some have based their estimates on the known characteristics of great runners, while others have used statistical analysis of existing records.

Crunching the numbers

In the early 2000s, Iranian-born mathematician Reza Noubary published an influential analysis of the 100 m world record. He looked at the rate at which athletes were improving, and extended the resulting curve into the future. Based on this progression curve, he estimated that we'd eventually hit our limits at about 9.44 sec some time in the 2050s. After Bolt set his current world record (a mark Noubary hadn't expected to be beaten until the 2030s), he conceded that he would have to revise his predictions.

Analysing the greats

By studying the bodies of great sprinters, we can work out the ways they're different from ordinary people. We can look at factors such as their reaction speeds (Bolt is actually very slow off the mark for a top-level sprinter) and the ratio of different types of muscle fibre in their limbs. The vital statistics to the left come from sports scientist John Brenkus, who researched the subject for his 2012 book *The Perfection Point*. He believes that this "perfect athlete" would be able to run the 100 m in just 9.01 sec under ideal conditions.

MIND OVER MATTER

Humans have an obsession with nice, round numbers. There's no major difference, for example, between a land-speed-record run of 398 mph and one of 400 mph (it's only 0.5% faster), but the latter just *feels* more significant. Given our fixation with these boundaries, it seems unlikely that we'll be able to cope with the 100 m record being 9.01 sec. And once it gets to 9.00, the race will be on for the first sub-9-sec run, which means 8.99 sec is almost inevitable.

MYTHCONCEPTION

USAIN BOLT LIVES ON CHICKEN NUGGETS

Bolt is well known for his love of chicken nuggets and spicy wings, often eating little else in the days after an Olympic final. So does this mean you can be a super-athlete and live on junk food? Sadly not. Bolt's typical diet is much more disciplined. During the day, when he's training, he eats small, carefully balanced meals prepared by a specialist chef, starting with an egg sandwich and then moving on to pasta and fish. He ends the day with a heaped plate of roast chicken and vegetables (even broccoli, which he hates).

FALSE

Picking up speed

Bolt makes up for his initial disadvantage with sheer power, exerting a massive 400 kg (880 lb) of force with each stride. When the other runners hit their peak speeds (usually at around the 50-m [164-ft] mark), Bolt is still accelerating. He doesn't reach his top speed until around 70 m (230 ft), at which point he's moving at 44.73 km/h (27.8 mph).

Slowing down

No runner can keep up this pace for more than a few steps. As their energy dwindles, the power in their stride drops. Each time they touch the ground, they slow themselves down a little. Bolt lengthens his stride to around 2.8 m (9 ft 2 in), touching the ground for less than a tenth of a second per step, and covers the last 30 m (98 ft) in only 10 strides.

Ask a...
Swarm Engineer

Sabine Hauert is not a scientist you want to mess with... Upset her and she could unleash a swarm of robots on you! We asked the lecturer from the world-renowned Bristol Robotics Laboratory (UK) about what the future holds for robots and us.

Robohub

A flock of starlings is known as a "murmuration"

Nature mastered swarming long before robots. Examples include flocks of birds such as starlings (above) that gather in their thousands to perform hypnotic aerial displays. It's thought that they do this to protect themselves from predators (the safety-in-numbers principle). They avoid colliding by maintaining a fixed distance from their immediate neighbours.

Is working with robots as cool as it sounds?
Working with robots is exciting because it brings together many disciplines. You need to design the robot, build it, program it, and make sure that it's helpful in the real world. Getting all of this right is no easy feat, so when your robot finally works, it's the best feeling. I really hope the robots we're designing today will improve the way we work, live and explore new frontiers.

Who inspired you?
I had two wonderful women as role models during my

Postdoc: Sangeeta Bhatia at MIT, and Radhika Nagpal at Harvard. They are both amazing scientists, leaders and entrepreneurs.

How do people react when you tell them what you do?
Usually it takes a bit of explaining, and then they're reminded of a TV show they've watched that featured a swarm of robots. *Black Mirror*, *Big Hero 6* or *Doctor Who* come to mind. This is usually the starting point for a discussion about how we hope to use the technology in the future, and what the current limitations are. We're still very far from the world of science-fiction.

How does it feel to be teaching the next generation of robot scientists?
It's a great time to be studying robotics; there's a real demand from industry. I teach Bio-Inspired Artificial Intelligence, and what I love most about this course is that we spend a

lot of time discussing the latest breakthroughs and the newest start-ups, as well as brainstorming about ethical and societal implications. It's a fast-paced field; the course changes a lot from year to year!

What's the hardest question a student has asked you?
The most difficult – but also the most rewarding – questions come from my PhD students. They're pushing the boundaries of robotics, and so I often don't have an answer. The best I can do is help them frame the question in the right way so that they can come up with their own answers, and make their own discoveries.

What particularly drew you towards swarm robots?
If you've seen a flock of birds or a trail of ants, you've seen swarming in action. I take

Kilobots only stand 3.3 cm (1.3 in) tall, so if they do try to take over the world, we could just step on them...

Taking part in the RoboCup – the robot equivalent of the World Cup – was one of Sabine's earliest interactions with robots. She told us: "You'd be amazed at how exciting it is to see a robot dog score a goal. I haven't left robotics since!"

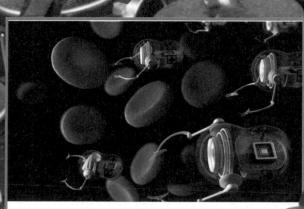

One possible application of swarm robots that Sabine is currently researching is the role that "nano-bots" could play in the field of medicine. These tiny robots could be injected into our bodies as a non-invasive means of diagnosing internal injuries/conditions, or even delivering targeted treatments to, say, cancer cells.

inspiration from these self-organized systems to design robots that work together. I'm fascinated by the complex behaviours that emerge from every robot following simple rules and only interacting with neighbours and their environment.

How much of swarm tech is based on nature?
Inspiration is taken from nature, but we have a variety of tools we use to engineer swarms. The puzzle is that we often know what swarm behaviour we want to achieve – to create a communication network using a swarm of flying robots, for example – but we don't know how to design the rules for the individual robots. For that, we can use bio-inspiration, but also trial and error, crowdsourcing, or machine learning.

What would you say is your most ambitious career goal?
Robot swarms mostly work in a laboratory environment. I want to see these robots having an impact in the real

world. In certain applications, this will require them to work in huge numbers, and so we need to think carefully about how we engineer robots so that they're safe by design, and even biodegradable.

I also think swarm engineering could transform the field of medicine, by helping us control tiny agents that work in huge numbers – for example, nanoparticles, bacteria or cells. This could lead to smarter, more personalized treatments.

What's happening in robotics?
Robots are finally leaving the lab and entering our daily lives. I'm excited by the mundane robots – for example, the robot vacuum cleaners, which took many, many years of development. I also think the robots we're developing today could have a real impact in autonomous driving, in medicine and care, in agriculture and in

industry. We're doing things with robots we just couldn't do before!

Why did you and Markus Waibel set up Robohub?
Robohub is a non-profit project dedicated to connecting the robotics community to the world. Years ago, we realized there was a lot of hype and misinformation about robots. This is important as it impacts public perception, policy, the diversity of students who enter the field, translation to industry and the uptake by users.

At the same time, those who were sharing high-quality information were spread out. Robohub solves this by encouraging roboticists around the world to tell their stories. We're a network of communicators, producing hundreds of podcasts, videos, blogs and tutorials. We're having an impact –

Robohub.org is now the main blog dedicated to robotics.

How do you think robots will have progressed by 2100?
Could robots ever be integrated members of society, like we see in sci-fi movies? Focus currently is on making robots that can perform specific tasks; they're therefore quite narrow in their abilities. We're very far from anything with capabilities as versatile as a human.

Rather than making human-like robots, I hope that in 2100 robots are ubiquitous, in the same way that dishwashers are today. We may not even think of them as robots, in fact, but just as tools that we use on a regular basis.

I DIDN'T KNOW THAT!

I sink, therefore I am

ROBOT PRO SKATER

This weird backwards beast is Handle, a hybrid wheeled/legged robot revealed in Feb 2017 by scary-robot builders Boston Dynamics. It combines the all-terrain abilities of human-like legs with the speed and efficiency of wheels to make a robot that can not only chase you down at running speed, but also follow you up stairs (Boston Dynamics CEO Marc Raibert described the design as "nightmare-inducing"). For now, however, Handle seems to be content to spend its days doing skateboarder-style stunts on its roller-skate feet.

PARANOID ANDROIDS

On 17 Jul 2017, Twitter user Bilal Farooqui snapped this picture out of his office window and lamented, "We were promised flying cars, instead we got suicidal robots." His office complex's free-roaming security robot – who was called "Steve" for some reason – appeared to have decided to end it all in an ornamental fountain.

Some suspected foul play (was Steve pushed?), while others thought he'd sadly given up on life. A little memorial was even created at his charging station (inset). According to Steve's operators (sinister-sounding robotics firm Knightscope), the truth wasn't nearly as dramatic: he was new and still learning his way around. He simply slipped on the wet bricks around the fountain and fell in.

CONFESSIONBOT

Unveiled in Hesse, Germany, on 30 May 2017, BlessU-2 is the world's first robot priest. Simply explain your troubles through the medium of the touchscreen on its chest and it will offer you a blessing to ease your mind.

These blessings can be delivered in five different languages and are accompanied by appropriate priestly arm-waving (and slightly inappropriate eyebrow-wiggling). Also, its hands light up and its nose flashes blue (just like a real priest!).

Er, what?

BIRDS VS DRONES

Drone operators in Australia have a unique problem with bird strikes. Drones, including the one whose last moments are pictured above, are falling prey to huge – their wings are 2.8 m (9 ft 2 in) across! – wedge-tailed eagles.

Like most Australian animals, wedge-tailed eagles think of nothing but killing all day. They're highly territorial and will attack anything – drone, aircraft or person – that they think is giving them sass.

Meanwhile, in the Netherlands, the eagles vs drones rivalry is being used to protect airports: trained anti-drone eagles (right) are hunting down unauthorized flyers.

HOUSE ROBOTS! Mayfield Robotics' Kuri (above) is a super-cute (too cute?) domestic robot, designed to serve as a hybrid of a digital assistant and a home-security robot. It doesn't do the dishes, but it does watch out for burglars with its all-seeing camera eyes. It even has an "automated home video" mode, in case you've always wanted to be followed around and secretly photographed by a slightly creepy robot child.

DUMB VS DUMBER

Ever wanted to take part in *BattleBots* (see pp.82–83), but don't have the know-how to make a killer robot? You should try Hebocon, the robot fighting league for the technically useless. This sport has its origins in Japan, where the first Hebocon event (held as part of a maker festival) took place in 2014.

Entrants pit their terrible robots against each other in sumo-style fights. The loser is the first one to fall over or leave the ring (the "winner" doesn't often have much to do with this). There are penalties for entrants seen to be trying too hard, or taking it too seriously.

WOULD YOU MARRY A ROBOT?

Q A According to a survey from Apr 2016, the answer is yes. When asked, 34% of young British adults said they would date a robot, so long as it looked and acted like a person. Making a robot that fits this description would be hard, but it might not really be necessary for human-robot romance. We humans already have a tendency to see human emotion and thought in robots when it isn't really there (see, for example, er... most of this chapter) and we know that people can fall in love with just about anything (a woman in Sweden "married" the Berlin Wall in the 1980s!).

Hey, baby, what's your IP number?

ROBOT INSECTS

As humans, we automatically assume it would be best if robots were human-shaped (see pp.64–65). Some people disagree, however, and think that we should be looking to creepy-crawlies for inspiration.

It makes sense when you think about it. Our six-legged neighbours have adapted to just about every environment imaginable and make up more than half of all known living creatures. The basic design is clearly a good one.

What's even more interesting to roboticists, though, is the way that insects often work as a group to achieve things that individual bugs couldn't do. Swarms of bees and colonies of ants are like intelligent creatures made from thousands of individual components, whose actions are governed by simple rules. This is also a pretty good description of how a computer works, incidentally.

The coming swarm
Swarms are a useful idea because tiny robots, like tiny insects, are never going to be very smart on their own; there's just not enough room for brains. To achieve anything useful, these bots need to work together and co-ordinate their actions (for a Q&A with a swarm engineer, see pp.70–71).

The creature pictured below is a BionicANT – created in Mar 2015 as part of a research project by German automation specialist Festo. We've flagged some of its key components.

Whether it's for undercover recon, rescue operations or saving the planet, mini robo-bugs clearly have the potential to make a *big* difference.

Some scientists have decided it would be easier to make robot-like insects than insect-like robots. They are doing this by wiring remote controls into the brains of living bugs. A freaky-looking cyborg beetle was coaxed into a zombie-like shambling walk back in 2009, and the **first controlled flight by a cyborg beetle** was demonstrated by Nanyang Technological University in Singapore in Mar 2015. "Cybugs" like this might be suited to search-and-rescue operations in confined spaces, such as fallen buildings or mines.

Festo's engineers found a clever way to make space for the ant's electronic brains. Rather than use circuit boards and put them inside the body, they 3D-printed circuits directly on to the body and mounted the chips there. This freed up space for the batteries.

Its electronic brain is in its bum!

Wireless antenna that allow the ants to communicate with each other

These circuit traces are 3D-printed on to the body of the ant

The antennae double as recharging connectors for the batteries

Twin cameras give the ant 3D vision, like us

Each ant has a pair of pincers to grab and hold things

MORE *STUFF!*

- The **smallest camera drone** is the Delft University of Technology's (NLD) DelFly Micro (below), which weighs 3.07 g (0.108 oz) and is 10 cm (3.9 in) long.
- Festo, the company behind the BionicANT, has a thing for animal robots. They started with a swimming jellyfish robot back in 2008, and followed up with a robot butterfly, a robot kangaroo and a 44-cm (17.3-in) robot dragonfly (pictured inset).

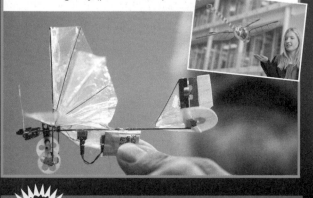

MYTHCONCEPTION

Heeelp!

AERODYNAMICALLY, BUMBLEBEES SHOULDN'T BE ABLE TO FLY!

This is only true if you are doing your calculations based on the principle that bees fly like aeroplanes, which they don't (the lack of engines is a clue). Bees' wings actually flex and twist in flight, creating tiny whirlpools of air that collide with each other in fantastically complex ways to create lift. We're still not certain of all the finer details of bumblebee flight, but the basic way they get about has been understood since the 1970s.

FALSE

INSTANT EXPERT

ROBOT BEES... In many parts of the world, farmers are running low on bees – they're dying off because of mysterious diseases and human changes to their ecosystem.

We need bees to pollinate flowers and make most crops grow. Without them, we'd have to eat broccoli and turnips with every meal. To avoid that fate, it's been suggested that we could make robot bees to do the job instead. This is possible – this picture shows a flower-pollinating drone – but it isn't a very good solution.

Each acre of apple trees, for example, needs about 35,000 bees to keep things going. This means that a typical farm would need hundreds of thousands of bee drones, costing millions of dollars to produce. Looks like we'll just have to be nicer to bees.

The furry bit is for rubbing on flowers

FOR THE RECORD

Developed by the Harvard Microbotics Laboratory (USA), the RoboBee is the **smallest tethered flying robot** and it achieved the **first controlled flight by a robotic insect** in 2013. Each one weighs under 0.1 g (0.003 oz) – about as much as a grain of sand – and is about half the size of a paperclip.

At the moment, the RoboBee has to be tethered to a power supply and guidance computer to fly, but the researchers believe that fully independent flight is only a few years away. The latest version of the RoboBee can stick to the underside of leaves using static electricity and even swim underwater.

Bzzzzz

MAN VS MACHINE

The list of things that computers can do better than humans gets longer every year. First it was maths, then chess, then videogames. What's next, and how long do we have before robots take over?

For most of human history, we've not really had much competition from outside our own species. Gorillas are rubbish at chess, tortoises write terrible poetry, and no elephant has ever got past the first level of *PAC-Man*. Now, however, we often seem to be fighting a losing battle against our own creations. The rise of the robots has begun, and we're happily encouraging it.

AlphaGo
On 29 Dec 2016, a player called "Magister" joined an online community for players of the strategy board game Go, and started playing informal games. Magister was good –

suspiciously good, in fact. The player recorded 60 wins in a week, beating the world's best players while apparently not stopping to sleep or eat.

On 5 Jan 2017, Magister was revealed to be an artificial intelligence called AlphaGo, created by a British Google subsidiary called DeepMind. A new era in AI had begun.

TIL
TODAY I LEARNED

Arm-wrestling robots are actually a thing. Obviously robots would win easily if they could bring, say, a house-sized industrial lifting arm to the table. But if they're restricted to something the size and shape of a human arm, people beat them every time. So far...

Ke Jie

This man is AlphaGo's piece-moving henchman
中国围棋协会

AlphaGo's secret practice sessions were part of DeepMind's preparations for a three-game match against the world's highest-ranked Go player, Ke Jie, on 27 May 2017. The contest ended in a decisive win for AlphaGo, adding Go to the list of things robots do better than humans.

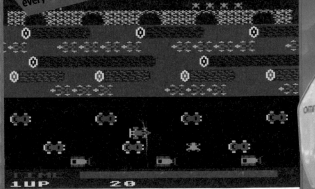

When it's not playing Go or plotting world domination, DeepMind's AI passes the time playing Atari 2600 games (such as *Frogger*, above). Like your parents, it finds the fancy graphics and tricky controls of modern games too confusing. Its speciality is block-smashing puzzle game *Breakout*.

✚ MORE *STUFF!*

- As well as beating humans in tests of mental agility, robots are also *replacing* humans in the world of camel racing (which is apparently a thing).
- DeepMind's current project involves showing its AI clips from *The Simpsons* and trying to get it to explain what Homer is doing in each scene.

⬟ FOR THE RECORD

In Feb 2011, a supercomputer named Watson won a series of special episodes of US TV quiz show *Jeopardy!*, achieving the **highest score on *Jeopardy!* by a computer** ($77,147; £47,853) in the process. Watson, who was designed specifically to win quiz shows, drew on four terabytes of stored information, including the entire text of Wikipedia.

◉ DEEP BLUE

On 11 May 1997, Deep Blue – a big black block of whirring fans and blinking lights about the size of a wardrobe – became the **first computer to beat a world chess champion under regular time controls**. It defeated former world chess champion Garry Kasparov in a series of high-profile exhibition games that shocked the world of chess (the world of chess, looking shocked, pictured above).

The most amazing thing about this is that Deep Blue – despite being one of the most powerful computers in the world in 1997 – has less processing power than a modern smartphone. Computer technology has now advanced to the point where most people are carrying devices capable of defeating even the greatest human chess players in their pockets – and using it to look at pictures of cats.

FOR THE RECORD

This alien-looking robot was developed for just one thing: killin... actually no, not killing, table tennis. The Omron Ping Pong Robot, revealed to the public in Oct 2015, is the **first robot table-tennis tutor**, capable of teaching even the worst rookie player.

The ping-pong robot started life as an in-house side-project at Japanese robotics firm Omron. Its designers chose table tennis because it's an interesting technical challenge.

Bzzzzzt

Return the serve or you will be exterminated!

OMRON

HOT SHOT

ROBOT DRAGON!
This strange mash-up of science-fiction and fantasy was created by German firm Zollner Electronik for the annual folklore festival in Zandt, Germany. At 15.7 m (51 ft 6 in) long by 8.2 m (26 ft 10 in) tall, this ferocious fire-breather is the world's **largest walking robot**. Beneath its scaly skin, the dragon (which is called "Fanny" for some reason) has a complex system of hydraulic pistons driven by a small turbo-diesel engine. The "naked" robot can be seen in the inset above.

DRONE RACING

Robots can react thousands of times faster than humans. They can also control vehicles with millimetre precision. But will they ever be able to beat a proper racing driver?

People enjoy racing things – horses, dogs, bicycles, cars. If you can make things go fast, people will inevitably race them against each other.

As racing technology gets better, however, human drivers start to look like a bit of a weakness. We're big and heavy, we tend to pass out in high-*g* corners, and we go all mushy when we crash.

The obvious solution to all this is to take the drivers out of the vehicles. Without people in them, cars (or drones) can go faster and be more dangerous. The vehicles can also be smaller, allowing them to be raced cheaply in small spaces.

There are two possible ways to do this. One is to have the drivers controlling the vehicles remotely, as happens in drone racing. The other is – dramatic music – let the vehicles control themselves, as will be the case in the Roborace championship...

The Robocar below is pretty, but it's not really practical for testing (you need space for prototype components and a safety driver). For the development of the self-driving AI, Roborace have been using this less elegant vehicle, called DevBot, which is a Ginetta LMP3 with an electric engine, lots of sensors and a cockpit for a human driver.

THE ROBOCAR

Unveiled in Feb 2017, the Robocar is a self-driving racing car designed to compete in the FIA's upcoming Roborace series. It is 4.8 m long and 2 m wide (15 ft 8 in x 6 ft 6 in), but only about knee high (the advantage of having no driver). With four 300-kW (402-hp) electric motors and a weight of just 975 kg (2,149 lb), it has a similar power-to-weight ratio to a Formula 1 car.

The car has a large number of sensors including lidar (laser range-finding), radar, optical cameras and GPS. The sensors feed data to an on-board computer, which decides on the best racing line to take. Each team will be supplied with the same cars, but will make their own guidance systems.

Front optical camera

Front radar (inside nose cone)

Cooling intake

At the moment, DevBot's lap times are still about 10-20% slower than those of a human driver, but it's catching up fast

Front side lidar

Side lidar

FOR THE RECORD

The World Drone Prix, held in Dubai on 11–12 Mar 2016, tempted racers from all over the world with a $1,000,000 (£698,778) prize pool – the **largest prize pool for a drone racing tournament**.

The overall winner, who went home with $250,000 (£174,695), was British teenager Luke Bannister (right) and his team, Tornado X-Blades. Luke started racing drones only a year before the event, using VR-style goggles to control them in first person.

• SCI-FI SCIENCE •

Does the Robocar look familiar to you? If so, this might be because it comes from the drawing board of German industrial designer Daniel Simon. He made a name for himself creating sci-fi vehicles, including the lightcars (below) in *Tron: Legacy* (2010). In that film, real humans race cars in a computer world, which is like Roborace in reverse (computers racing cars in the real world).

360° camera and radio antenna

Rear-facing lidar

CHARGE

GPS receiver

Carbon-fibre bodywork

Top view

DRONE RACING LEAGUE

Founded in 2015, the Drone Racing League (DRL) is one of the biggest names in the world of drone racing. Unusually, all the drones used in DRL events are designed and made by the league's organizers, creating a level playing field and saving the racers from being too worried about crashing them.

The model currently in use, the Racer3 (pictured), has a top speed of 80 mph (128 km/h) and is covered in brightly coloured LEDs for visibility. On 13 Jul 2017, a prototype version of the Racer3's successor, the RacerX, reached an average speed of 165.2 mph (265.8 km/h) – the **fastest ground speed by a battery-powered RC quadcopter**.

DRL

Ask a...
Robot Warrior

When his robot is in the battle arena, it's no more Mr Nice Guy!

Tombstone pulverized its rivals to be crowned victor of *BattleBots* in 2016. Now its lead creator, Ray Billings of Hardcore Robotics, tells us about the highs and lows of robot warfare.

TOMBSTONE

The robot that triumphed in 2016 is a culmination of 16 years of small incremental changes. Ray has built many horizontal spinning robots, some of which have done well and some less so. But in each case, he learned something to improve the design. The philosophy has always been the same: deliver the biggest hit, reliably. One thing that has remained consistent throughout is that terrifying steel bar weapon. It can store 106 KJ, which is roughly 50 times the energy stored in an AK-47 round!

Would you say building battle bots is a family activity?

Combat robotics is very much a family activity. There are many teams where the entire family is the team, and it's something that can be enjoyed by kids and adults alike. It has also been a great father/son project for me and my son Justin. He's a grown man now, but we still compete together.

Also, building is one of the best learning activities you could ever get kids involved in. Kids will always astound you with how smart they are – if you can get them motivated!

Tell us about your workshop.

Our build strategy has always been a home garage activity. But the size of the garage and the tools in it have changed substantially over the years! Originally, all I had was some hand tools and a small wire feed welder. Now, the garage has two large milling machines, a lathe, five different welders, plasma cutter, an electronic rework station and

Titanium chassis

Drive powered by 32-V lithium polymer battery; weapon powered by a pack of 96 cells

Rubber shock insulation mounts – a new addition in 2016

Chain on which blade spins

38-in-long (96.5-cm) steel bar; rotates at 2,770 rpm

Max speed: 10 mph (16 km/h)

10-in-diameter (25.4-cm) tyres

Not all of the machines that Ray makes are classic combat bots... Take the first iteration of the Great Pumpkin (left), for instance. It featured a huge inflatable pumpkin lawn decoration on top. Ray thinks that makes it unique, and he considers it the strangest bot he's built.

a large amount of tooling for it all. It has grown beyond a hobby into an obsession!

Where do you get inspiration for designs?

Most of the time, designs start as nothing more than a concept in my head. I'll refine the idea for a while before I

commit to the next step, which is mock-up. This can be done in software or sketches.

But it can also be done by laying out the pieces on the workbench and arranging the puzzle in front of me. Frequently you will design things in software that look fine, but when you start

On that bombshell, I'm outta here!

Team Hardcore (left to right: Rick Russ, Ray's son Justin Billings, Ray himself and, of course, Tombstone) posing with the Giant Nut trophy (which is now kept in Ray's games room). Inset is Bombshell, the robot they defeated in the final of *BattleBots* 2016.

setting the parts into place you find out that access for tools (or hands!) is lacking.

Which rival robot do you wish you had built?
Oh, so many great choices! I could see me building a full shell spinner like Megabyte or Shrederator. And I have to admit that a hammer-style robot like The Judge or Beta (below) would be fun too!

How does your team decide on your robots' names?
Naming a combat robot is almost an art form. Many top teams will have a "theme", with robot names relating to that somehow. In the case of Hardcore Robotics, our logo is the Grim Reaper, so bot names usually revolve around death.

How do you strike a balance between attack and defence?
Many would argue that I *don't* strike a balance, as I almost never give much thought to defence! This is one of the best parts of this sport. You want a super-big weapon and no defence? Build it! You want an armoured brick with minimal or no weapons? Build it! There are no wrong answers here.

Does your team do anything before a match for luck?
I have a specific tool I use for powering up the robots – it's the "lucky key". It really isn't special in any way, but we still use it before every match!

What's the most thrilling battle you've been part of?
One was the match between Tombstone and Beta at 2016's *BattleBots* (below). It went the full three minutes, which is unusual. Although I caused a great deal of damage, Beta was in control of most of the fight, so when it went to the judges I had no idea which way it would go. The uncertainty added a lot of drama!

How devastating is it to see your robot being destroyed?
Every single combat robot will take damage, and they all will die a violent death eventually. If you haven't accepted that before going in, it may not be the sport for you. Figuring out what broke and how to not have it break again is what engineering is all about!

What qualities do you need to be a combat robot engineer?
Fabrication skills are a huge help – more so than electronic skills in my opinion. And having a budget to buy parts that you know 100% are going to be destroyed eventually is also beneficial!

But you can offset those things by building smaller robots, without breaking the bank. You can have a great time competing with the ant-weight class, learning all of the skills and hanging out in the pits with the larger bots.

The basic skills for success are a desire to do well, and the enthusiasm to work really hard.

ROBOTS

BATTLEBOTS

BattleBots invites (generally amateur) engineers to construct destructive robots, which are then pitted head to head in a specially built arena. The US series first aired in 2000 and ran for five seasons, before making a comeback in 2015–16. Hardcore Robotics first entered Tombstone into *BattleBots* in 2015. Although they walked away with the "Most Destructive" award and as runner-up that year, the overall champ – based on a nail-biting judges' decision – was Bite Force.

Pictured above is Tombstone beating hammer-bot Beta in the quarter-finals of the 2016 series, which it went on to win.

ROBOTS IN SPACE

If science-fiction movies have taught us anything, it's that no spaceship crew can be considered complete without at least one robot on board.

This is the actual camera the robot uses to see

These illuminated "eyes" were put on so astronauts can easily see which way the robot is looking

Humans are not well suited to space exploration. We need food and water, drop dead if we run out of air, and *really* don't respond well to the vacuum of space. Robots, by contrast, need only a power source and some way of receiving instructions from Earth. Given all the problems involved with sending people to space, would we not be better off just using robots?

Mars rovers and similar robots (see pp.28–29) are all science, all the time. They don't need to sleep or eat and can stay on a planet for years. It's an easy win, right?

Not necessarily so: robots are persistent, but they're also really slow. What a robotic rover can do in a day, an astronaut could do in a few minutes. In their short time on the

Moon, for example, the Apollo astronauts generated so much data that scientists are still sifting through it to this day.

The robot vs astronaut balance might shift, however, as robots get better. Future rover concepts such as NASA's Spidernaut (below) combine an all-terrain spider body with the humanoid upper body of the Robonaut (right) to create a freaky science centaur.

👤 INT-BALL

This adorable little guy is the JEM Internal Ball Camera ("Int-Ball" for short): a free-floating, melon-sized robot helper that arrived on the *International Space Station* on 5 Jun 2017.

The Int-Ball's purpose is to take over the time-consuming photo- and video-monitoring of experiments on the *ISS*. It autonomously moves between experiment stations – using small air-blowing fans to steer itself around – and takes pictures at regular intervals. Int-Ball can navigate its way back to its charging station when its batteries run down.

It can also be manually operated by mission controllers and experts on the ground, giving them an "avatar" that allows them to hover over an astronaut's shoulder and whisper "You're doing it wrooooonng" when they're fixing things or carrying out complicated experiments. They'll love that.

The Int-Ball isn't the first floating robot assistant to go into space: that honour goes to a 14-in-wide (35-cm) device called the AERCam Sprint, which was designed to be used for remote inspections of the exterior of the Space Shuttle. It only flew once, on Shuttle mission STS-87 in Nov 1997.

In addition to the Int-Ball, the *ISS* is also home to a cluster of indoor satellites called the Synchronized Position Hold Engage and Reorient Experimental Satellite (a really convoluted

AERCam Sprint

SPHERES

Astrobee

way to get the cool acronym SPHERES). The SPHERES drift around the *ISS* gathering data on zero-g environments.

In autumn 2017, the SPHERES are being replaced by a pair of new Astrobee robots. These

will operate in a similar way to Int-Ball – autonomously drifting around the station, taking inventories of equipment and filming astronauts as they do their work, but will also carry snap-in experiment modules.

These floating drones are shown to scale with each other

JUST WHAT IS A ROBOT ANYWAY?

The dictionary definition of a robot is "a machine that carries out actions automatically". This rather vague and general description covers lots of things that don't fit into our "humanoid with beeping noises and flashing lights" image of what a robot should be. In South Africa, for example, traffic lights are called robots – as in, "turn right at the robot" – because they're automatic.

This more general description means that almost all satellites – including the **most remote man-made object**, *Voyager 1* (pictured left) – are robots. They carry out actions such as adjusting antennas or deploying solar panels on their own, without human input. If you count communications satellites and earth-observation satellites (below) as robots – and almost all of them are technically robots – then there are more than a thousand robots in space right now, circling the globe, watching you... listening to your phone calls...

Interesting...

ROBONAUT

"Anything you can do..."

Robonaut is a weird-legged humanoid that arrived on the *ISS* in Feb 2011. It's designed to remotely (or autonomously) carry out experiments or repair tasks, using its dexterous hands to manipulate the same tools and equipment used by the human crew. The current version of Robonaut (the R2) can only be used inside the station, but it's hoped that later versions will be able to venture outside.

Weeeeee!

The *ISS* has a second, smaller robot arm that tends to the outside science experiments on the Japanese Kibō module.

FOR THE RECORD

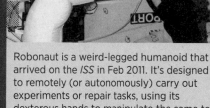

The most high-profile robotic device in space right now is the Canadarm2 – the **largest robotic arm in space**. This 17.5-m-long (57-ft 8-in) robotic boom is fitted to the *ISS* and can be used with either an astronaut on the end (as shown) or with a set of hand-like manipulators called Dextre. The robot arm can do everything from tweaking solar panels to grabbing passing spacecraft.

FASTEST TIME TO SOLVE A RUBIK'S CUBE

By the time you've read this sentence, Feliks Zemdegs would have solved the world's most famous puzzle. Find out how…

If you've tried to unscramble a Rubik's Cube, there's a good chance you'll have suffered from "Rubik's Rage", which usually ends with you throwing it against a wall! With that in mind, imagine the skill and dedication it takes to complete one in less than five seconds!

Feliks Zemdegs (AUS, right) – who has set 110 Rubik's Cube records over his speed-cubing career to date – is a member of the exclusive sub-5-sec club.

His lightning-fast time of 4.73 sec set a new record for the **fastest time to solve a Rubik's Cube** in 2016 – a mark that has since been beaten by Patrick Ponce (see below)!

Here we look at some of the key facts and figures behind Rubik's Cube feats, as well as the origins of the toy that has inspired its very own genre of puzzles and records.

LEAST YOU NEED TO KNOW

Name: Patrick Ponce
Nationality: USA
Age: 15
Fastest 3x3x3 solve: 4.69 sec (beating Feliks' record of 4.73 sec)
Event: Rally in the Valley in Middletown, Virginia, USA
Date: 2 Sep 2017

No. of turns: 17
Type of cube used: Cubicle Valk M
World records currently held: 1
Medals won at World Cube Association events: 97 (54 golds, 31 silvers, 12 bronzes)
No. of solves at World Cube Association events: 1,694

4.69 sec
The fastest time to solve a Rubik's Cube (3x3x3, by a human)

0.63 sec
The fastest time to solve a Rubik's Cube (3x3x3, by a robot)

43 quintillion
Total possible permutations of a 3x3x3 cube – or 43,252,003,274,489,856,000 to be precise

1.4 trillion years
Time it would take to realize every configuration, if turning a 3x3x3 cube once every second

KNOW YOUR CUBES

Classic 3x3x3 cube

2x2x2 cube

4x4x4 cube

5x5x5 cube

6x6x6 cube

9x9x9 cube

FOR THE RECORD

There's more than one way to crack this twisty puzzle... Multi-record holder Feliks also holds the title for **fastest one-handed completion**: 6.88 sec. The **fastest time to solve a Rubik's Cube with the feet**, meanwhile, is 20.57 sec, set by Jakub Kipa (POL) on 27 Jun 2015. Some have mastered this skill without even being able to see the cube: Kaijun Lin from China achieved the **fastest time to solve a Rubik's Cube blindfolded** – 18.5 sec – on 5 Nov 2016. Others can multi-task: for instance, the **most Rubik's Cubes solved while running a marathon** is 254, by Blair Williamson (NZ) on 4 Jun 2017.

ERNŐ RUBIK

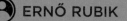

The iconic mechanical puzzle was the brainchild of Hungarian architect and professor Ernő Rubik. The original cube was devised as a tool to help teach students on his architecture course about 3D geometry. However, after sharing his creation, its scope as an addictive plaything quickly made itself apparent.

After a number of iterations, the prototype patented in 1974 was made of wood and rubber bands, and had faceted corners (below). Rubik had done such a good job that it was a month before he was able to solve his own invention!

Magic Cube

The colourful plastic toy that we're familiar with today was born a year later. Originally called the "Magic Cube" ("Bűvös Kocka"), the product was rebranded as Rubik's Cube in 1980, when it was launched globally; people were scared the Magic Cube sounded too occult!

Little could Ernő Rubik have known back then that his classroom teaching aid would become one of the best-selling toys of all time.

INSTANT EXPERT

RUBIK'S CUBE MATHS...
So what's the secret to solving a Rubik's Cube faster than it takes most of us to get out of bed? With more than 43 million trillion configurations, it's quite tricky!

Extensive research by scientists – such as MIT professor Erik Demaine (right) – and decades' worth of computational calculations have determined that the most moves needed to solve any 3x3x3 cube is 20. This is known as "God's number".

As to *how* you get God's number (and thus a fast solve time) varies between cubers. There are several techniques based on the order or pattern (i.e., algorithm) used, e.g., corners first, layer by layer or even good old-fashioned intuition. The most popular method – and the one used by Feliks Zemdegs during his record – is "CFOP". This starts with a cross pattern on one face, then progressively gets more complicated... Check out Feliks' own website – **cubeskills.com** – for tutorials.

261 light years
Distance of every configuration of a 3x3x3 cube laid end to end (or 294,660 return trips to Pluto)

1.5 million
Sales of *You Can Do the Cube* (1981), a guide written by 13-year-old Patrick Bossert

20 moves
Fewest turns needed to solve a 3x3x3 cube starting in any random combination, i.e., God's number

400 million
Estimated classic cubes sold since the toy was released internationally in 1980

Mirror cube

6x3x3 cuboid

Square-1

Pyraminx

Megaminx

Skewb

MAKE & BREAK
10 COOL EXPERIMENTS TO TRY AT HOME

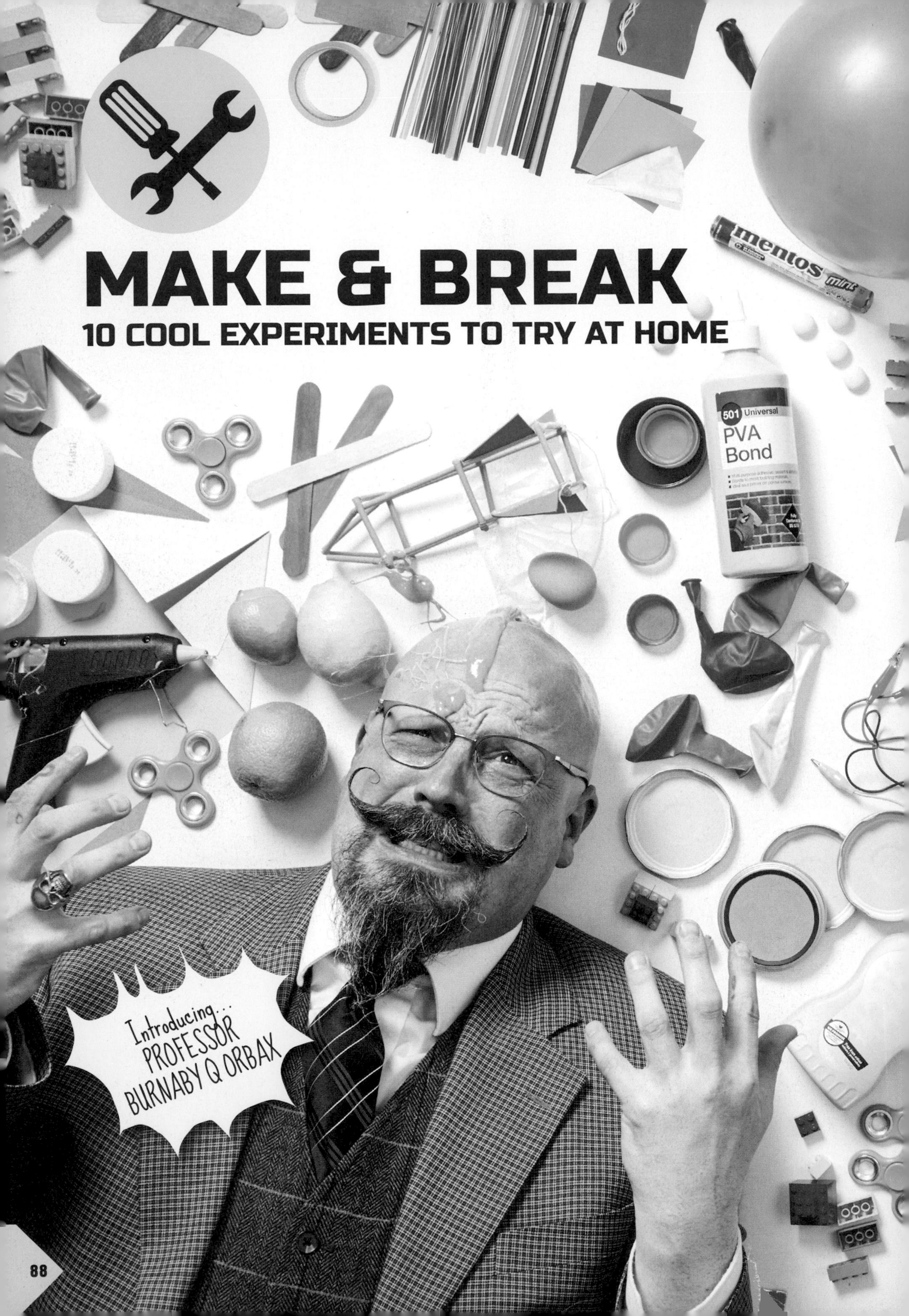

Introducing...
PROFESSOR
BURNABY Q ORBAX

mentos mint

501 Universal
PVA
Bond

...and his lab assistant
SWEET PEPPER
KLOPEK

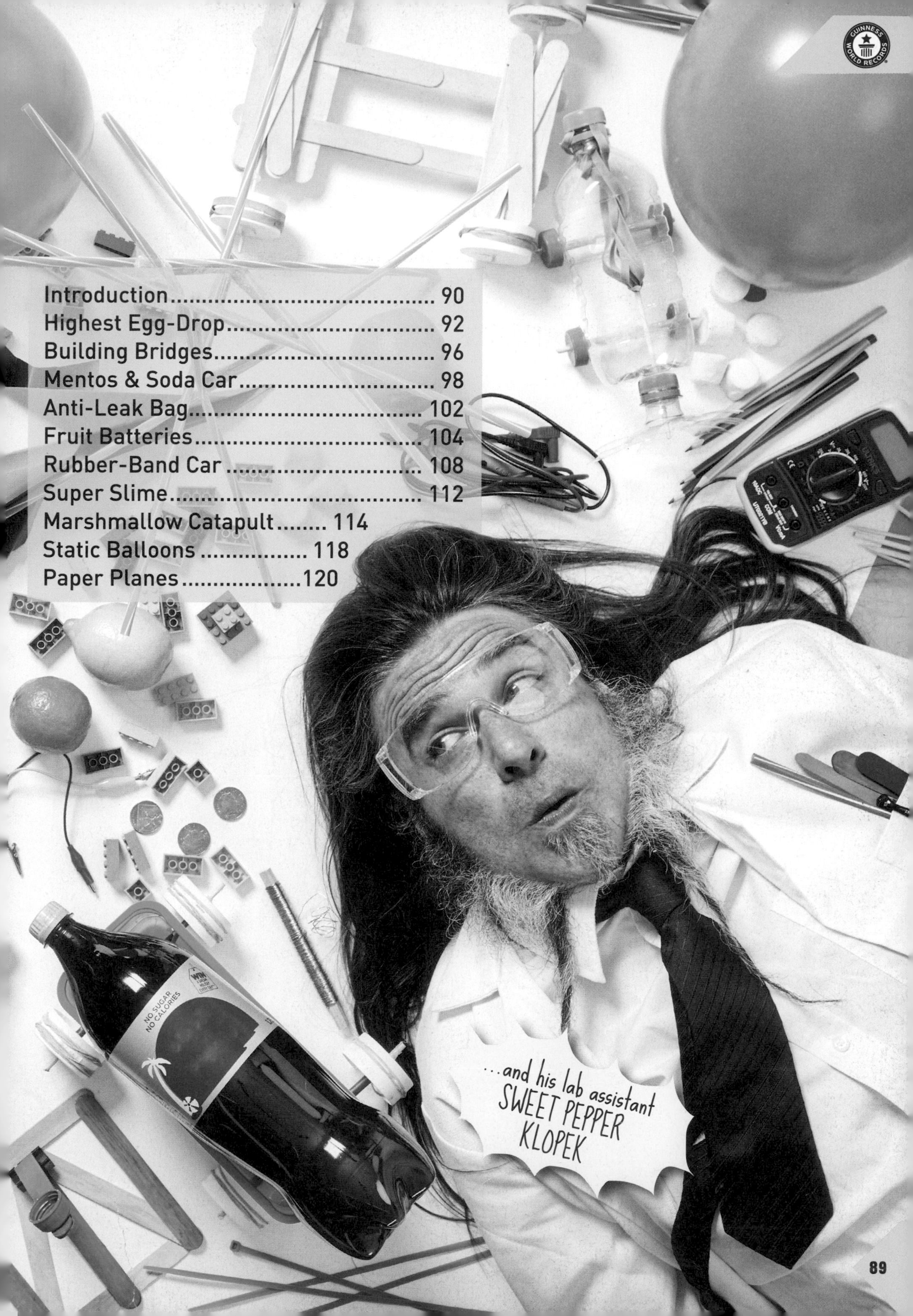

Introduction

Welcome to the **Make & Break** chapter! This is *your* opportunity to get hands-on with science... and stuff. Before you dive in, meet the hosts of this special section and learn about the craziness that lies ahead...

Greetings, science fans! We're Professor Burnaby Q Orbax and Sweet Pepper Klopek. "Who?" you might be asking. Well, we'll be your guides through the exciting world of *making* stuff and (hopefully) *breaking* records.

Reading books and watching classroom demos can only get you so far. To really understand a scientific principle or theory, the best method is always to see it in action for yourself. So we've come up with 10 science challenges that you can try at home using common household objects.

To make things more exciting – if that's even possible – the good folks at GWR have paired each of the experiments with a brand-new world record. How cool is that?

Whether it's getting balloons to stick to walls, designing cars that run on "alternative fuel" or squeezing electricity out of lemons, there's a **Make & Break** record for everyone...

As well as being a daring double act in the lab, Burnaby Q Orbax and Sweet Pepper Klopek regularly perform amazing feats on the stage. These side-show legends have set many records, involving everything from mousetraps and baking trays to meat hooks. *Ouch!*

PAGE **114**

This DIY chapter isn't just about getting messy (and, okay, learning a few things about science). It's also a chance to set your very own record! That's right: it could be *your* name appearing on that super-official Guinness World Records certificate we're modelling here.

But hold up: before you start raiding the kitchen cupboards and hounding your parents for supplies, let's talk about the process. Don't yawn: it's important!

There's a proper way to apply for a record – trust us, we're veterans at it.

The very first thing you should do is visit **www.guinnessworldrecords.com/science**. From there, you can make an application for any of the records you'll find in this chapter.

You'll then be sent all the guidelines for that particular record. Make sure you follow these rules exactly or you risk your attempt being disqualified. And be sure to collect all of the evidence that's required.

If you have any questions, the GWR records team is there to help; you can contact them via your online application. Good luck with your attempts...!

What Professor Orbax doesn't know about polymer physics isn't worth knowing...

...while Lab Assistant Klopek is an expert at pointing at things

We're delighted to introduce you to the ~~beards~~ faces – and more importantly, the heart and soul – of the **Make & Break** chapter: Professor Burnaby Q Orbax (left) and his long-suffering partner in *grime*, Sweet Pepper Klopek (right).

This plucky pair from Canada have set a number of Guinness World Records titles in their time, so they're well qualified to guide you through the journey of attempting – and hopefully achieving – your own.

What's more, Professor Orbax isn't just rocking that tweed-jacket-and-specs look for kicks – he's a genuine, bona fide physics lecturer at the University of Guelph in Ontario, Canada. His specialty is polymer physics, so the Anti-Leak Bag experiment (see pp.102–03) was familiar territory for him.

Although Sweet Pepper Klopek has no formal science training, he brings something just as important to these try-at-home experiments: enthusiasm. Let's face it, even the likes of Newton and Da Vinci wouldn't have got very far without a little help from their lab assistants. Plus, as you'll soon discover, an extra pair of hands never goes amiss!

STUFF YOU'LL NEED:

Each experiment has a shopping list of specific equipment required, but here are some basic tools/items that will be handy across the whole Make & Break chapter:

- GLUE GUN — and plenty of refills!
- SCISSORS / CRAFT KNIFE
- STOPWATCH
- GOGGLES
- STICKY TAPE
- WEIGHING SCALES
- RULER / MEASURING TAPE
- PAPER / PEN / PENCIL
- VIDEO RECORDER / SMARTPHONE / CAMERA — for documenting your record attempts

See Professor Orbax and Lab Assistant Klopek making this Mentos soda car at www.guinnessworldrecords.com/science

PAGE 102

PAGE 98

PAGE 112

⚠ PARENTAL GUIDANCE

Some experiments involve potentially hazardous things that are sharp (like a craft knife), hot (like melted glue) or itchy (like chemicals). You may want to get a responsible adult to help with these steps. Regardless of your age, take extra care whenever handling dangerous equipment. And don't do anything silly like eating slime – we're looking at you, Sweet Pepper!

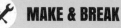

Highest Egg-Drop

This *egg*-streme endeavour is a classic try-at-home experiment: how high can you drop an uncooked egg without it cracking? Luckily, the lovely people at GWR will let you use some household items to build a parachute or protective cage. Still, this is a tricky record to *beat*...

THE RECORD: Greatest height to drop a protected egg without breaking

THE CHALLENGE: Take one raw hen's egg and a selection of items from around the home, then combine in such a way that the egg can be dropped from a great height... and remain intact!

As the saying goes, you can't make an omelette without breaking eggs. The same could be said of record-breaking, at least when it comes to this *eggs*-tra tricky challenge.

Even without anything to protect it, it's possible to drop an egg an awful long way without it breaking – if you get the technique right. Check out David Donoghue's incredible record-breaking drop in For the Record (right). So just imagine how far an egg can fall safely if you could protect it with something!

To help you with this record, you can use some or all of the items listed below for prot-egg-tion. [Editor: an *oeuf* with the egg puns!] These include plastic drinking straws, cardboard, string, a sheet of plastic and sticky tape.

Consider encasing the egg in a straw-and-cardboard cage. Or you could perhaps fashion a parachute from the string and plastic. Or what about a series of protective spikes made from straws?

On pp.94–95, you'll find some of the options we explored. You don't have to copy them – see how creative you can be. Whichever route you choose, good cluck!

FOR THE RECORD

On 22 Aug 1994, the UK's David Donoghue dropped fresh eggs 700 ft (213 m) from a helicopter on to a golf course at Blackpool in Lancashire, UK, and they *didn't* break; it's the **greatest height to drop an egg (unprotected)**. David, who had served in the British Army, studied the science of the "bouncing bombs" – used in the famous World War II Dambusters raid in Germany in 1943 – to perfect the angle and speed of his drops. "Organically farmed eggs are the strongest," he helpfully suggests.

YOU CAN USE:

1 × PLASTIC SHEET (MAX. SIZE 40 × 40 cm or 15.7 × 15.7 in)

4 × PIECES OF CARD (MAX. SIZE 10 × 10 cm or 4 × 4 in)

2 × PIECES OF CORRUGATED CARD (MAX. SIZE 10 × 10 cm or 4 × 4 in)

1 × PIECE OF FOAM (MAX. SIZE 10 × 10 cm or 4 × 4 in)

20 × DRINKING STRAWS

1 × PIECE OF ELASTIC STRING (2 m or 6 ft 6 in)

1 × PIECE OF CLEAR TAPE (30 m or 100 ft)

RAW HENS' EGGS (4 g or heavier)

SHOPPING LIST

A thin plastic bag works well for a parachute canopy

It has nothing to do with this record, but in the Philippines, one of the most popular national dishes is *balut* – a fertilized egg that's boiled and eaten just a few days before the chick hatches! If you indulge, watch out for the feathers and bones! Yuk!

Mama?

HOW DOES IT WORK?

$$\text{Gravity} = 9.8 \text{ m/s}^2$$

$$\text{Time} = \sqrt{2 \times 100 \text{ m} / 9.8 \text{ m/s}^2}$$
$$= 4.52 \text{ sec}$$

Height: 100 m

Weight of egg: 60 g

Air resistance

$$\text{Velocity at impact}$$
$$= \sqrt{2 \times 9.8 \text{ m/s}^2 \times 100 \text{ m}}$$
$$= 44.27 \text{ m/sec}$$

$$\text{Energy at impact}$$
$$= 0.06 \text{ kg} \times 9.8 \text{ m/s}^2 \times 100 \text{ m}$$
$$= 58.8 \text{ joules}$$

Gravity is not the friend of eggs. This fundamental force will pull the egg towards certain destruction, unless you can slow its descent or cushion its inevitable impact. In the example above, an egg dropped from 100 m (328 ft) would hit the ground in 4.52 sec, at a final velocity of 44.27 m/sec. So how can you improve the odds and reduce the energy (58.8 joules, as it happens) of the impact?

To slow down the egg, you need to increase the surface area – the larger the area, the more that air resistance acts against the egg. One effective way of doing this is to add a parachute, which increases the surface area significantly.

To reduce the force of the impact, think about how you make the egg the last thing that touches the ground. Consider cushioning it to absorb and spread the force – for example, using a star-shaped arrangement of straws to take the impact, rather than the egg.

GUIDELINES

• The egg must be a commercially available raw hen's egg weighing a minimum of 42 g (1.48 oz).

• All or some of the items listed opposite can be used to encase the egg or assist in the flight of the egg only; it's not permitted to create a landing pad on to which the egg lands.

• You may only drop the egg by hand.

• The measurement must be taken from the bottom of the egg to the ground – using a steel tape – *before* the egg is dropped.

• After the attempt, the egg must be cracked open to prove that it's raw.

Highest Egg-Drop (continued)

Eggs-terminate!
Eggs-terminate!

THE ELEVATOR: In the first of our suggested designs, we've crafted a closed-end tube from the foam and filled it with shredded pieces of the corrugated cardboard. The tube is then housed in a supportive frame made from the straws. The cardboard "fins" at the top are designed to increase surface area and slow down the descent. The straws also absorb some of the impact – in theory! Consider adding a parachute, as per later designs (right).

THE ROBOT: Use your imagination (goodness knows you'll need to!) for this one – it's a quadrupedal "robot" design that's built to absorb the shock of landing. The theory is that the straws take all the impact – the energy is driven up the "legs" and dissipates before reaching the egg. The egg itself is wrapped in the foam and secured with tape to cardboard sides. It's important that this design falls straight down, but just to be sure, we've stuck some "arms" through the "body" for extra protection.

THE MUMMY: It's a crazy idea but it might just work. Use scissors to cut the foam, the cardboard, the corrugated cardboard, the straws and the string to shreds. Make a little bag from the plastic sheet and fill this with the fluffy stuffing. Place the egg in the midst of the stuffing before using the sticky tape to bind it all together. Just keep wrapping until you've used up all the tape, like you're making an Egyptian mummy. The hope is that the filling will act as a shock-absorbing cushion, keeping your egg from harm. Yeah, good luck with this...

THE PARATROOPER: Here's the first of our designs using a parachute. Firstly, to protect the egg, we've used the cardboard (both types) and the foam to create a squidgy platform. On to this, we've built a pyramid from the straws – this holds the egg in place and gives you something to attach the string to. The string, in turn, is tied (or taped) to the plastic sheet, forming the parachute. The pyramid should be tight enough to stop the egg falling out when you make the drop. You might want to wait for the wind to drop before releasing this one!

1

2

3

4

TOP TIP!
FROM PROFESSOR ORBAX

• Try *eggs*-perimenting with different types of eggs. You can only use hens' eggs, but consider spending a little more of your pocket money to buy free range and organic eggs. For one, it's nicer for the hens, but also you might find that organic eggs have tougher shells than the non-organic variety.
• Find the strongest drinking straws that you can, and experiment with different kinds – some have bendy tips, which might (or might not) help!
• Whichever design you settle for, it will probably work best with a parachute, so consider adding this every time.
• To avoid smashing your way through your family's breakfast, practise with a rubber egg (you can find them on sale on the web) or a hard-boiled egg (much less messy).

THE SPIDER: This design keeps the egg as far as possible from the point of impact by suspending it at the axis of a handful of straws. The theory is that the straws hit the ground first, taking the brunt of the impact and absorbing energy built up during the descent. With the "spider legs" going off in all directions, it also shouldn't matter how the egg falls, or if it's blown off course by the wind. On saying all this, in the test we did by dropping it on Pepper's head, it failed. Oh well, better luck n-*eggs* time...

THE DRAGSTER: The four-sided pyramid also features in this design. Here, it's used upside down to act as a shock absorber. Fins at the rear should, theoretically, keep the contraption straight as it falls, and the parachute adds the much-needed drag. If nothing else – and given the amount of eggs we broke testing this one, it *will* be nothing else! – it looks cool and aerodynamic.

Wobbly

Not wobbly

Triangles – like the sides of a pyramid – make other shapes stronger. This is why you see triangular shapes on the trusses of bridges or in scaffolding. Triangles spread a force evenly across all three sides. A cube can wobble but a pyramid can't!

5

6

95

Building Bridges

How far can you extend a bridge span before it collapses? We'd like you to work this out the old-fashioned way – by building your own bridges with LEGO® and watching them fall down until you find a design that works.

THE RECORD: Longest span of a LEGO brick bridge made in three minutes

THE CHALLENGE: Build a LEGO bridge in 3 min (with no help from anyone else) that is at least 10 cm (3.93 in) off the ground and that will stand for at least 10 sec.

This deceptively simple record requires you to manipulate LEGO at high speed. Just erect two towers and span them with a bridge deck. Easy, right? Well, your ambition must be matched with a steady hand and a good understanding of the physics involved – if you're too quick, or if the span gets too long without sufficient support, it could all come crashing down.

This is a great record if you're planning on a career in engineering. Now's the time to put your designs to the test – before you start building *real* bridges!

SHOPPING LIST

YOU CAN USE:
- LEGO BRICKS -
  NO LONGER THAN
  4 cm or 1.57 in
- BASE PLATES
  (OPTIONAL)

FOR THE RECORD

The LEGO recreation of London's Tower Bridge is one of the largest sets available, with a dizzying 4,295 individual pieces to lose, accidentally eat or tread on in the dead of night. The set's complexity has made it a popular target for speed builders. The current record for **fastest time to complete the LEGO Tower Bridge set (team of five)** is held by British LEGO nerds Team Brickish – who put the whole thing together in just 1 hr 20 min 38 sec on 30 Nov 2014.

Compression (squeezing)

Tension (stretching)

Torsion (twisting force)

Lateral thrust (outward push)

HOW DOES IT WORK?

In this record, you're fighting against the force of gravity. The longer you make the span, the more of its own weight the span has to support. The weight of the span puts pressure on the links between bricks in the centre of the span, and as they buckle, it stresses the joins between the span and the towers.

GUIDELINES

- The LEGO bricks used must be no longer than 4 cm (1.57 in).

- The bricks must be laid flat on a surface prior to the attempt, and may not be pre-joined in any way. Once laid out, the bricks may not be touched until the attempt begins.

- The bridge must have two towers on either side and a deck connecting the two.

- There must be at least 10 cm (3.93 in) clearance between the underside of the deck and the ground.

- You have 3 min to complete the bridge and it must stand unsupported for 10 sec after the time is up.

TIL
TODAY I LEARNED

The oldest still-standing bridge is a small single-arch stone bridge over the Meles river near the city of Izmir (formerly Smyrna), in what is now western Turkey. It was built by Ancient Greek settlers some time before 850 BCE, making it around 3,000 years old.

1

With the clock ticking, you're going to need to move fast. The first bits you should construct are the towers at either end. These must be big and strong, but you can't take too long to make them.

2

Next you'll need to make the bridge span. Here, you've got to balance stiffness with weight. More bricks means more strength, but are they fixed firmly enough to support their own weight?

3

Finally, join it all together and stand back. If it's still standing after 10 sec, then you've got yourself a valid record attempt. Be sure to film everything clearly, including the stopwatch used to time the attempt.

Deck

Length

Height (10 cm min.)

Tower

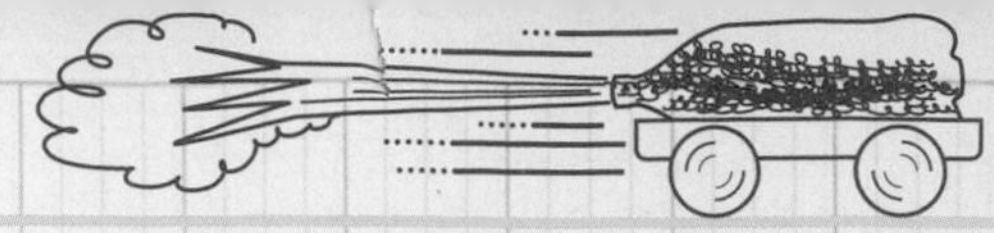

Mentos & Soda Car

In the pursuit of science (and records), sometimes things have to get messy... And when you mix Mentos with a fizzy drink, mess is one thing that's guaranteed! Head outdoors and witness one of the coolest reactions you'll see beyond the lab.

WE USED:
- SODA BOTTLE
- JAR LIDS
- FIDGET SPINNERS
- PLASTIC TUBES
- PLASTIC TUB
- CABLE TIES
- COPPER WIRE
- MENTOS

THE RECORD: Farthest distance by a Mentos and soda bottle vehicle

THE CHALLENGE: Build some kind of "car" (we're talking in its most basic form, so a platform with four wheels). Then use the explosive power of Mentos mixed with soda to propel it as far as it will go.

Surprisingly, the easiest thing about this record is setting off the Mentos and soda reaction (we've used diet cola).

The more complicated elements are creating a stable vehicle that doesn't fall apart a few centimetres into its journey (trust us, it'll happen), finding a bump- and obstacle-free stretch of ground (harder than it sounds) and getting the car down on the floor *before* you get a face full of soda!

SHOPPING LIST

GUIDELINES

- The vehicle can be of any design, but must have four wheels and be propelled *solely* by a Mentos and soda fountain. Part of the challenge is finding the best design.

- A start line must be marked on the ground where the attempt takes place. The surface the car travels on must be flat, reasonably hard and level – no slopes allowed!

- There must be no interference with the vehicle once the attempt has begun. If the vehicle hits any object during the journey, the attempt is disqualified.

- A clear video of the complete record attempt and measuring process must be submitted as evidence.

- The distance must be measured in a straight line from the start line to the closest edge of the vehicle once it has come to a rest.

HOW DOES IT WORK?

$$A_1v_1 = A_2v_2$$

$$0.006362 \text{ m}^2 / 0.0000785 \text{ m}^2$$
$$= 81 \text{ m}^2 (\times 0.08432 \text{ m/s})$$
$$v_2 = 6.83 \text{ m/s} (24.6 \text{ km/h; } 15.3 \text{ mph})$$

v_2

CO$_2$ bubbles

Close-up of a Mentos sweet, showing its rough surface

Nucleation points

Velocity at which soda leaves the bottle

The reason that soda is so bubbly is because carbon dioxide gas (CO_2) is pumped in to give the drink its fizz. The CO_2 binds to the water molecules (H_2O) in the soda, but only lightly. It doesn't take very much for the CO_2 to escape; that's why the drink always foams up when you take off the lid – and also why record-breaking burpers swear by it (see pp.126–27)!

One thing that can speed up the release of the CO_2 is dropping something into the soda. At first glance, Mentos appear smooth, but under a microscope (see inset) you'll find that their surface is covered in tiny bumps and pits.

The suspended CO_2 is able to break away from the water molecules by forming bubbles on another surface – a process known as "nucleation". That's why you always see a few bubbles clinging to the inside of the soda bottle. Despite their small size, the rough-coated Mentos sweets provide a huge surface for lots of bubbles to form very quickly.

This sudden build-up of foamy liquid has to go somewhere and, naturally, it seeks to get out of the bottle. Forced out of the narrow neck means it comes out at high velocity, thanks to the wonders of fluid continuity (see equation left). That's what *should* give your bottle car its propulsion.

TIL
TODAY I LEARNED

Many people assume that the explosive reaction between Mentos and soda is a result of chemistry. But it's actually down to physics. The rough texture of the sweets provides the perfect surface for lots of bubbles to form very quickly (see more in "How Does It Work?" above).

Maybe we'll be driving life-sized Mentos-soda cars one day...

Probably not...

MAKE & BREAK

99

Mentos & Soda Car
(continued)

Start by making the main chassis of your "car". You want to strike a balance between weight (keep it as light as possible) and strength (it needs to be able to support a full bottle of soda without getting crushed). We opted for an empty plastic tub, but you could use anything from lolly sticks to LEGO bricks – just run it by GWR's records team first. Very carefully cut the top off (**1**) until you're left with just the shallow base of the box (**2**); the lower to the ground that the bottle sits, the more sturdy the vehicle will be. Next, glue on your axles (**3**) – we've used a couple of plastic tubes originally used to hold vitamin tablets.

With the axles attached to the chassis (**4**), it's time to turn your attention to the wheels. It's worth really thinking about your wheel design because success hinges on them turning freely – and not falling off! We dusted off some old fidget spinners (these toys are built for rotating, just like wheels) and glued them inside some jar lids (**5**). Then we glued the spinners to the axles (**6**); take care not to get any glue on the ball bearings in the centre as this will stall your car before it even gets started.

Ideally, you want the nozzle to point slightly downwards to get the most out of Newton's Third Law (i.e., the foam jet pushing against the ground)

To stop your bottle tumbling off when your car (hopefully!) speeds away, add a cable tie or two to secure it in place.

TOP TIP!
FROM PROFESSOR ORBAX

To help our car travel farther, we added some rubber bands to the rims of the jar lids. These are essentially performing the same role as the rubber tyres covering the wheels of your family car or bicycle. *Traction* is the friction that occurs between the wheels and the ground, ensuring the car "bites" into the road. This resistance enables a vehicle to transfer rotational energy from the axles (torque) and turn it into forward motion. No matter how powerful your Mentos-soda fountain is, if your wheels aren't gripping the ground, the car won't go very far.

8

Place a lump of Plasticine/modelling clay on a flat surface and use it to carefully poke a hole in the lid of your bottle. You might need to adjust the size of this to get the most efficient stream, but it's best to start small; after all, you can always make it bigger, but not vice versa.

A stretched-out paperclip will also do the trick

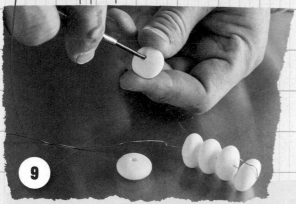

9

Rather than dropping the Mentos in one at a time, which will set off the reaction before you're ready, it's best to create a pre-formed string; six to eight sweets should do it. We poked holes through the middle, then threaded them on to a piece of copper wire.

10

Pour out just enough of the soda so that you can suspend your string of Mentos through the lid without them touching the liquid. With the bottle still standing up, screw the cap back on. Keep a tight hold on the wire or you'll get an unwanted soda shower! When you're ready to roll, drop all the Mentos in and lay the car flat, pointed in the general direction you'd like it to travel.

THIS is why this record should be done outdoors

Don't handle the Mentos too much or you'll rub off the rough surface

We used diet cola, but try a few different types of soda to see which one works best!

As the size of the hole increases, so does the size of the stream; but for power and duration, you'll need a smaller aperture

Anti-Leak Bag

There's nothing quite so satisfying as poking pencils into a watery bag. Trust us on this, we're scientists! But your wits will need to be as sharp as your pencils if you're going to earn a record out of it – spill just one drop and it's game over.

TIL
TODAY I LEARNED
Plastic is a type of man-made polymer, generally made from hydrocarbons – a by-product from processing crude oil. However, not all polymers are artificial. Examples of natural polymers include leaves (cellulose), leather (collagen) and even our very own DNA!

THE RECORD: Most pencils pierced through a water-filled bag in one minute

THE CHALLENGE: Fill a resealable plastic bag – a sandwich or freezer bag is perfect – with water and ram as many pencils through it as you can in 60 sec without springing a leak. Impossible, you say? Think again! Thanks to the wonders of science, you should be able to pierce both sides of the bag without soaking your legs, your lab assistant or your bedroom carpet. (But just to be sure, you should probably attempt this record outside!)

Adding a few drops of food colouring doesn't change anything scientifically but it looks cool, so why not?

GUIDELINES

- Any wooden graphite pencils can be used; plastic pencils are not permitted.

- The plastic bag must be no larger than 25 cm (9.8 in) wide and 30 cm (11.8 in) high. When filled, the water level in the bag can be no lower than 3 cm (1.18 in) below the resealable strip.

- On the start signal, the participant must pick up one pencil at a time and pierce the bag; each pencil must go through both sides of the bag.

- The bag must be held over coloured paper (or similar), which clearly shows up if water drops on to it. If the bag starts to leak at any time during the minute, the attempt is disqualified.

Sheet of coloured paper to detect water droplets

SHOPPING LIST

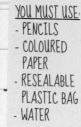

H₂O

Maximum bag size:
25 x 30 cm
(9.8 x 11.8 in)

TOP TIP!
FROM PROFESSOR ORBAX

You can only use wooden graphite pencils for this record – it's one of the rules. But the shape and length of the pencils are totally up to you, so feel free to experiment with a few different types. Make sure you read up on all the guidelines before you give this record a go at **www.guinnessworldrecords.com**.

Something else that you're recommended to do before the attempt is to sharpen your pencils – a *lot*. It's worth investing in a new pencil sharpener for this, because the finer you can get the tip, the cleaner the point of penetration will be. The smaller the holes made, the lower the likelihood of a leak!

MAKE & BREAK

1

Hold the bag in one hand over the piece of coloured paper. (The paper will help show any water droplets that might trickle out during the attempt.) When you're ready, your lab assistant should start the stopwatch.

2

Pierce the plastic with a single swift movement. If you do this too slowly or too gently, the hole is more likely to leak. It will help if the plastic bag is held taut.

3

Continue pushing the pencil all the way through the bag until the nib emerges on the other side. Then repeat! Try to keep the pencils as far apart from each other as possible to avoid forming weak points. If any water leaks, the attempt is over.

HOW DOES IT WORK?

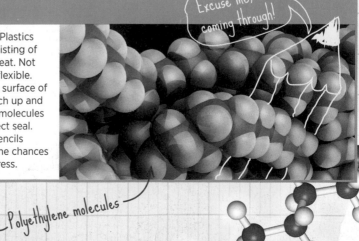

Excuse me, coming through!

The secret to this trick lies in the make-up of plastic. Plastics are made of large molecules, called "polymers", consisting of many repeating units that are forced together with heat. Not only are these molecule chains strong, they are also flexible.

When the fine tip of the pencil presses against the surface of the bag, the polymers don't break; instead, they bunch up and nudge to the side. As the pencil passes through, the molecules mould themselves around it, forming an almost perfect seal.

Plastic is only so strong, though. Poke too many pencils through the same area of the bag and you increase the chances of a leak, as the polymers are put under too much stress.

← Polyethylene molecules

Fruit Batteries

Did you know that your fruit bowl is brimming with electrical potential? When life gives you lemons (and a few other household odds and ends), forget about making lemonade – generate home-made electricity instead. *Mwahahaha!*

The levels of electricity are so low that it's safe to touch – you'll just feel a slight tingle. Avoid putting it in your mouth, though!

THE RECORD: Fastest time to light an LED with a fruit battery

THE CHALLENGE: Combine some citrus fruit, copper coins and a few nails to make your very own bio-battery in the fastest possible time.

As cool as it is, this experiment isn't just about generating electricity out of seemingly nothing. Speed is also key. You'll need a steady hand and a well-thought-out plan *before* you begin.

Over the page is a step-by-step guide to how we made a fruit battery, but don't feel bound by this method. You're welcome to try using different fruit and electrodes; remember, science is about experimentation, after all.

Admittedly, you won't be powering your house (or even your phone) with lemons any time soon. Nevertheless, this classic experiment never fails to impress.

Well, we were impressed!

FOR THE RECORD

Professor Saiful Islam (PAK/UK) and his team at the Royal Institution in London, UK, took this experiment to another level on 13 Dec 2016.

Hooking up 1,013 lemons cut in half (left), they drew 1,275.4 volts – the **highest voltage from a fruit battery** – as part of a demonstration for the annual BBC Royal Institution Christmas Lectures.

The **highest *power* from a fruit battery**, meanwhile, is 1.21 watts, achieved by Da Vinci Media (DEU), using 1,500 lemons in 2013. The power generated was used to light an LED display.

GUIDELINES

- A typical fruit battery uses citrus fruit, copper coins, galvanized nails and crocodile/alligator clips; other materials can be used, but you must get approval from the GWR records team first.

- All fruit incisions must be made *before* the attempt.

- The mini LED diode used must have a forward voltage between 1.6 and 4.2 V.

- The bulb must be fully lit, with a voltmeter used to measure the output. The reading must match the forward voltage stated within a 0.1-V margin of error.

- The attempt must be overseen by two independent witnesses and timed by an experienced timekeeper.

A (tiny) light bulb moment!

WE USED:
- CITRUS FRUIT
- COPPER COINS
- CROCODILE/ALLIGATOR CLIPS
- GALVANIZED (ZINC-COATED) NAILS
- LED BULB
- VOLTMETER

- - - - SHOPPING LIST - - - - -

Limes and oranges work, too

UT0021YB

MAKE & BREAK

HOW DOES IT WORK?

Anode   Wire   Cathode

Zn   Cu

Electrolyte

All batteries (including bio-batteries, like this) consist of three key parts: a positive electrode (cathode) that is looking to shed electrons, a negative electrode (anode) that is looking to pick up electrons, and some form of fluid/solution (electrolyte) connecting the two. Once the electrodes are linked up (usually by a wire), the electrons begin to flow and hey presto, you have electricity.

Reacting to the citric acid in the lemon, the zinc (nail) is "oxidized" (i.e., it loses electrons), whereas the copper (coin) is "reduced" (i.e., it gains electrons). The lemon juice serves the role of "electrolyte" – a conductive pathway through which positive ions can flow. Electrons then travel through the external crocodile clips to complete the circuit.

The whole process is known as a "redox reaction"

Fruit Batteries (continued)

1

First, give your lemons a quick roll to make sure the insides are extra juicy. Carefully use a knife or scissors to pre-cut two slots/holes in one side of each lemon – this must be done *before* attempting the **fastest time to light an LED with a fruit battery**.

Give your coins a clean to remove any built-up grime

2

Once the timer starts, the first thing you'll need to do is insert all of your electrodes into the pre-made holes. We've begun with the cathodes (the positive electrodes): the copper coins.

4

Join up all of the electrodes with crocodile clips. Each time, make sure that one end is attached to a nail and the other is attached to a coin.

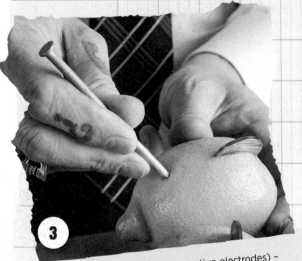

3

Next, add your anodes (the negative electrodes) – we're using galvanized nails. Both the coins and nails need to go in deep enough to be in contact with the pulpy centre, but leave enough metal exposed to easily attach the clips.

In a "batteries in series" configuration, each cell (or lemon in this case) contributes to the total voltage

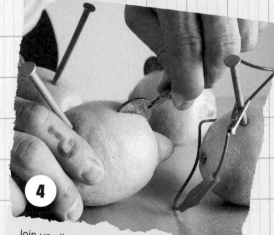

5

Once you've joined up all the lemon batteries, you should be left with two free clips at the ends – one coming from a nail and the other from a coin. These will hold the LED.

DING!

6

To complete the circuit, attach the clips to the diode. The lead from the coin should go to the negative "leg" (often indicated by a flattened edge on the plastic casing). As soon as the LED is fully lit, the timer can be stopped.

The forward voltage of an LED is typically between 1.8 and 3.3 volts

TOP TIP!
FROM PROFESSOR ORBAX

The components we have used here are just one way of making a fruit battery. Why not try experimenting with other types of fruit? Acid is essential to the process, so it's best to stick with citrus fruit, such as limes, grapefruit and oranges. It won't qualify for this particular record, but you can also create a battery out of potatoes (this relies on phosphoric, rather than citric, acid). It's possible to use alternative copper/zinc objects for the electrodes, too – or even different metals altogether. Just make sure that you run your equipment list past the records team at **www.guinnessworldrecords.com** first.

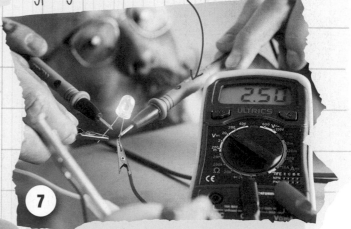

2.50

7

Before you pack up, there's one last job. With the voltmeter, take a reading of the output and photograph the display to send as evidence. It must be within 0.1 volts of the LED's stated forward voltage to be valid.

Rubber-Band Car

Gasoline cars are on the way out; the future is alternative fuels, such as electric batteries, hydrogen cells and, er, giant rubber bands...? Well, perhaps not that last one. Rubber-band cars do work, though, and they can cover record-breaking distances.

THE RECORD: Farthest distance travelled by a home-made rubber-band vehicle

THE CHALLENGE: Build a four-wheeled car from random stuff you have lying around at home. Add some rubber bands for power and see how far it goes!

For this record, we're not that bothered about how you make the car – just as long as it has four wheels and gets its power from a stretched rubber band. Over the page, we've put together a set of instructions for a basic design to give you somewhere to start, but you can change some of the elements or come up with your own design. Get creative!

For the record attempt, you're going to want to find a super-flat surface, such as the floor of a school hall or gym. For the initial tests – if your car runs as badly as ours did at first! – you can probably just make do with your hallway or even a dining table.

We're assuming you never throw anything away, you filthy animal!

SHOPPING LIST

WE USED:
- MUSTARD BOTTLE
- RUBBER BANDS
- BOTTLE CAPS OF VARIOUS SIZES
- SKEWERS

GUIDELINES

- You can make your car from any combination of the items, such as rubber bands (duh!), plastic bottles, bottle lids, wooden lolly sticks, straws, toothpicks, wooden kebab skewers, glue and tape. Other household items may be used, but they must be pre-approved by GWR.

- The car must have four wheels and must derive its power solely from the energy stored up in the rubber band(s).

- The rubber band(s) may only be wound by hand – no mechanical or electrical aids are allowed.

- The record attempt must take place indoors.

- The car must be released behind a clearly marked starting line, and must travel along a flat surface.

- The distance is measured as a straight line between the starting point and the closest edge of the car to the start line when it stops.

HOW DOES IT WORK?

By stretching out an elastic band, you're transferring energy (elastic potential energy) into the rubber in the same way that you transfer energy (gravitational potential energy) into something when you lift it up. The rubber used in elastic bands is made from long polymer chains (see p.103) that are, in their natural state, all wrinkled up. When you stretch or twist a piece of rubber, the chains are pulled straight – which they don't like. The moment you let go, they snap back to their wrinkled state – releasing all that stored energy in the process.

Chain molecules unstretched...

...and stretched

108

Same weight as SIX dairy cows!

AAAAaaaaahhhmoooo

In Apr 2004, Joel Waul (USA) started making a rubber-band ball at his home in Lauderhill, Florida. He started with office supplies, but soon reached the point where those little bands wouldn't stretch far enough to cover his ball.

By 2007, he was knotting together massive industrial rubber straps. and by the time it was measured in Nov 2008, Joel had the world's **largest rubber-band ball**.

The ball, which he calls "Megaton", was 2 m (6 ft 7 in) in diameter, weighed 4,097 kg (9,032 lb) and contained some 700,000 individual rubber bands!

MAKE & BREAK

The word "rubber" was coined in 1770 because of the substance's ability to rub out pencil marks. The rubber band was patented in 1845 by British inventor Stephen Perry.

T.I.L
TODAY I LEARNED

Elastic bungee cords are one of the most common causes of serious eye injury in the USA, although they can't compete with falling on things (ouch), fights (ouch) and accidents involving sharp objects (oooouch... some people still haven't learned not to run with scissors!)

NOW TRY THIS...

Stretchy things can power cars in more ways than one... You can also make a rocket-style car with a balloon. To build this, you'll need to replace your rubber-band motor with a balloon and a nozzle of some kind (a drinking straw works pretty well). First, feed the nozzle into the mouth of the balloon and bind it up as tightly as you can with rubber bands and tape. Then stick the nozzle/balloon assembly to the car with the nozzle pointing out the back.

Inflate the balloon by blowing (or pumping) air down the straw and then let it go. The force of the air coming out of the balloon will push the car forward like a rocket, except slower, and with a farting noise instead of flames.

→ Direction of travel →

Balloon

Straw

Air

Wheels

Every action has an equal and opposite reaction

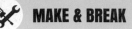
Rubber-Band Car (continued)

Professor Orbax is holding the bottle like this to show the camera – you'd be better off laying it flat on the table

Keep fingers well out of the way when cutting – or get an adult to help with this bit

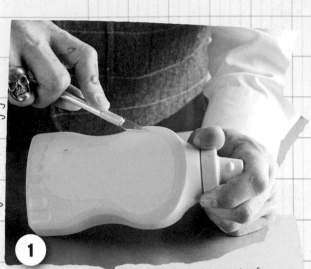

1

For our design, we started by cutting out one side of a mustard bottle. It's best to use a sharp craft knife for this, cutting very carefully to avoid weakening the bottle (don't cut into the sides) or stabbing yourself in the hand!

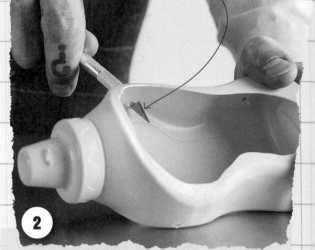

2

Poke holes in the sides for the axles to pass through. When cutting holes with a knife, constantly ask yourself, "What's on the other side of this? Is it my other hand?" You don't want the answer to this question to be yes!

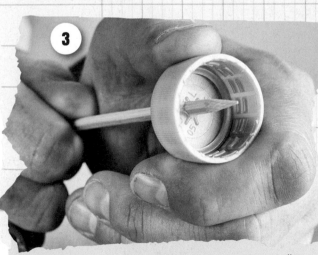

3

Poke the wooden skewers through the smaller, sturdier bottle lids – depending on the sort of lids you've found, you may need to start this by making a hole with the knife or a metal skewer. Needless to say, don't stab yourself in the hand with the skewers!

Hot glue is hot! (duh!)

4

Secure one end of each axle to the wheel using hot glue (don't do both ends now or you won't be able to push it through the car). Make sure the parts are well glued together, and that none of them are glued to your hands!

Axle: rod/shaft that passes through the centre of a wheel, allowing the wheel to spin

5

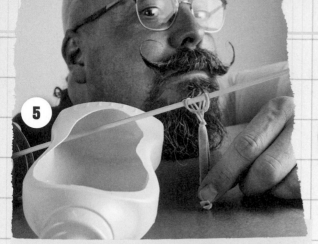

Pass the rear axle through one side of the car and tie on the rubber band (see Top Tip!, right). You want your rubber-band motor to be fairly tight and stretched out between the axles.

TOP TIP!
FROM PROFESSOR ORBAX

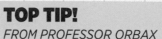

For this to work, you need to attach the rubber band to the axle in the correct way. The way we did it was using a knot called a "cow hitch". Here's how to make one:

1. Put one end of the rubber band over the axle. **2.** Wrap that end around the axle. **3.** Tuck the other end through the bit that goes around the axle. **4.** Pull the whole thing tight.

MAKE & BREAK

6

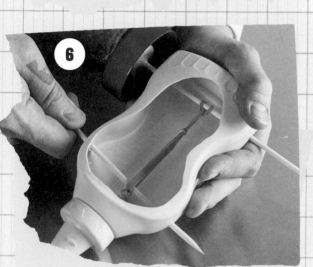

Push the front axle through and loop the other end of the rubber band around it. If your rubber band is too long and slack, tie a knot in it past the front axle to use up any extra rubber.

7

Trim the axles to the right length with wire cutters. You want the wheels to be reasonably close to the body, but not so close as to make it impossible to glue in the wheels (repeating stage 4) on the other side.

8

Stretch some more rubber bands over each wheel to give them more grip. Now it's time to test your creation. How far will it go?

To power the car, turn the back wheels so that the rubber bands tighten. Then simply let go!

Super Slime

Slime, gunge, goo... It doesn't matter what you call it, few things will gross out your parents more than this wonder material! You can roll it, squash it or hang it off your nose like a booger – but for this record, it's all about stretching it.

TIL
TODAY I LEARNED

Silly Putty was invented during World War II by a chemist who was trying to make artificial rubber for the US military. He came up with a blend of chemicals that was bouncy, non-toxic and gooey at room temperature – all fun things, but no use to the war effort.

THE RECORD: Longest distance to stretch home-made slime in 30 seconds

THE CHALLENGE: This is a record of two halves. First, you have to channel your inner mad chemist to make the slime. This will probably take a few tries to get the perfect recipe – you're aiming for elastic, but not too runny.

Second, you have to stretch a piece of your slime as far as it will go without breaking. For this part of the attempt, you only have 30 sec, so you have to work quickly!

Things can quickly get messy when working with slime, so it's best to attempt this record on a wipe-clean surface like tiles or lino – NOT carpet!

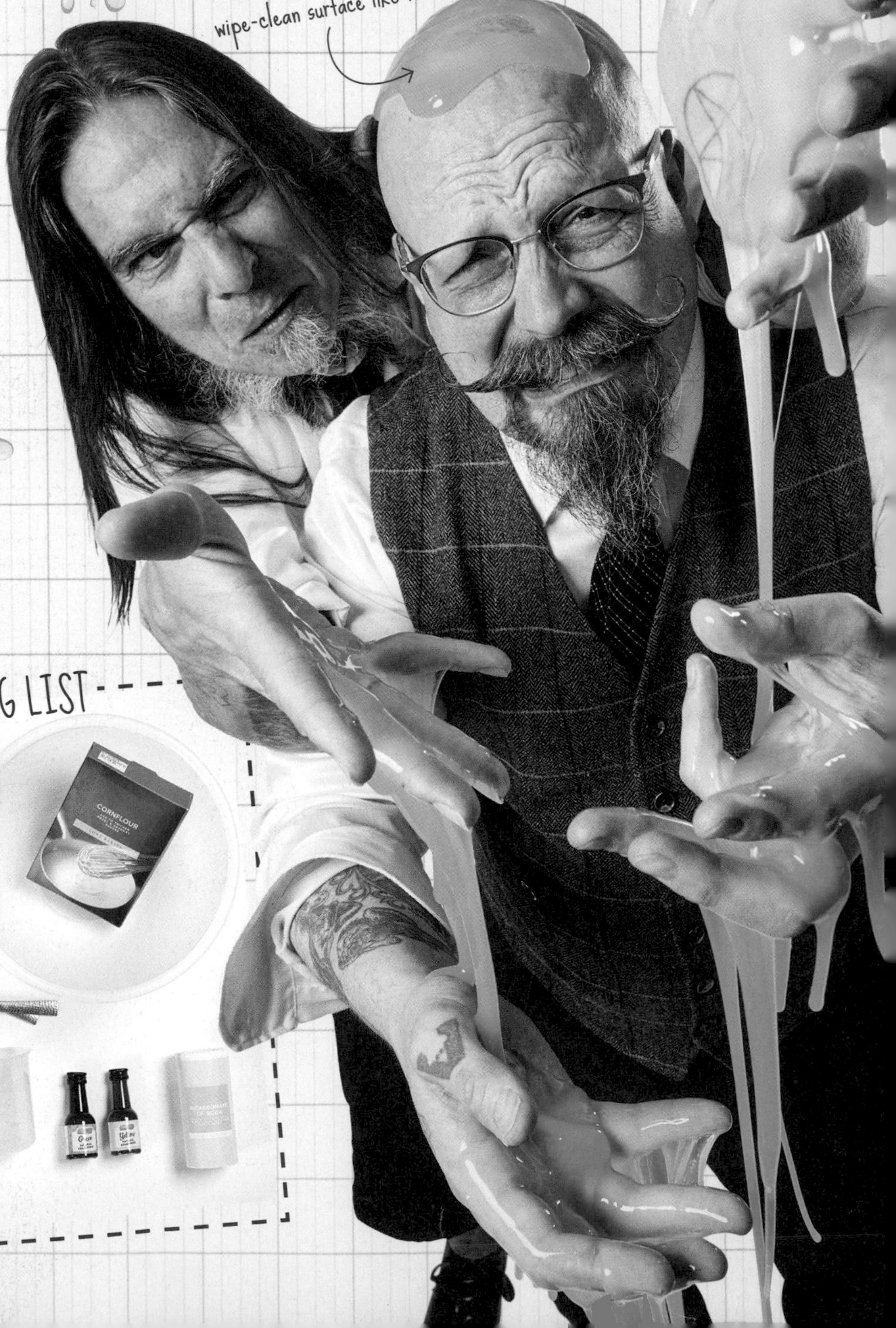

WE USED:
- PVA GLUE
- BAKING SODA
- FOOD COLOURING
- BOWL & SPOON
- LAUNDRY DETERGENT (WITH BORAX)

SHOPPING LIST

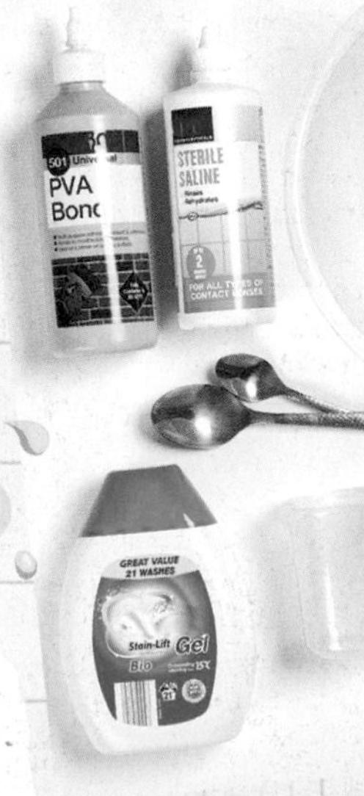

GUIDELINES

- The following ingredients can be used to make the slime: glue, water, borax, cornstarch/flour and food colouring. The ingredients list and methodology must be submitted as evidence, along with video footage.

- The slime used must weigh no more than 50 g (1.7 oz). Its weight must be recorded on a scale.

- The challenger starts with their hands flat on a surface. When the time starts, the slime must be stretched with the hands. After 30 sec, the challenger must stop touching the slime; it should be left to rest for 10 sec before any measurements are taken.

- There can be no complete tears/breaks in the slime, otherwise the attempt is invalid.

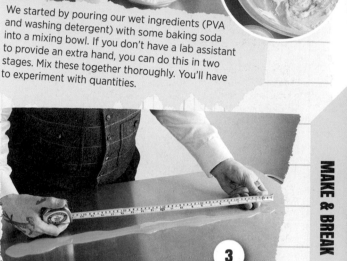

1 We started by pouring our wet ingredients (PVA and washing detergent) with some baking soda into a mixing bowl. If you don't have a lab assistant to provide an extra hand, you can do this in two stages. Mix these together thoroughly. You'll have to experiment with quantities.

2 Food colouring isn't obligatory to the recipe, but it certainly makes the slime more... well, slimy. Once you've stirred this in, you may need to add a bit more powder to counter the gloopiness (see Top Tip! below).

3 Once you're happy with the consistency of your slime (not too wet, not too dry), you're ready to try for the record. Start with it as a ball/blob, then carefully tease it out on a smooth, flat surface. The floor is probably best unless you have a *really* long table. Remember, you're against the clock so work fast!

MAKE & BREAK

HOW DOES IT WORK?

The key ingredient in this is borax. It sounds like a Pokémon character, but is actually a chemical compound used in detergents, contact-lens solution and a few other household products. You'll need to find a detergent with borax (not all of them do) – otherwise your slime will be a bit rubbish.

The borax – also known as sodium borate – makes the slime slimy by bonding with the PVA (polyvinyl acetate) glue. The vinyl acetate polymers are cross-linked (joined together) by the sodium borate molecules, creating massive interconnected molecule chains.

It's these long chains that give slime its unusual non-Newtonian properties. It's a liquid most of the time, but acts more like a solid if struck or put under pressure.

At rest, the loose structure of the molecules gives slime its soft and flexible feel – behaving much like a liquid.

Under pressure, (e.g., squashing), the molecules lock together, acting more like a solid; when the pressure stops, they return to their "liquid" state

1 Soft & flexible **2** Locks on shock

TOP TIP!
FROM PROFESSOR ORBAX

Is your slime too slimy? Is it running all over the place and generally not co-operating with your attempts to break records? What you need is a thickening agent. We used a bit of cornflour (*not* cornmeal – that's something completely different) to get our slime to behave.

A tablespoon or two is enough to get things looking right. Just sprinkle it into the mixture and stir it in.

If you go too far and stiffen your slime into a thick, unbending goop, you'll need to add a little more PVA glue and detergent to balance things out. Careful, though; add it a little at a time or you might end up back where you started!

113

Marshmallow Catapult

You'll need a good aim and a faithful lab assistant (or at least a willing buddy) to take on this *sweet* experiment. Perhaps don't mention that their role will mainly involve having marshmallows fired at them... Heads up, Sweet Pepper!

Minimum marshmallow size

2.5 cm
2.5 cm

THE RECORD: Most marshmallows caught in the mouth with a home-made catapult in one minute

THE CHALLENGE: Construct your own catapult out of everyday items, such as lolly sticks and bulldog clips, then use it to hurl marshmallows at a friend (or enemy). How many sweets can your partner catch in their mouth in a minute?

Be warned – this trick is, well, tricky. *Really* tricky. You're going to need a lot of practice to nail the right technique.
No surprise, science is the key. Wrap your head around how energy works and you'll be hitting your target every time. Well, sometimes... Even if you don't, at least you can console yourself with marshmallows. Siege warfare never tasted so good!

GUIDELINES

• The details – and diagrams – of your proposed design must be submitted to GWR for approval *before* you make the catapult.

• The marshmallows can be cuboid or cylindrical, but each must be at least 2.5 cm (1 in) in all dimensions.

• The person catching the marshmallows must be standing at least 2 m (6 ft 6 in) from the catapult at all times.

• Only one marshmallow can be fired at a time. It's up to the challenger whether they eat or spit out a marshmallow once it's been caught in the mouth.

SHOPPING LIST

WE USED:
- BULLDOG CLIP
- BOTTLE CAPS
- LOLLY STICKS (TWO SIZES)
- MARSHMALLOWS

You'll also need a glue gun and scissors!

We made our catapult with two types of wooden lolly stick (glued into a framework), a bulldog clip and a lid from a milk bottle. But that's just one way of doing it. Other things you can use to harness that crucial potential energy are clothes pegs, springs and elastic bands.

HOW DOES IT WORK?

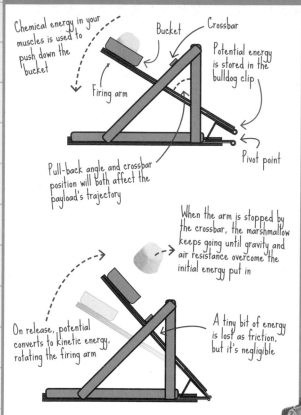

Chemical energy in your muscles is used to push down the bucket

Bucket

Crossbar

Potential energy is stored in the bulldog clip

Firing arm

Pivot point

Pull-back angle and crossbar position will both affect the payload's trajectory

When the arm is stopped by the crossbar, the marshmallow keeps going until gravity and air resistance overcome the initial energy put in

On release, potential converts to kinetic energy, rotating the firing arm

A tiny bit of energy is lost as friction, but it's negligible

The first law of thermodynamics states that energy can neither be created nor destroyed – only transferred. This experiment is a perfect demonstration of that law in action.

When the catapult is sitting on a table at rest, it's in an energy-neutral state. You use chemical energy (which we get from the food we eat – including marshmallows, incidentally) to depress the arm. Once the levered section is down, it's under tension, with energy stored in the compressed bulldog clip. As soon as you let go of the end, the potential energy converts into kinetic energy, swinging the arm until it hits the crossbar, at which point the payload is propelled forward. The marshmallow will travel in an arc at the same speed the arm moved, until other forces counteract it. The velocity of the sweet and how far it will travel are both determined by how much energy you put in, i.e., how far you pull back the arm.

FOR THE RECORD

Working on the same principle of rapidly converting stored energy into kinetic energy was this record-setting trebuchet. These medieval weapons (see *TIL*, below left) actually had a far greater range than catapults. They get their power from a counterweight attached to a long arm, with the payload suspended from the opposite end with a sling. When the weight is released, the arm rotates and the projectile is flung forward. The **most powerful trebuchet (20+-kg projectile)**, built by Nova FM – Partridge (AUS) in 2011, tossed a VW Beetle car weighing 766 kg (1,688 lb) a distance of 76.9 m (252 ft).

Probably best not to do this with your parents' car...

Goggles are also recommended – because no one likes getting a marshmallow in the eye!

TIL
TODAY I LEARNED

During the Middle Ages, weapons such as catapults and trebuchets were all the rage for throwing rocks at things. They were the go-to solution for storming enemy fortresses. As well as being good at smashing down walls, they could also be used to toss diseased animals into towns – one of the first forms of biological warfare.

Marshmallow Catapult
(continued)

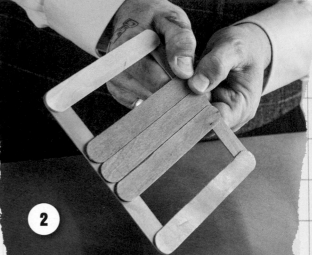

1 HOT!!!

No matter what you use to make your catapult, you're going to need a way of sticking things together. A glue gun is the fastest and most secure way of doing this. Take care when working with hot glue as it's very... burn-y. Not quite as hot as "blue lava" (see pp.34–35), but it feels close! In fact, you might want to ask a responsible adult to help you with this bit.

2

With the glue gun loaded and ready, the first thing to do is build the base. Whatever shape you go with, the main thing you want it to be is sturdy. With this in mind, we went for a square design, with a reinforced strip in the middle to hold the firing arm.

3

4

Now, we turn our attention to the firing arm. This is the bit that will launch the marshmallow. We made ours from four more lolly sticks. Carefully cut one end off each stick, and make sure that they're all the same length!

Glue the four sticks on to the bulldog clip, sandwiching the metal arms between the sticks. Don't be shy with the glue at this stage as you want the firing arm to be solid. Remember to set it aside to dry for a few minutes before you continue.

PAC-Man would be awesome at this record...

...as would a pelican

5

Attach one side of the firing arm to the central plate on the base. While that's setting, you can start making the two side panels. We created two right-angles out of six smaller lolly sticks (see Top Tip!, right, before you begin).

TOP TIP!
FROM PROFESSOR ORBAX

One of the hardest parts about this record is consistency. Even when you've aimed a marshmallow into your partner's mouth once, it's pretty much as difficult the second time, and the third...
A trick to help with this (which is completely within the rules!) is to measure and mark out some lines on the catapult framework, so you know you're putting the same energy into each launch. You could even use geometry equipment such as a protractor or set-square as part of your catapult's design.

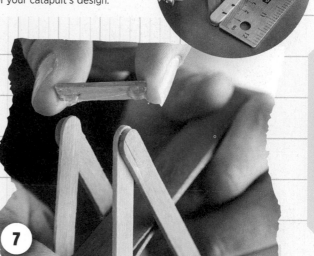

6

The catapult is really starting to take shape now. Glue the two triangular struts either side of the firing arm. It's worth leaving these to dry and then applying some additional glue to make sure the joins are strong. This will help extend the life-span of your candy chucker.

7

It doesn't look like much, but this small piece of lolly stick – or whatever you opt to use – is crucial. Without a crossbar, the arm keeps swinging and your marshmallow is doomed to a mediocre flight.

8

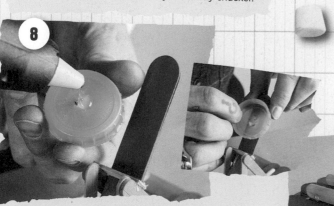

The final step is to add the "bucket" that will hold your tasty projectile. You want something deep enough so that the marshmallow won't keep falling out, but not so snug that the payload might get stuck when firing. Before sticking, lightly score the base of the lid for extra grip.

I regreeeetttt noooothing...

MAKE & BREAK

Static Balloons

Most people think all electricity is good for is turning on lights and tasering criminals. But did you know it also has sticking power? All you need to do is use your head and think positive (well, and negative).

THE RECORD: Most balloons consecutively suspended by static electricity

THE CHALLENGE: Stick as many balloons as you can to a wall or ceiling with static electricity. How many can you make stick before one falls off?

The first step is to blow up as many balloons as you can without passing out. Next, put on something woolly such as a sweater or a scarf. Why? So you can rub the balloons on it and get them charged with static. Finally, stick 'em to a wall. Simple!

Alternatively, you can just rub the balloons on your hair…

Stick with it, people!

Balloon

Not a balloon

GUIDELINES

• The record must take place in a room with a plastered wall or ceiling.

• You can use as many balloons as you want, and they can be of any variety of shapes and sizes.

• All balloons must be inflated with lung power and may only contain air – no helium or other gases allowed.

• At a given signal, you may pick up a balloon and rub it on your head or clothing to build up a static charge. It can then be transferred to the wall or ceiling.

• The attempt ends when one of the balloons loses its static and slips or falls from the wall/ceiling to the floor.

SHOPPING LIST

YOU MUST USE:
- BALLOONS

Any shaped party or modelling balloons will do

TIL
TODAY I LEARNED

Ever wondered why a Van de Graaff generator (below) makes your hair stand on end? The machine gives your body an overall positive charge. Because like charges repel, each strand of positively charged hair does all it can to get away from its neighbours, sending your locks flying.

HOW DOES IT WORK?

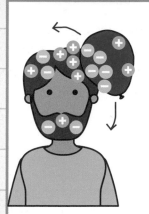

The balloon will only be "sticky" on the side you rubbed

As you rub the balloon against your head or your clothes, something is happening – or rather lots of little things are happening – at a subatomic level. As a result of friction, electrons from your hair/fabric move on to the surface of the balloon, giving it an overall negative charge. (Because your hair has lost some of its electrons, it becomes temporarily positively charged – this is why strands of your hair stick to the balloon.)

A surface such as a wall is normally neutral in terms of charge. However, placing the net-negative balloon against it causes the positively charged particles to gather at the surface. As we all know, opposites attract, and so the balloon "sticks" – until, at least, the electrons begin to dissipate, at which point the balloon falls. Sad times.

⭐ FOR THE RECORD

For a truly hair-raising display of static electricity, you need a Van de Graaff generator. These machines pass a revolving rubber belt over rollers to create their differential in charge. The belt accumulates electrons (giving it a net negative charge), while the rollers (and the surrounding metal sphere) become positive. When enough static builds up, the sphere attempts to dispel the charge by firing out sparks at the nearest object – whether that's another metal sphere or you!

Invented by Dr Robert Van de Graaff (USA), the **largest Van de Graaff generator** (below) was demonstrated to the public on 28 Nov 1933. Each of its columns stands at 25 ft (7.6 m), topped by a 15-ft-wide (4.5-m) orb. Now housed at the Boston Museum of Science in Massachusetts, USA, it reportedly produced lightning-like discharges of up to 7 million volts.

NOW TRY THIS...

If you still want proof that static electricity is real (it's not magic, we promise!), this trick is pretty neat. Start the same way by rubbing a balloon against your preferred surface (sweater, cloth, etc.) for a minute or two. You can use your hair to test that it has acquired a strong negative charge. Run a tap and slowly move the charged side of the balloon towards the stream. As it gets closer, you should see the water defy gravity and bend! This is the result of the balloon repelling the electrons in the water, giving the H_2O in its immediate vicinity a slightly positive charge. Just as happens with the wall, opposites attract. Unlike the wall, the water is light enough to be manipulated and so is drawn towards the balloon.

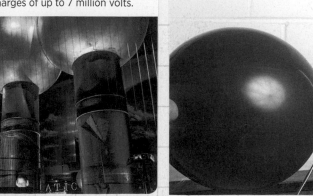

Woo – science!

Paper Planes

This record-breaking challenge is really taking off – how many home-made paper aircraft can you throw into a target area in three minutes? Be warned: time flies when you're against the clock.

THE RECORD: Most times to hit a target with paper aircraft in three minutes

THE CHALLENGE: Fold one or more paper planes – the design is up to you, as long as it conforms to GWR guidelines – and then start that stopwatch. You've got three minutes to lob as many of them into a target zone as you can.

GUIDELINES

- The planes you use must be a classic paper aircraft design with recognizable wings and made from A4 paper (210 x 297 mm) or US Letter paper (8.5 x 11 in).

- The target range must consist of a circle with a diameter of no less than 6 m (19 ft 8 in). A bucket with a maximum diameter of no greater than 30 cm (11.8 in) must be placed in the middle of this circle to ensure that the distance between the outer circle and the bucket is 3 m (10 ft) from all points along the circle.

- Any planes that bounce out of the target bucket will be discounted from the total.

Paper planes – the bane of school teachers everywhere – are actually a good way to learn about aerodynamics. Some planes are designed for long flights and some for accuracy. It's the latter you'll need here, as this record is about repeatedly hitting a target. We've suggested one design (overleaf) but you don't have to use it – why not get creative and try a few designs of your own?

With normal aircraft, wings are shaped in such a way that air travels over the top of the wing at a higher speed than the air beneath. The faster air above the wing results in a drop in pressure compared with below the wing. The *difference* in pressure is what causes the wing – and the aircraft – to lift (see below).

HOW DOES IT WORK?

As with regular big, metal planes, paper aircraft are affected by a number of forces as they fly:

Thrust: This is the energy you apply when you throw the plane, giving it its power.

Lift: What the flying plane experiences as air moves over and under the wings, keeping it aloft.

Weight: Gravity is always acting on the plane, pulling it towards the ground.

Drag: Friction with the air slows your plane's forward momentum.

Experiment with the size and shape of your plane's various elements – a heavier nose, longer wings or sleeker body will affect its flight.

You

30 cm
3 m

Lift

Wing (experiment with angles)

Nose (a heavy nose = a stable flight)

Thrust

Drag

Weight

Fast air above wing = lower pressure

Consider tearing and folding up an "elevator" on each wing for extra lift

Difference in pressure = lift!

Multiple record-breaker Ashrita Furman (left) of New York, USA, holds a paper plane record... in his mouth! Ashrita and his friend Bipin Larkin (USA) broke their own record for the **most paper aircraft caught in the mouth in one minute**, with 17 – or one every 3.5 sec! Bipin did the throwing, while Ashrita did the catching, improving on their record for the second time. They first achieved 14 planes back in 2011, then 16 in 2012. Can *you* beat the unflappable Ashrita?!

Engineering students often use paper aeroplanes to learn the principles of flight and aerodynamics. That's why students and employees of the Braunschweig Institute of Technology in Germany built the **largest paper plane** in 2013. It had a wing-span of 18.21 m (59 ft 9 in) – as long as a bowling alley!

Planes must hit the bucket - NOT your lab assistant!

TIL
TODAY I LEARNED

Throwing paper planes is an extreme sport! Since 2006, x-sports fanatics Red Bull have hosted the Red Bull Paper Wings world paper plane championships. Three disciplines are contested: distance, hangtime and aerobatics. Could you be the next champ?

Paper Planes (continued)

You can only use one sheet of paper per plane, and you're not allowed any glue or sticky tape. You can use the same design or as many different designs as you want (other ideas pictured below). Here's one that we've used to get your attempt off the ground (**1**). To make it, start by folding the sheet in half along its length (**2**), then unfold (**3**).

Take the top-right corner and fold it down to the centre fold to form a triangle (**4**). Repeat with the top-left corner (**5**). Then fold this newly formed triangle down, giving you a square (**6**).

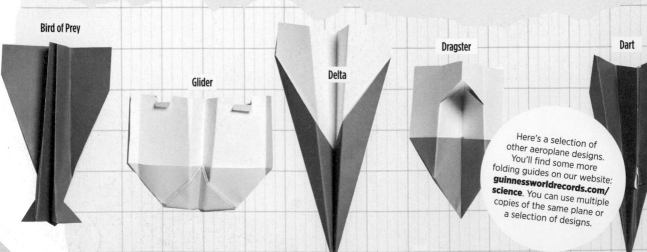

Bird of Prey

Glider

Delta

Dragster

Dart

Here's a selection of other aeroplane designs. You'll find some more folding guides on our website: **guinnessworldrecords.com/ science**. You can use multiple copies of the same plane or a selection of designs.

Fold the top-left corner over so that the corner touches the centre fold (**7**). Repeat with the top-right corner (**8**). You should be left with a small triangular point, which can be folded back (**9**).

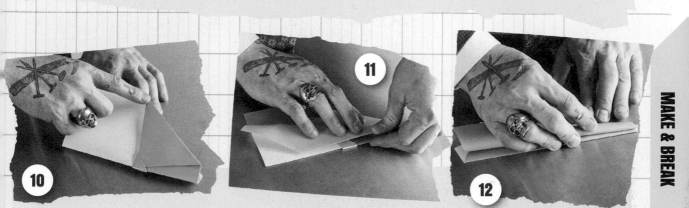

Flip the plane over and bring the two halves together along the centre fold (**10**). Next, fold the right-hand wing down until it aligns with the centre fold (**11**) and repeat for the left wing (**12**).

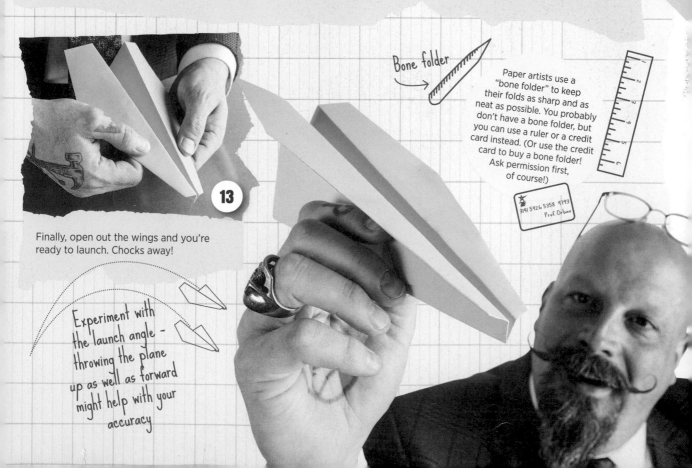

Finally, open out the wings and you're ready to launch. Chocks away!

Bone folder

Paper artists use a "bone folder" to keep their folds as sharp and as neat as possible. You probably don't have a bone folder, but you can use a ruler or a credit card instead. (Or use the credit card to buy a bone folder! Ask permission first, of course!)

3141 5926 5358 9793
Prof Orbas

Experiment with the launch angle – throwing the plane up as well as forward might help with your accuracy

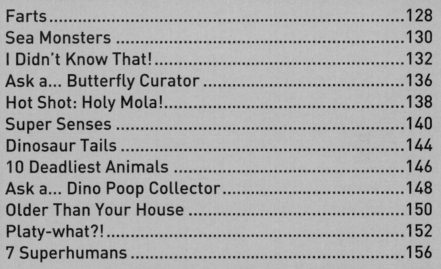

IT'S ALIVE!

SMALLEST NEMATODES

"Aaargh, what is it?" you might scream. "Kill it with fire!" But no, don't run away, shrieking with terror – this ugly-looking critter is just 80 micrometres long. That's about the same size as the diameter of an average strand of human hair. The world's **smallest nematodes**, or round worms, have no common names. They live in marine sediments and they're mostly harmless to humans. Unless they burrow into your skin or eyeballs and lay their eggs... in which case, still don't kill them with fire!

Aaarrrrrghhhh!!!

Run for your life!

LOUDEST BUUUUURP!!

We've all embarrassed ourselves by burping loudly, but have you ever wondered just how loud you could belch if you *really* went for it?

It starts with a large bottle of soda – cola, preferably. Two or three big gulps later and Paul Hunn is ready to make his record attempt. He bends at the waist, his hands lock into his hips. It's all part of the preparation, like a sprinter settling into the blocks. If you listen closely, you might hear a low rumble. Paul takes one last deep breath, then it's time...
BUUUUUUURRRRPPP!
Roaring out of his mouth, hauled up from the depths of his belly, is the most ear-rupturing eructation you'll ever hear. The sound technician standing 2.5 m (8 ft 2 in) away confirms it with his sound meter: 109.9 decibels – the **loudest burp** by a human being. But how does a humble legal assistant from London (that's him on the left) make a sound louder than a motorcycle... from his gut?!

INSTANT EXPERT

LISTEN UP... Clap your hands together. The noise you hear is the result of air particles vibrating. The energy in the clap transfers to particles in the air, which begin to vibrate. These energetic particles bump into other particles, travelling like an ocean wave. The bumping continues until the particles reach your ear (or run out of energy).

Pressure waves in air

| HIGH AND LOUD | Sound wave shape | LOW AND QUIET |

You hear a sound because the vibrating waves cause your eardrum to vibrate. The eardrum then channels the sound down your ear canal to the auditory nerves, which send signals to the brain. In a split second, your brain knows that you've just been belched at.

Decibels

Sound is measured on the decibel scale. Readings increase on what's called a *logarithmic* scale. This means that a sound pressure level of 30 dB is 10 times higher than 20 dB and 100 times higher than 10 dB.

It also matters how close the sound meter is to the thing it's measuring. The closer you are to the source of a sound, the louder it will seem. That's why sound-related records need to all be measured from the same distance – in this case, 2.5 m (8 ft 2 in). The decibel scale on the left gives some common measurements – where would *your* burps register?

NORMAL CONVERSATION

FRIDGE HUM

TOILET FLUSH

LAWNMOWER

MOTORCYCLE

COMPUTER FANS

AMBULANCE SIREN

WHISPER

FIGHTER JET

FIRECRACKER

SHOTGUN BLAST

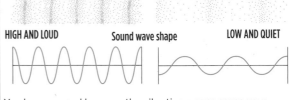

DECIBELS
A-WEIGHTED, MEASURED FROM A DISTANCE OF 1 M

REDLINE CAUSES HEARING DAMAGE

10 20 30 40 50 60 70 80 90 100 110 120 130 140 150 160 0

I need to burp.

You can burp through your nose too!

Mouth

BURP

Upper sphincter

HOW DO YOU BURP...? The process of turning food into energy is a long and complicated one involving bacteria, enzymes and acid. Over the course of its long, twisty journey from your mouth to your butt, the food you eat breaks down, producing gas in the process.

It's not a little bit of gas either: on a typical day, the average adult's innards create about 25 litres (6.6 gal) of gas – that's enough to inflate a beach ball! The reason we aren't all huge wobbling balloons is that most of this gas – which was created by bacteria – is re-absorbed by other bacteria. Only about 2.5 litres (0.6 gal) is left over and has to be expelled.

The gas that's produced in your intestines (which is most of it) tends to leave by going, er, down – emerging as farts, in case you hadn't guessed. Generally, only the gas that's produced in your stomach and the top of your digestive system is expelled out of your mouth as a burp. This small amount of digestive gas gives burps their stink, but most of what comes out is just air that you swallowed while eating, or carbon dioxide from fizzy drinks.

3

As the gas reaches the top of your oesophagus, you can either allow it to fill your mouth and release it discreetly, or open wide and let rip!

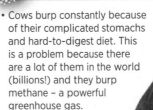

WHAT MAKES A BURP SO LOUD?

THE BIG QUESTION

You don't make a burping sound when you breathe out (thankfully!), so why is a burp different? It's because the burp is pushed out with such energy that it causes the flappy tissue at the top of your oesophagus to vibrate – in the same way that a whoopie cushion makes a fart noise.

Some people can burp words or even the entire alphabet by controlling their oesophagus. The medical term for burping words is "esophageal speech".

If you want the loudest possible burp, record-breaker Paul Hunn recommends that you drink fizzy pop – through a straw might also help – and breathe in as much air as possible. Then, use your stomach muscles to push that burp out!

2

When your body detects a big bubble of gas in your stomach, it opens the sphincters (little gates made of muscle) at the top and bottom of your oesophagus, allowing the gas to move up to your mouth.

Oesophagus

aka "food pipe" or "gullet"

1

You've eaten some food and it's all settled in your stomach. After the initial sloshing and splashing, the air and gas tends to rise to the top. (In a weightless environment this doesn't happen, so astronaut burps are unpleasantly damp. Ew, gross!)

Lower sphincter

+ MORE *STUFF!*

- Cows burp constantly because of their complicated stomachs and hard-to-digest diet. This is a problem because there are a lot of them in the world (billions!) and they burp methane – a powerful greenhouse gas.
- In grazing animals, being unable to burp out gas can be fatal – this sometimes happens when they eat too much gassy food. The expanding gas can burst their stomachs!
- Squirrels can't burp.

Stomach

Gas

Food

Acid

To the butt (see p.128)

FRTS

Farts are funny. They always have been and they probably always will be. But what are they, where do they come from and why do they smell so bad?

Everyone farts, and they fart a lot. Unless we live far from civilization, we spend our days wafting through clouds of invisible, generally odourless fart gas. It fills every school and office like a fog.

While everyone farts, however, no two farts are alike. Every person's body has its own distinctive balance of different bacteria that work in unique ways and create a one-of-a-kind, bespoke stench.

Human farts are mostly made up of hydrogen (H_2) and carbon dioxide (CO_2), with smaller amounts of oxygen (O_2)

and nitrogen (N_2). Methane (CH_4) levels vary massively from one person to another, making up anywhere between 0.002% and 28% of fart gas.

These gases constitute the bulk of a fart, but aren't responsible for the smell. The foulness of a hot fart comes from a selection of different compounds (scientists can't exactly agree which ones), with the key ingredient being hydrogen sulphide, which smells of rotten eggs. These eggy gases make up only a tiny fraction (less than 1%) of a fart, but a little bit goes a long way.

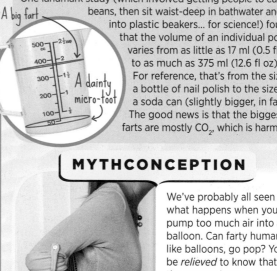

Farts smell bad, but they aren't actually toxic. They are flammable though – because of the hydrogen and methane that they contain!

No naked flames!

HOW BIG IS A FART?

THE BIG QUESTION ?

Scientists who have studied farts (yes, that's a thing) have found that the volume and frequency of farts varies hugely from one person to another. One landmark study (which involved getting people to eat beans, then sit waist-deep in bathwater and fart into plastic beakers... for science!) found that the volume of an individual poot varies from as little as 17 ml (0.5 fl oz) to as much as 375 ml (12.6 fl oz). For reference, that's from the size of a bottle of nail polish to the size of a soda can (slightly bigger, in fact). The good news is that the biggest farts are mostly CO_2, which is harmless.

A big fart

500 cc / 2½ cup
400 / 2
300 / 1½
200 / 1
100 / ½
50

A dainty micro-toot

INSTANT EXPERT

CONTROL YOUR STINK... You've probably noticed that not all farts are created equal. On some days you can bottom-burp for hours without offending anyone, while on others you have to stand in a well-ventilated field and hope the wind carries your terrible deed away from the nearest town. Why?

Some of this is down to the unique population of your gut – everyone's innards are home to food-munching bacteria, and some people have more of the types that create stinky farts than others – but it's also related to your diet. Certain foods – particularly beans, red meat and cabbage-like vegetables – contain lots of sulphur (which is bad). The smelliness of these farts can be made worse by poor diet, which slows the speed at which things move through the gut, giving them more time to really brew up.

Fluuuuurrrrrp

MYTHCONCEPTION

We've probably all seen what happens when you pump too much air into a balloon. Can farty humans, like balloons, go pop? You'll be *relieved* to know that the answer is no, we can't. If we hold our farts in, they either seep out – silent and unnoticed – or they come out in great trumpeting blasts once we go to sleep, when we no longer have the ability to control them. Coughing and sneezing may also set them free. Some fart gases, particularly CO_2, even get reabsorbed into the bloodstream over time.

HOLDING IN A FART CAN KILL YOU

FALSE

To BURPING
on pp.126-27

Food goes in

The small intestine is actually much, much longer than it looks here - about 6 m (19 ft 8 in) in a normal person (we didn't have space)

1

Make a hole in this and you'll probably die

Still food-like at this point

Pretty much just poop now

Mushy past here

Yep, definitely poop

2

Poop-like paste

3

Butt →

Fart factory

WHAT GOES ON IN THERE?... The human digestive system is a really long tube that goes all the way through your body. It starts at your mouth and ends at your anus.

The first stage of your food's magical transformation into poop takes place in the stomach (**1**). Here, the chewed food is bathed in a vat of corrosive liquid (mostly hydrochloric acid), which begins the process of breaking it down.

We're assuming you chew your food, and don't just swallow things whole, like a snake

From the stomach, what is now a sort of paste passes into your small intestine (**2**). Here the food is broken down by a combination of resident bacteria and "digestive juices" (that's actually what they're called) supplied by your pancreas and liver. The nutrients are absorbed through the walls of the small intestine as it squeegees the mixture along using muscle movements called *peristalsis*.

By the time your "food" reaches the large intestine (**3**; also known as the colon), your body has extracted most of what it wants from it, leaving just stinky brown goo (we're talking "worst smell imaginable" stinky here). As it passes through to your anus, the large intestine squeezes out the water (waste not want not) and the last bits of nutrition. It is now officially poop!

FLATULISTS

Other terms include "fartiste" and "farteur"

Farting for laughs may not be high art, but it's never going to go out of style. Professional fart artists, properly called "flatulists", once plied their trade in the royal courts of Europe, tooting away to the delight of kings and princes. In the 19th century, a French performer called La Pétomane regularly sang opera using only his butt. Today, the world's leading flatulist is Mr Methane (aka Paul Oldfield, right), whose act includes an all-fart rendition of the "Blue Danube" waltz.

IT'S ALIVE!

➕ MORE *STUFF!*

- Herring (shoal pictured) communicate with each other by farting. Well, not exactly farting – they're technically venting their swim bladder (an air bag they use to regulate their buoyancy) – but it looks and sounds like farting and probably stinks of fish.
- The **oldest known joke** – which was written down in Sumeria (present-day Iraq) some 3,900 years ago – is about farts. It reads as follows, "Something which has never occurred since time immemorial; a young woman did not fart in her husband's lap." Ha... Yeah, we don't get it either.
- The speed of a fart in an unventilated room has been clocked at about 7 mph (11.2 km/h), but it varies with temperature, composition and humidity. Generally speaking, however, you can outrun a fart.
- The largest farts in the world are thought to be those of the blue whale (not surprising as it is the **largest animal**); they've not been properly measured, but whale biologists say they're real, go on forever and smell horrifying.

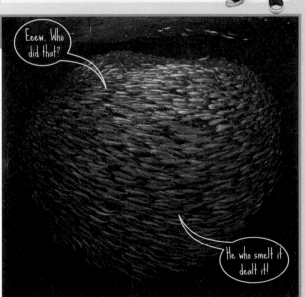

Eeew. Who did that?

He who smelt it dealt it!

SEA MONSTERS

In Feb 2007, the crew of the New Zealand-based fishing boat *San Aspiring* had a nasty shock when their line pulled up not a fish, but a big squid... a really, *really* big squid!

This is what the crew of the *San Aspiring* saw when they looked over the side. We've added the outline of a man to give a sense of how big it is.

The colossal squid and its close relative the giant squid (which is actually only a little bit smaller) are some of the most mysterious and least understood animals in nature.

Scientists have known about them for centuries, but only indirectly. They would come across whales with big, sucker-shaped cuts on their skin and find the occasional giant, rotting tentacle on a beach somewhere.

Even today, with all our cameras and submersibles, the number of confirmed human encounters with colossal squids can be counted on the tentacles of one cephalopod. The accidental capture of a colossal squid by the *San Aspiring* represented a rare opportunity to learn more about the strange, elusive and record-breaking creatures.

FOR THE RECORD

The specimen caught by the crew of the *San Aspiring* in 2007 is the **heaviest colossal squid** ever caught, and one of the first to ever be brought to shore intact.

Recognizing just how unusual their catch was, the crew hauled the squid on board and froze it in the hold. It was then taken to Wellington, New Zealand, where scientists at the Te Papa Natural History Museum defrosted it and carried out a full autopsy (process pictured below).

They calculated the final body length was 4.2 m (13 ft 9 in) – though it may have shrunk in the freezer – and that it weighed 495 kg (1,091 lb). That's about the size of a semi-trailer!

Alarmingly, the scientists who examined the squid were also sure that this specimen was nowhere near fully grown. Based on the sizes of beaks found in the stomachs of whales, it is thought that an adult colossal squid weighs around 750 kg (1,650 lb) and measures some 14 m (45 ft) long. That's roughly the size of a city bus. Some scientists believe they may grow even larger than that – as long as 18 m (59 ft).

This wouldn't really work, but it gives you an idea of scale

The rear part of the mantle is shaped into a fin that the squid uses to steer itself

The "body" of a giant squid is properly called its "mantle"

The red skin is seen here peeling off during the autopsy

FOR THE RECORD

Colossal and giant squids have the **largest eyes** in the animal kingdom. The example caught by the *San Aspiring* in 2007 had eyes that measured 27 cm (10.6 in) across, estimated to have been at least 40 cm (15.7 in) in diameter when it was alive. That's bigger than a full-sized basketball. The lens alone (pictured right, being held – *eew* – by one of the researchers who carried out the autopsy) was about the size of a large orange. And remember: this wasn't even a fully grown adult!

Eye

The plural of squid is squids, which looks silly but is fun to say out loud

MORE STUFF!

Eyes!

Not eyes!

Colossal squids are not the only oceanic oddities...

• The Pacific barrel-eye fish (above) lives in the gloomy deep, but hunts jellyfish that swim in the clearer waters above. It has evolved so that its eyes point up, allowing it to easily spot prey against the light. The eyes are the green orbs on top, not the lumps on the front.

• The vampire squid (below) lives at depths of 900 m (2,952 ft). To see down there, it has the **largest eyes (in proportion to body)** of any animal. It also has glow-in-the-dark ink – black ink isn't much use if you live in darkness!

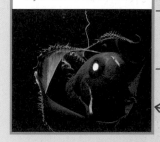

IT'S ALIVE!

It's technically more of an octopus than a squid

INSTANT EXPERT

Hooked suckers

Beak

DEEP-SEA PREDATORS...
Giant squids and colossal squids have eight arms covered with hooked suckers, two long "tentacle clubs" and a razor-sharp beak where arms and body meet. They hunt by grabbing things with the tentacles and then pulling them in towards the beak. Once something has been hooked by the suckers on the arms, escape is impossible.

Surprisingly, given their weaponry, giant squids are quite shy creatures. They only attack their favourite prey (fish, crustaceans and smaller squids) and hide from almost everything else (they're even scared of electric submersible motors).

Also, rather than rending and tearing their prey like sharks, they take delicate little nibbles from what they catch, eating slowly. The reason for this is that each squid's throat goes straight through the middle of their doughnut-shaped brain. Taking too big a bite of something would kill them!

Head

Arms

Tentacle clubs

TIL
TODAY I LEARNED

Giant squids have bodies that are optimized for the crushing pressure of the deep sea. Taking them out of the water has a similar effect to throwing a person into the vacuum of space – they tend to rupture. The aftermath looks pretty gross, as you can see.

I DIDN'T KNOW THAT!

ACTUAL SIZE

CATS IN BOXES

Why does Maru, the **most watched cat on YouTube**, love boxes so much? There are a few possible reasons: the main one is that cats like Maru prefer to be much warmer than people – 35°C (95°F) is a comfortable temperature for a cat. Sitting in a box, with nice insulating cardboard all around, helps keep Maru's furry body warm. Boxes also provide good hiding places, which are important for ambush predators (that's what cats are). He might not look fearsome, but Maru is primed and ready to pounce.

Mi-wow! Maru's videos on YouTube have racked up almost 350 million views!

ITSY BITSY SUNFISH

Have another look at the gigantic *Mola mola* on pp.138–39. You're back? Right, now look at the weird thing on the left here. This is a baby sunfish! More specifically, it's a picture of a baby sunfish blown up to 20 times its actual size. Those massive fish actually grow from that tiny speck shown above left. They grow really fast: one specimen in the USA's Monterey Bay Aquarium grew from 26 kg to 399 kg (57–879 lb) in just 15 months!

PUNCHABLE FACES! Recent studies have suggested that early hominids (the ancestors of modern humans) evolved stronger faces at around the same time that they evolved the ability to form their hands into fists, and that these things are (unsurprisingly) connected. This "facial buttressing" was most pronounced in the crucial weak points around the eye sockets and jaw. Later hominid evolution saw facial bones slim down a bit, although this was probably because our punches got weaker and not because we got less violent.

PLEASE FORM AN ORDERLY QUEUE

If a hermit crab finds a nice shell that's a bit too big, it will sometimes hang around nearby, waiting for another, bigger crab to come along. When that crab climbs into the big shell, the first crab gets first dibs on the slightly smaller one the big guy discarded. Occasionally another, even smaller crab will see the first crab waiting and hang around in the hope of getting a new shell itself. Sometimes queues form on the seabed.

Also, when we say "shell", we're simplifying things slightly: in today's rather polluted oceans, hermit crabs will use anything they can find, including human garbage such as glass bottles, ping-pong balls and bits of pipe.

HIPPOS CAN'T SWIM!

Despite living most of their lives in or around water, hippos have never moved past the "running along the bottom" stage of learning to swim. They walk or run along the bottom of lakes and rivers, periodically jumping up to the surface to take a breath.

Claw marks

It's not still in there, is it?

This is how big a person would be by comparison

GIANT BURROWS... This cave, located in southern Brazil, isn't actually a cave: it's a burrow! Around 10,000 years ago, an elephant-sized giant ground sloth (illustrated, inset) carved this tunnel through solid rock using its huge claws – the marks of which can still be seen scratched into the walls. The fact that these giant creatures were hiding in burrows is a bit creepy, though: what were they so scared of?

Feeling like you need to yawn? Yawning may be contagious as it's a primitive form of communication or herding behaviour.

Q A WHY DO WE YAWN?

Well, there are many theories, but the short answer is that we don't know. Yawning has been observed in most animals including mammals, reptiles, birds and even fish. Weirdly, there may be a link between the duration of an animal's yawn and the size of its brain. This was discovered in 2016 by psychologist Andrew Gallup, who spent hours watching videos of animals on YouTube, stopwatch in hand, timing their yawns.

He found – among other things – that an average lion yawn lasts 2.76 sec, a gorilla's lasts 3.59 sec and a hedgehog's lasts 2.45 sec. Gallup's theory is that yawning serves to cool the brain, so it makes sense that bigger brain = longer yawns.

Boring!

INSECT ATHLETES

Pound for pound, ants are some of the strongest creatures on the planet. They can lift 50 times their own body weight (akin to a weightlifter carrying a small truck), run 100 times their body length every second (Usain Bolt can only manage six), and jump 2 cm (0.7 in) into the air (equivalent to a human high jump of 13 m/42 ft 7 in). This picture, taken in 2016 by photographer Eko Adiyanto, shows a weaver ant wrestling with the weight of a dead bee about 40 times its size. (It's cool, but we're pretty sure the picture is upside down!)

LONGEST FINGERNAILS

Wolverine can retract his claws, but not Ayanna... Find out what it's like living with mega-nails, exactly what they're made of, and if biting them can kill you...

In an average lifetime, each of our fingernails has the potential to grow around 2.6 m (8 ft 6 in). Of course, most of us never let them get beyond a few millimetres, but that won't cut it if you want a record.

Ayanna Williams (USA, right) hasn't trimmed her nails in over two decades. She knows what it takes to *grow* the distance! She puts her nail-growing success down to acrylic nail varnish, sleeping on her side and taking care during daily tasks such as washing-up.

But as we'll show you here, every one of us has the potential to nail this record. Unless you're a zombie...

Ayanna's nails = 576.4 cm = 1 giraffe!

INSTANT EXPERT

NAIL ANATOMY... From before we're even born until the day we die, nails are living, growing parts of us. Much like our skin, fingernails are constantly undergoing a process of regeneration. To understand how these modified claws really work, you have to scratch beneath the surface...

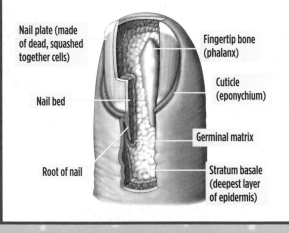

Nail plate (made of dead, squashed together cells)

Fingertip bone (phalanx)

Nail bed

Cuticle (eponychium)

Germinal matrix

Root of nail

Stratum basale (deepest layer of epidermis)

LEAST YOU NEED TO KNOW

Name: Ayanna Williams
Nationality: USA
Total nail length: 576.4 cm (18 ft 10.9 in)
Longest individual nail: Left thumb: 68 cm (2 ft 2.7 in)
Duration to grow: 20-plus years
Time to paint her nails: 20 hr – using one bottle of nail polish per hand

WHAT NAILS ARE MADE OF... While on the surface our fingernails appear to be one solid layer, take a look under a microscope and you'll see that they comprise lots of mini-layers – a bit like the surface of a pine cone.

The material they are made of is a tough protein called keratin. It's the same stuff that forms our hair, as well as numerous parts of animals, including the horns of rhinos, the shells of turtles and the beaks of birds.

Nails begin to grow from tissue under the skin called the germinal matrix. This continually produces new cells, forcing older ones to the surface. The external plate is actually a layer of compressed, hard, dead cells not connected to any nerves – that's why it doesn't hurt when you cut your nails.

MYTHCONCEPTION

YOUR NAILS KEEP GROWING AFTER YOU DIE

We've all heard horror stories about skeletons found with wild hair and long, gnarly nails... But is there any truth in the grizzly tale that parts of our body continue to grow *post-mortem*?

The simple answer is: no. In order to function, cells need a steady supply of glucose, which is transported by our blood. So the moment the heart stops beating and blood is no longer pumping, our cells only have enough energy reserves to last a few hours.

The most likely explanation for this myth lies not in how the body grows after we die, but rather in how it *shrinks*. As a corpse becomes dehydrated, skin begins to tighten around the bones. This causes skin to retract on the fingers, creating the impression that nails are growing. The same process makes it look as if hair and beards have grown.

FALSE

With the **longest nails on a pair of hands (female)**, Ayanna Williams is the latest member of the GWR "Fingernail Hall of Fame".

Another taloned talent is Lee Redmond (USA), the female holder of the **longest nails ever**. Her nails measured 865 cm (28 ft 4.5 in) in 2008, but she sadly lost them in a car accident a year later.

Shridhar Chillal

The undoubted "King of the Claws", though, is India's Shridhar Chillal (left). His impressive nails added up to 909.6 cm (29 ft 10.1 in) in 2014 – as long as a London bus: the **longest nails on a single hand ever**.

It all stemmed from a challenge by a teacher, who accused Shridhar of being impatient. To prove him wrong – and to wind up his parents! – Chillal put away his nail-clippers for good.

It hasn't all been plain sailing, though. Chillal told us his noteworthy nails have worked against him when looking for jobs – and love. Sleeping is also awkward – when he turns in the night, his wife needs to be on hand to move the giant mass of nails.

CAN BITING YOUR FINGERNAILS KILL YOU?

THE BIG QUESTION ?

It might sound far-fetched, but biting your nails – a condition known as onychophagy – is more than just a bad habit; in the most extreme cases, it can be fatal. In Sep 2013, amateur soccer referee John Gardener from the UK died after a heart attack triggered by a septic infection. The cause of his blood poisoning was excessive nail-biting – to such an extent that he had caused them to bleed, allowing bacteria in, which led to the infection.

We all know it's not good for us, so why do so many people chomp on their nails? Although there are multiple psychological theories, none of them have been proven. The common consensus seems to be that it's a readily available form of stress relief. But boredom, OCD and "over-grooming" have also been blamed.

Ask a...

Butterfly Curator

Hailing from biodiversity hotspot Colombia, Dr Blanca Huertas is Senior Curator of Butterflies at London's Natural History Museum (NHM). She reveals what it's like working with some of the animal kingdom's most colourful characters.

What drew you to working with butterflies?

I'm originally from Colombia – unofficially the country with more butterflies than any other country in the world. Since I was a small child, I used to travel with my family to the countryside, seeing loads of insects, plants and landscapes. I got very interested in nature and in collecting, but it was only when I started university that I found a mentor to help me to turn my passion for butterflies into a career.

How does it feel to work for an institution like the NHM?

A real privilege. It's a magical place. From the very moment you start your day, walking across the galleries and the most extraordinary building,

helping people to understand the world, you feel privileged. It still feels a dream working in the place I always wanted.

What does a typical day involve for you?

There are no typical days – every day is completely different. Although we have long-term projects and priorities with the collections, almost every day I receive an interesting question, task or project to get involved with.

I spend some days in the collections, looking at specimens collected over 100 years ago; other days, I'm attending or giving talks to colleagues or the public; other days

still, I'm helping people with the most obscure questions. Sometimes I'm in a remote location anywhere in the world chasing butterflies, and sometimes I'm writing a paper describing a new species quietly at my desk.

What's the most common question you get asked?

There's actually quite a few, but the most frequent one is: "What's the difference between a butterfly and a moth?" It's hard to explain – they're so closely related that if you look in detail, their differences are not as substantial as many still think.

I'm always asked which my favourite butterfly is. That's also a tricky question as being in charge of millions in the museum collections, I have many, many favourites!

Where in the world have you conducted fieldwork, and where would you recommend amateur lepidopterists to go?

Because of my area of expertise and the greatest concentration of diversity of butterflies is in the tropics, I tend to travel most often there for fieldwork. The tropical forests in Central and South America have over 40% of the world's butterflies.

Temperate areas (e.g., Europe) are good to start watching butterflies, as

DISCOVERING NEW SPECIES

One of the most exciting parts of any lepidopterist's job has to be venturing into the wilderness in search of undescribed butterflies.

The places Dr Huertas visits are often so remote that the only way to reach them is by helicopter! This main picture was taken on a field trip in 2016 to Chiribiquete National Park in Colombia. However, not all great discoveries are made trekking through the jungle.

Although living in the Chiribiquete Mountains, a new species of ringlet butterfly (right) was found by Dr Huertas and an international team in the archive drawers at the Natural History Museum, where it had been lying uncatalogued for over 100 years. The species was named *Magneuptychia pax* – in honour of an ongoing peace process in Colombia.

Sometimes it's possible to make discoveries that you're not even looking for. For instance, in 2006, Dr Huertas and a colleague found a colourful new bird in Colombia, since named the Yariguies brush finch.

they're well-studied and have many resources available to identify local species such as field guides and monitoring programmes. However, the tropics in Asia and South America are fascinating. There are still many new species to find and describe there.

How do you find butterflies?
Butterflies are ubiquitous and found almost everywhere in the world, except Antarctica. The rainforest is one of the favourite places for butterflies because of the large diversity of resources available. You can always find butterflies in forest clearings, near riverbanks or wherever there is sunlight and food. I usually catch butterflies using a net, but also as some are very fast and high flyers, I use bait traps to catch them.

What are the biggest challenges/dangers when hunting for butterflies?
Despite what you might think about butterflies fluttering slowly by, I assure you, they don't let you catch them easily!

Running and not looking at the terrain is dangerous as you might fall off a cliff! Also, you get badly distracted and usually don't notice snakes or other animals. When I set up bait traps, I've been bitten badly by ants, stung by wasps and even chased by large mammals! I tend to visit remote and lonely areas,

String to suspend the trap from a branch

Zip in one side for easy access to butterflies

Trap barrel made of light-coloured fine mesh

Butterflies enter at the bottom; their instinct is to fly up, where they become trapped

Bait is something sweet, e.g., rotten bananas or sugar-water

Weighted base platform to reduce swaying in wind

The idea of catching butterflies in the wild probably conjures an image of someone chasing fluttering bugs with a long net – and this *does* still happen! Another method (which involves less running into things) is to use a bait trap hung up high in the rainforest canopy.

which can be unsafe in terms of access, but also because of illicit groups or landmines.

Tell us about your latest trip to Colombia in Aug 2017.
I just returned from a field trip to Chocó, one of the rainiest places on Earth. This trip was quite different to what I usually do. I normally go to the mountains and very remote areas where I know no humans have been collecting butterflies before. However, in this case,

we set up an expedition with an artist to a remote place where the forest meets the sea. We wanted to explore the relationship between science and art.

What can we do to encourage butterflies to our gardens?
First and golden rule: don't use pesticides in your garden. Most people plant lovely flowers that might attract butterflies, but when they use chemicals, they are killing not only the pests

Nom nom nom

Poo

Asked to tell us something about butterflies that is shocking, Dr Huertas said: "Some don't feed on sweet, colourful flowers, but instead on the juices of dead animals, rotten fruit or even poo" – such as the purple emperor (above).

but also caterpillars and other harmless wildlife. Butterflies are attracted to wild flowers, herbs and nettles. Buddleia is one of their favourites.

Are there any butterfly-related citizen science projects?
Some of the most important ones are run by Butterfly Conservation in the UK and Europe. Citizens contribute with records to monitor the state of butterflies in different countries. The scheme provides large, up-to-date sets of data that scientists can analyse and use to map current trends, endangered species and propose action plans.

IT'S ALIVE!

Sensational Butterflies

As well as some 5 million preserved specimens, the NHM also has a live exhibit (above). Dr Huertas said: "It's a great exhibition that I'm very proud of! Visitors get a real feel of the tropical jungles where some of the most spectacular butterflies come from."

FOR THE RECORD

The butterfly at the very top of Dr Huertas' "to see in the wild" wishlist is the Queen Alexandra's birdwing (*Ornithoptera alexandrae*), native to Papua New Guinea.

With female wing-spans reaching in excess of 28 cm (11 in) – about the length of a rugby ball – they are the world's **largest butterflies**.

Pictured here is the brightly coloured male Queen Alexandra's birdwing. If you think he looks big, bear in mind that their wings average

"just" 16–20 cm (6.2–7.8 in) across, so they are dwarfed by the brown-and-yellow females.

As well as having size on their side, Queen Alexandra's birdwings are also poisonous. They obtain their toxicity from the pipevine plant that they eat as caterpillars.

ACTUAL SIZE

HOLY MOLA!

The ocean is full of weird things (see pp.130–31), but few are weirder than the sunfish (*Mola mola*). These vacant-looking creatures measure up to 3 m (10 ft) from fin tip to fin tip and weigh in the region of 2 tonnes (2.2 US tons), making them the **heaviest bony fish**.

Their lives are mostly spent drifting aimlessly and eating whatever ends up in their mouths. Although they're fish, which you'd expect to be good at this sort of thing, they're not strong swimmers. In aquariums, they tend to hurt themselves, even in very large tanks, because they swim into walls a lot.

SUPER SENSES

Eyes and ears are also scaled up with the super-sized head, indicating the large areas of our brains dedicated to processing visual and auditory information

Our senses are our windows to the world around us. Without them we'd be constantly walking into things, missing important announcements and trying to eat things that aren't food.

You've probably been told that humans have just five senses: sight, hearing, taste, smell and touch. Those are the most obvious ones, but we actually have quite a few more than that.

Other senses include thermoception (how we know if we're hot or cold), equilibrioception (how we know which way up we are), proprioception (how we know where our limbs are without looking) and nociception (how we know we've been injured).

Those senses are joined by less easily defined senses such as chronoception (how we know that time has passed) and interoception (how we know when we're hungry, or out of breath, or need to wee).

Depending on how you define a sense, we have as few as eight or as many as 20.

TIL
TODAY I LEARNED

Weirdly, humans are slightly better at detecting the scent of bananas than dogs are, despite dogs having a much better sense of smell generally. Also, our sense of smell works better in the spring and summer, when there's more moisture in the air.

Your tongue and lips have a huge number of neural connections

This is why babies put everything in their mouths

Our hands are our main means of interacting with the world, so have lots of nerve endings; in fact, our fingers are the **most touch-sensitive part of the body**

More about platypuses on pp.152–53

INSTANT EXPERT

THE HOMUNCULUS... This strange-looking (fictional) creature is Penfield's Homunculus, one of the oddest residents of London's Natural History Museum (and they have a platypus, so that's saying something!).

To understand why he looks the way he does, have a look at your hands. A normal person's hands aren't very big compared with, for example, their legs (you can check this yourself, we'll

wait). However, they have a huge number of sensory nerves by comparison, and require a much larger area of the brain to keep track of all that information.

Penfield's Homunculus shows what we'd look like if our body parts were scaled to match the proportions of our brain's sensory perception regions. So sensitive areas are bigger than insensitive ones.

The calves are among the least sensitive body parts

Our feet have a large number of sensory connections because we need detailed feedback to stand and walk

We've not shown genitals (private parts) here because, well, it's a bit much. Suffice to say they're a lot larger than actual size.

This is Nick Stoeberl, owner of the world's longest tongue; it's 10.1 cm (3.97 in) long!

INSTANT EXPERT

COLOUR BLINDNESS...

We usually have three cells (called cones) in our eyes that detect colour, but if any one of these is defective, we are "colour blind".

People with colour blindness are usually either dichromats (i.e., they have two cones) or monochromats (just one cone). These forms of colour vision are tested using patterns like the ones below and right, which are called "Ishihara plates".

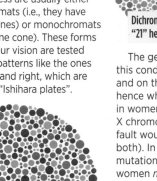

Dichromats see the number "21" here (rather than "74")

The genes related to this condition are recessive and on the X chromosome, hence why it's much rarer in women (they have two X chromosomes, so the fault would have to be on both). In fact, a similar mutation may grant some women *more* colour-sensing cells – a condition called "tetrachromacy". This enables them to see a wider range of colours than most people, though it's not clear how common this might be – only a few proven cases exist.

Dichromats see only a "4" or a "2" here

MYTHCONCEPTION

YOU TASTE SWEET THINGS WITH THE TIP OF YOUR TONGUE

The taste buds on your tongue are capable of perceiving five basic flavours – sweet, sour, salty, bitter and umami. The last one is the savoury or meaty taste of things such as soy sauce or Marmite. You have between 2,000 and 8,000 taste buds, but they're spread evenly over the tongue and are capable of perceiving all the flavours equally. No one part of your tongue is any more sensitive to a particular flavour than any other.

FALSE

IT'S ALIVE!

This is what taste buds look like up-close

✚ MORE *STUFF!*

- Dogs can have as many as 300 million olfactory receptors (smell-sensitive neurons) in their noses. Humans, by comparison, have *only* 6 million. Despite this handicap, our sense of smell is actually pretty good. Those 6 million smell receptors are capable of telling the difference between either 10,000 or 1 trillion smells (scientists are still arguing about this point).

All the smells

- In 2006, researchers from the University of California, Berkeley, USA, blindfolded people and got them to track a scent trail (a drizzled line of chocolate oil) across a field. You'd think this would be impossible, but the volunteers (who got down on their hands and knees and snuffled through the grass like dogs) turned out to be surprisingly good at it. They were slower than dogs, obviously, but they tracked the trail just fine.

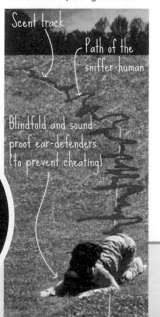

Scent track

Path of the sniffer-human

Blindfold and sound-proof ear-defenders (to prevent cheating)

- What we think of as our sense of taste is mostly just our sense of smell being interpreted in a different way. Some researchers believe that our noses account for as much as 90% of a food's perceived flavour.
- Our sense of smell comes from a structure called the olfactory bulb. This filters particles out of the air and assigns different sensations of smell to different chemical compounds. This means that when you smell a fart, you've just inhaled molecules that were recently in someone's butt. Gross.

Brain

Olfactory bulb

Nasal cavity

Olfactory nerves

That's what your tongue looks like!

MOST VENOMOUS SPIDER

A killer is lurking in the suburbs of Sydney, an arachnid with a venom that is powerful enough to kill you in less than an hour.

This terrifying creature is the Sydney funnel-web – the world's **most venomous spider**. Its venom is deadly in concentrations as low as 0.2 mg for every kilogram of a victim's bodyweight. That means 16 mg (less than two one-hundred thousandths of a gram) could be enough to kill an adult human.

For a long time we thought the most venomous spider was the Brazilian wandering spider, but in 2015, after consulting with venom experts, Guinness World Records awarded the record to the Sydney funnel-web.

The reason for this is that while the Brazilian wandering spider has been shown to be more deadly in studies on mice, its venom isn't particularly effective against people. The venom of the Sydney funnel-web, meanwhile, is even more venomous to us than it is to mice.

These huge fangs can bite through a fingernail!

MYTHCONCEPTION

SUCKING OUT THE VENOM SAVES LIVES!

It makes a sort of sense, doesn't it? Something has put venom in you, so surely taking that venom back out will stop it from doing any damage. In reality, it's not that simple. The venom will have already started to move through your body by the time you manage to suck it out, so it won't help much. More importantly, doctors need to be able to extract venom from the bite so that they can match it to the right antivenom and stop it killing you.

FALSE

FOR THE RECORD

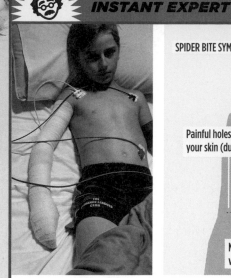

LEAST YOU NEED TO KNOW

Name: Sydney funnel-web spider (*Atrax robustus*)
Range: Found in the area around Sydney on the east coast of Australia
Leg-span: 6–7 cm (2.3–2.7 in)
Fangs: Up to 1 cm (0.4 in)
Favoured habitats: Under logs and in small crevices; has been known to hide in people's shoes
Known fatalities: At least 14 between 1927 and 1981

SPIDER BITE SYMPTOMS

Respiratory distress

Tachycardia (rapid heartbeat)

Painful holes in your skin (duh)

Nausea and vomiting

Muscle twitching

ONCE BITTEN... A Sydney funnel-web bite is a nasty experience. It begins with a sharp, stabbing pain, and the unpleasant sight of a hand-sized spider hanging to your skin by its 10-mm-long fangs.

The bite really, really hurts, but that's just the beginning. Within about 30 min, your heart rate will start to rise and you'll start to sweat. Your muscles will then start twitching and jerking painfully.

Next, you will begin to have trouble breathing and severe nausea will set in. As the pain worsens, you'll start vomiting. Eventually, you'll lose consciousness, go into circulatory failure, and die.

You don't want that, obviously...

How to survive

The first thing you should do is apply a bandage tightly to the area around the bite. It's best to wrap the entirety of the limb that was bitten (as you can see in the picture above left, which shows bite survivor Matthew Mitchell shortly after his brush with a funnel-web in Feb 2017).

You should then seek medical treatment straight away. A hospital can give you antivenom, which helps you to fight off the toxin.

If you get treatment quickly, you'll survive with no lasting damage done. That's not the case with certain other types of spiders that have what's called necrotizing venom. This isn't as toxic, but it burns away your flesh as it takes hold (a necrotizing spider bite, below). Bleurgh!

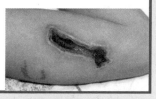

MILKING SPIDERS?!

The world's **largest spider** is the Goliath bird-eating spider of South America: it isn't particularly venomous, but it is really scary. Fully grown, its leg-span can be as much as 28 cm (11 in) – that's about the size of a dinner plate.

It's an opportunistic predator, meaning it will have a go at anything that gets close enough, including scorpions and, famously, small birds (left). Usually, however, it prefers to eat earthworms and toads, and is generally quite docile.

Venom glands

Suction pipette for extracting venom

We can't synthesize funnel-web antivenom in the lab. The only way to make it is to extract venom from live spiders through a process known as "milking" (left), then inject very small amounts into rabbits. This venom sample isn't enough to kill, but it does provoke an immune response. Vets draw blood from the animal and extract the antibodies its immune system created. These pre-made antibodies make up the antivenom that gives people's immune systems a boost after a bite.

DINOSAUR TAILS

Dinosaurs: they're big reptiles with dull-coloured, scaly skin... right? Wrong! It turns out that the most famous dinosaurs were a lot stranger and less lizard-like than we thought.

Studying dinosaurs is like staring at the world through a keyhole – we can only see tiny pieces of a huge and complex ecosystem. This means that every new discovery has the potential to completely upend what we thought we knew about these ancient animals.

Over the last few decades, we've learned that dinosaurs were probably a lot more like birds than lizards. Most therapods (meat-eating dinosaurs) had feathers, for example, and some of them might even have been able to fly. The so-called "Land Before Time" becomes a very different place when you replace those terrifying giant lizards with honking, feathery, giant chickens.

Yes, honking. Scientists now think dinosaurs probably sounded like geese

THE DINOSAURS ALL DIED OUT

You won't see a *Tyrannosaurus rex* wandering down the street, but the age of the dinosaur has never quite gone away. You'd probably not be surprised to learn that crocodilians (such as crocodiles and alligators) are cousins of the dinosaurs, and that they've been around in some form for 200 million years.

More surprising are the direct descendants of dinosaurs that have been hiding in plain sight the whole time: birds! They evolved from therapods about 120 million years ago. Once you know about the connection, it seems obvious – just look at the picture of a velocirap... we mean baby heron, below.

FALSE

This is the tail itself

Up close, the feathers look more like hairs

FOR THE RECORD

In Dec 2016, palaeontologist Dr Lida Xing published a paper revealing the discovery of the **first fully preserved dinosaur tail**, which had been sealed in a piece of amber (pictured above) for around 99 million years.

Fossils like this are Lida's speciality. He does a lot of his field work in jewellery markets, rather than fossil beds, hoping to find small dinosaurs that got caught in sticky tree resin. He came across this specimen in an amber market in Myitkyina, Myanmar.

It's not possible to say exactly what sort of dinosaur this tail came from (there's not enough of it), but it was almost certainly from a very small therapod. It would have been similar in appearance to a velociraptor, but only about the size of a sparrow. The picture to the right is an artist's impression of what it might have looked like. Its feathers were not adapted for flight and were most likely either for thermal regulation or purely for display.

TIL
TODAY I LEARNED

In 2014, a group of scientists demonstrated that you can almost perfectly replicate a *T. rex*'s likely gait (way of walking) by strapping a length of wood to the tail of a chicken. The weight of the "tail" makes the chicken walk in a more upright position.

SCI-FI SCIENCE

In *Jurassic Park* (1993) and its sequels, velociraptors are 2 m (6 ft 6 in) tall and use their claws and razor teeth to hunt humans. Real velociraptors were rather different: they stood around 50 cm (1 ft 7 in) tall and were covered in feathers.

The movie versions have no feathers because we didn't know velociraptors had feathers when the first film was made (that wasn't discovered until 2007). The film-makers also made their velociraptors much bigger – probably because a turkey-sized monster isn't very scary!

+ MORE *STUFF!*

They looked a bit daft, but velociraptors were still scary things. In 1971, palaeontologists found the fossilized remains of a velociraptor in the process of taking down a *Protoceratops andrewsi* – a horned herbivore about the size of a large sheep. The dinosaurs were buried by a collapsing sand dune mid-fight.

Protoceratops

Velociraptor

T. rex is more closely related (in both time and genetics) to a sparrow than a stegosaurus

IT'S ALIVE!

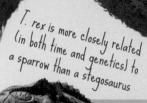

KING OF THE DINOSAURS

Tyrannosaurus rex has been pop culture's favourite dinosaur since its discovery in 1905. This is partly because it has an awesome name (it means "tyrant lizard king"!), but mostly because it's a 3.6-m (12-ft) monster with teeth the size of bowling pins. The rising tide of feathers is threatening to knock *T. rex* off the top spot, however – after all, would it still be scary if it had lots of brightly coloured plumage?

In Jun 2017, researchers found samples of fossilized *T. rex* skin (inset right) that proved they had scales, not feathers. Which means that, for now at least, *T. rex* is likely to retain its image as the most scary dinosaur.

ACTUAL SIZE

145

10 DEADLIEST ANIMALS

In 2014, technology magnate and the world's **richest man**, Bill Gates (USA), sought to pin down, once and for all, which is the **deadliest animal**. He posted his findings on his blog and the results were more than a little surprising...

He's worth about $85.7 bn, give or take a million

You might not naturally put dangerous animals and Microsoft founder Bill Gates together. But given his extensive charity work in the developing world, he has good reason to be blogging about nature's most wanted.

There are lots of myths around this subject. Certain animals are so often in the media spotlight, it seems as if they're on non-stop killing sprees. While other, guiltier critters slip under the radar.

Gates' list confirms that the creature claiming the most lives in an average year is also one of the puniest: the mosquito (or "little fly").

On their own, mosquitoes aren't much of a threat to us – they're easily squished! But combined with the lethal parasites that some carry, they become the **deadliest animals**.

The most serious disease that these parasites can cause – malaria – claims around 600,000 lives a year by itself.

Bugs with even tinier "bugs" living inside them are a common theme in this top 10. So forget big, bitey beasts like sharks; often, the wildlife most likely to kill us is no larger than the tip of your little finger!

10,000

Native to Africa, tsetse flies are blood-sucking bugs with a painful bite. Certain species carry *Trypanosoma* parasites, which cause "sleeping sickness". Symptoms of this disease include fatigue, confusion and eventually death. Their mortality hit rate is around 10,000 people per year.

=5

10,000

You'd be able to outrun a freshwater snail, but what makes them so dangerous are the nasty parasites they release into water. These flatworms can damage our liver, bladder and kidneys – causing an illness known as bilharzia, or "snail fever".

10,000

Yet another reason to run away from creepy-crawlies is the aptly named assassin bug. It sneaks up in our sleep and bites our faces! If that weren't bad enough, parasites in its poo cause Chagas disease – a condition that can lead to heart failure.

=5

2,500

Ascaris roundworms are the **most successful parasitic worm in humans**, infecting as much as 25% of the world population. Although generally not lethal, their presence can cause serious issues, such as a blockage of the small intestine or pneumonia.

8

=5

1,000

10

Considering that these reptiles have one of the most powerful bites, perhaps it's no surprise that crocodiles make the list. Most attacks are opportunistic and take place in hot weather (when cold-blooded crocs are more active).

9

Tapeworms get into our systems via eggs or larvae living in raw food or dirty water. They can go undetected in our guts for years – reaching several metres long – but become more lethal if they spread to other organs such as the brain.

2,000

■ = 1,000 deaths

25,000

"Man's best friend" is the fourth most likely beast to take your life. Responsible for 90% of rabies bites, dogs (mainly strays) are blamed for 25,000 deaths annually. So you may want to think twice about asking Lassie for help...

4

TIL
TODAY I LEARNED

Just as surprising as some of the animals that feature in this top 10 are some of the animals that don't. Tales of surfers and swimmers being attacked by sharks are never far from the news. But in this data set, they were attributed with just 10 deaths a year on average.

3

50,000

Serpents use chemical warfare to take out their victims. Various venoms work in different ways, paralysing muscles, clotting blood or simply necrotizing (killing) cells. Some are so potent that they can take effect in a matter of minutes.

2

475,000

Humans may seem like an odd inclusion in this list, but we are animals too. As a result of war, crime and accidents, nearly half a million are taken out by their fellow *Homo sapiens* each year. Lesson to take from this? Trust no one.

1

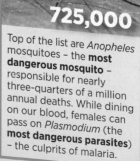

725,000

Top of the list are *Anopheles* mosquitoes – the **most dangerous mosquito** – responsible for nearly three-quarters of a million annual deaths. While dining on our blood, females can pass on *Plasmodium* (the **most dangerous parasites**) – the culprits of malaria.

147

Ask a...
Dino Poop Collector

Watch where you step! George Frandsen (USA) is the proud owner of the **largest coprolite collection**, with 1,277 pieces of prehistoric poo as of 2015. His fossils are housed at a museum in Florida for all to see/sniff...

TIL
TODAY I LEARNED

The dung from prehistoric carnivores was more likely to form coprolites than that from vegetarians, owing to their diet. The calcium-rich droppings – from their prey's bones, teeth and scales – took longer to decompose than plant matter, allowing more time for burial.

How did the collection begin?
The collection started when I was in college, aged about 18. I was asked to make a fossil collection for a palaeontology class and came across a coprolite. I thought it was the neatest thing in the world.

Since then, I've collected more and more. I applied for the record because I wanted to bring coprolites to the forefront. They're a fascinating fossil that I think everyone should know about.

What is it about coprolites that makes them so important?
What got me interested in finding and collecting coprolites is the story they tell of prehistoric life. No other fossil can tell you as much as a coprolite can.

Inside you can find inclusions, which are pieces of plants and animals, such as bones. This information can tell us about what animals were eating and their metabolism, as well as prehistoric ecosystems.

In coprolites from my collection, I've discovered a tooth plate from a prehistoric fish called a pycnodont, a toe bone from a prehistoric deer, fish fins, shark teeth, and microscopic pieces of plants.

How do people react to your fossilized poop?
When people see coprolites for the first time, they're often in shock. A lot of people don't even know there's such a thing as coprolites until they see them. Watching the public view coprolites is very interesting. Kids want to touch them – they want to know if they're still soft or smelly! We're able to hand them coprolites to show that they are indeed rocks. Often when children see the collection, they're keen to learn more. They want

FOR THE RECORD

The **largest coprolite from a carnivore** was most likely produced by a *T. rex* some 65 million years ago. It's not part of George's collection, but owned by the Royal Saskatchewan Museum in Canada. The fossilized faeces measures 50 cm (19.6 in) across and weighs in excess of 7 kg (15 lb 7 oz).

Potentially the longest coprolite overall (below), at 40 in (101.6 cm) long, sold at auction for $10,370 (£6,064) in 2014. It's debated, however, if the specimen really was dung.

INSTANT EXPERT

HOW COPROLITES FORM... Not every prehistoric poo is destined to become a coprolite. It all depends on where the dino (or other creature) did their do. Ideal sites included floodplains, swamps and even the sea, where the poop was immersed and quickly buried in sediment or mud. Over millennia, anaerobic (non-air-breathing) bacteria broke down the poop, converting the organic matter into minerals. What's left behind is a stone copy of the original dung, sometimes with tougher materials, such as bone, encased inside.

Here's something for the person who seems to have everything: jewellery made from petrified poo! Like other stones, coprolites come in a range of shapes, sizes and colours – each one is unique. They can even be cut and polished like gems.

to go home and find out which dinosaur made the coprolite. Or what the dinosaur ate. So we give them recommendations of websites where they can find out more.

How do you tell the difference between a coprolite and a rock?
This is one of the most frequently asked questions I receive! Well, sometimes it's really difficult and other times it's really easy. For example, some coprolites retain the distinct shape of faeces, such as "Precious" [pictured above left]. These are known as "true to form", as they have changed very little since the day they were made. For other coprolites, you have to look inside to try to find bits of plants and animals.

Can you figure out which animal a coprolite is from?
It's very difficult to tell which species made a coprolite, as so many specimens look very similar. We can take an educated guess based on the time period it's from and other fossils that are associated with it.

It's far easier to tell what the creature ate, owing to the inclusions inside. There are many coprolites in my collection that are a mystery as to who made them. They come from the same era as dinosaurs, so the most likely culprits are dinosaurs of all shapes, sizes and varieties – as well as crocodilians and marine reptiles such as mosasaurs.

Do you think the identification process will become easier?
I think in the future, as technology progresses, we may be able to determine which animal made a coprolite, rather than just what they were eating and how old they are.

How do you age a coprolite?
Gauging the age of a coprolite can be tricky. Most often, this is determined from the layer of sand, soil or rock that it's found in. The oldest coprolites can date back as far as 400 million years. Anything less than 10,000 years old is a bit [suspect] and should probably be left for a few more thousand years.

Do you plan to build on your collection?
Since the official count in 2015, I've acquired many more coprolites and I'm planning to beat my own record in the near future. My goal right now, though, is to find the largest coprolite in the world.

Coprolites have been found on every continent, and anyone can find them – as George told us: "The majority of my collection comes from south-east USA, but I have examples from all over the world." Here, he is holding a pile of small coprolites unearthed from the Pleistocene epoch (2.5 million–12,000 years ago).

OLDER THAN YOUR HOUSE

Most people can expect to live perhaps 70 or 80 years, but there's a select group (there's about 40 of them alive right now) who live beyond 110 years. These amazing people are called supercentenarians, and you have the chance to be one...

Could humans live forever? As a species, we've been searching for eternal life since ancient times. That goal is one of the few things modern scientists have in common with medieval alchemists who once prescribed "elixirs" for long life that often caused madness or, ironically, death.

Surprisingly, despite all the medical advances we've made since the boiling-mercury days, the maximum life-span of a human hasn't changed much.

The **oldest person ever** – Jeanne Calment (FRA) – lived to the age of 122 years 164 days. She died more than 20 years ago and no one has come close to her record since. Can we ever push that record further? And what can *you* do to join the supercentenarian club?

INSTANT EXPERT

GETTING OLD... So you want to avoid dying for as long as possible? Here's some advice on how to achieve this.

The key bits are pretty obvious: you need to eat lots of fruit and vegetables and avoid fatty foods. Also, get lots of exercise – like Jim Arrington, the **oldest bodybuilder**, pictured right in 2015 (aged 83!). You should also strive to be chilled at all times; make friends, get lots of sleep, don't worry about things.

While you're at it, boost your levels of RNA molecule CCCAAUCCC and suppress the genes involved in growth-factor signalling (but be careful you don't go too far). In case you'd not guessed, neither of those options are actually possible right now. But they might be when you're older, especially if you live a really long time.

The rate at which your brain regenerates slows as you age, which can cause memory problems

Your ears never stop getting bigger, but your head stays the same size

Unless you maintain a very active lifestyle (like Jim), your muscles will get smaller and weaker

As you age, the amount of collagen in your skin will decline, making it thinner and less elastic

Bones lose density as calcium levels decline

Joint tissues get thinner

1

2

3

4

JEANNE LOUISE CALMENT

The **oldest person ever** was born in Arles, France, on 21 Feb 1875. She received an extensive education (for a woman of that era), completing school when she was 16. She married when she was 21 (in 1896) and had one child, a daughter called Yvonne, in 1898. Her husband, Fernand, was a successful merchant, and she lived a fairly leisurely life – never having to work and being attended to by servants.

She remained active throughout her life: cycling, going on long hikes in the mountains and even hunting with her husband (until his death at 73 in 1942). She ate reasonably healthily, but didn't stick to any particular diet. She did smoke, but her habit never exceeded two cigarettes per day. She lived alone until 1985, when she was moved into the nursing home where she spent the rest of her life. Jeanne lived through two World Wars, the development of television, the modern motor car, aeroplanes, computers and numerous other technologies that are taken for granted today. She died on 4 Aug 1997 at the age of 122 years 164 days.

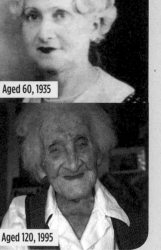

Aged 60, 1935

Aged 20, 1895

Aged 120, 1995

FOR THE RECORD

Just as we were going to press, the **oldest living person** passed away at the age of 117 years 189 days. Violet Brown (right) was born on 10 Mar 1900 in Jamaica, then part of the British Empire, making her the last living subject of Queen Victoria. She had six children, four of whom were still living as of Jul 2017.

Violet also jointly held the record for **highest combined age for a parent and child** until her son Harland's death – at the age of 97! – in Apr 2017.

Imagine your mum still being alive if you get to 97!

TIL
TODAY I LEARNED

The longest-lived rodent is the naked mole rat, which can live for as long as 28 years. This isn't really relevant to what we're talking about here, but we wanted an excuse to show you a naked mole rat. I mean, look at it, it's got no fur! What's with that?

OLDEST...

1 **Male stripper:** Bernie Barker (USA, 66 years 233 days)

2 **Acrobatic salsa dancer:** Sarah "Paddy" Jones (UK, 75 years 246 days)

3 **YouTube gamer:** Shirley Curry (USA, 81 years 26 days)

4 **Gymnast:** Johanna Quaas (DEU, 86 years 144 days)

5 **Wing walker:** Thomas Lackey (UK, 93 years 100 days)

6 **Abseiler:** Doris Long (UK, 101 years 55 days)

7 **Competitive sprinter:** Hidekichi Miyazaki (JPN, 105 years 1 day)

8 **Competitive cyclist:** Robert Marchand (FRA, 105 years 39 days)

IT'S ALIVE!

5

6

7

8

PLATY-WHAT?!

Wait... what?

The platypus is half mammal, half reptile, half bird and all weird. It looks like nature's idea of a joke, made from all the left-over bits of the animal kingdom. And it sweats milk...!

In 1799, the governor of New South Wales, John Hunter (pictured), sent a preserved platypus – bagged on a hunting trip – to the British Museum in London, UK. The museum's zoologist, George Shaw, was a little baffled by this latest discovery, which he noted, "[resembles] the beak of a Duck engrafted on the head of a quadruped". He even suggested that it might be a "deceptive preparation by artificial means" – a hoax, in other words.

It's easy to see why people thought the platypus was a hoax. It has the body of an otter, the tail of a beaver, the bill and webbed feet of a duck, the claws of a reptile and the spurs of a cockerel.

Along with the almost-as-strange echidna, the platypus is the sole surviving example of a group of mammals known as the monotremes. They lay eggs like reptiles, but nurse their young like mammals – though they have no nipples so they "sweat" milk instead.

The more we learn about this funny little creature – which lives quietly in the rivers and lakes of eastern Australia – the stranger it seems. We now know, for example, that females have five X chromosomes but only one working ovary, that the males have venomous spurs on their hind feet, and that they all "see" using electromagnetic fields. So yeah, it's pretty weird!

They growl when they feel threatened, like dogs

They're born with teeth, but then they fall out. Adults grind up their food by swallowing gravel

The duck-like bill is incredibly sensitive. The platypus can pick up tiny electrical signals that guide it to its prey

Platypuses swim with their eyes shut

LEAST YOU NEED TO KNOW

Latin name:
Ornithorhynchus anatinus ("duck-like bird-nose")
Other names: Duckbill or water-mole
Native habitat: The rivers, lakes and ponds of eastern Australia and Tasmania
Conservation status: Not currently under threat
Weight: 700 g to 2.4 kg (1 lb 8 oz to 5 lb 4.6 oz)
Length: Typically 50 cm (20 in) for males, 43 cm (17 in) for females
Diet: Worms, freshwater shrimp and insect larvae

The platypus' skeleton is extremely dense, and serves to provide the otherwise cork-like animal with enough ballast for it to dive to the bottom of rivers.

Seems legit...

HOAXES

People have been inventing hybrid animals and fantastic beasts for thousands of years. For as long as these stories have been around, people have been willing to have a go at making one – for laughs or cash. It's hardly surprising some people thought the platypus was a hoax.

The "Fiji mermaid" (top) was an obvious fake, created by gluing together the rotting remains of a dead monkey and the tail of a fish (which must have been fun). Despite this, it drew huge crowds when presented to the public in New York, USA, in 1842.

This beaver-like coating of brown fur covers most of the body and helps to keep the platypus warm

The tail is used a little when swimming, but is mostly just a place to store fat

The females secrete milk through the skin, leaving their puggles to lap it up as it collects in the folds in their abdomen

Back feet

The venom injected by these spurs causes intense pain that isn't dulled by normal painkillers.

Front feet

On land, the platypus walks on its knuckles with its feet curled up into fists. This protects the webbing.

With females weighing in the region of 0.7-1.6 kg (1 lb 8 oz-3 lb 8 oz), platypuses are the <u>lightest</u> egg-laying mammals

TIL
TODAY I LEARNED

As it produces both eggs and milk, the duck-billed platypus is, in theory, the only creature in the animal kingdom that could produce custard on its own. It'd be really hard to get the proportions right, though, and you probably wouldn't want to eat it!

The jackalope (right) is a legendary American beast with the body of a jackrabbit and the horns of an antelope. The first was created by a hunter in Douglas, Wyoming, in 1932.

As if Australian wildlife wasn't deadly enough, locals have long maintained that the koala (below) has an evil sibling called the "drop bear". It supposedly lurks in trees and plunges on to unsuspecting tourists. The mythical beast has its own exhibit at the Australian Museum in Sydney.

Easily avoided by smearing yourself in Vegemite and speaking in an Australian accent, apparently

153

HEAVIEST MANTLE OF BEES

Meet the brave record holder who took the art of "bee bearding" to a whole new level by smothering himself in a buzzing cloak (aka "mantle") of hell... Unleash the bees!

In the days before Netflix, YouTube and (dare we say it?) *Buzz*Feed, one way to keep entertained was to watch someone covering their face in bees. Admittedly, even today, this amazing act – known as "bee bearding" – is still pretty compelling to watch!

According to record bee-bearder Ruan Liangming (pictured below) from China,

the secret to his success is keeping a cool head, as well as being able to "read" the bees' mood... Which is all well and good until you have several hundred-thousand of them swarming over you!

How are apiarists (bee experts) and bee-bearders not stung to death? And what happens to you – and the bee – when you're stung?

FOR THE RECORD

Ruan Liangming is currently "lord of the bees". In 2013, he achieved the **longest duration with the head fully covered with bees**: 53 min 34 sec.

A year later, he buzzed back into action, donning a cloak of bees (see below) that by the end weighed in at 63.7 kg (140 lb 6.9 oz) – the **heaviest mantle of bees**.

INSTANT EX

1

2

Queen

| MOST SMALL BEES 2 min | WESTERN PAPER WASP 2 min | MEXICAN TWIG ANT 5 min | RED FIRE ANT 5 min | SONORAN BUMBLE BEE 5 min | YELLOW JACKET 10 min |

LEVEL 1   LEVEL 2

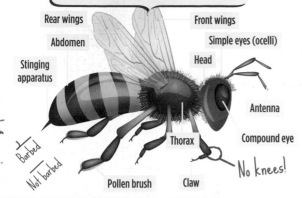

Rear wings
Front wings
Abdomen
Simple eyes (ocelli)
Head
Stinging apparatus
Antenna
Thorax
Compound eye
Barbed
Not barbed
No knees!
Pollen brush
Claw

Ouch!

BEES DIE AFTER THEY STING

If you get stung by a worker honey bee, spare it a thought, as it's not long for this world. Honey bees are the only bees to have backwards-facing barbs on their stingers. This means that as they fly away after attacking you, their entire back end wrenches out – ouch! This trauma inevitably leads to death. In contrast, most solitary bees and queens (and also wasps) have smoother stingers, so they live to sting another day.

TRUE -ISH

WHY DO BEE STINGS HURT?

THE BIG QUESTION ?

Bees will only sting as a last resort if they feel under threat. In some cases, it will be the last thing they ever do (see Mythconception, left), but for all bees it's a dangerous and highly draining ordeal.

Only female bees can sting. The stinger is, in fact, a weaponized form of "ovipositor" – an organ typically used for laying eggs. Once this has pierced the skin, up to 0.1 mg of toxic venom is injected, which fires up your pain receptors.

Depending on the victim, the toxins trigger varying effects. In most cases, these include a burning sensation, slight swelling and redness, all of which pass after a few hours. But in severe reactions, a bee sting is much more dangerous; it can cause dizziness, nausea and even affect respiration.

FOR THE RECORD

BEE BEARDING...
Wondering how "bee whisperers", like She Ping pictured here, attract their winged friends? The process starts by capturing a queen or two and placing them in little cages around the body (**1**). Worker bees are then released in waves. The irresistible chemicals, known as pheromones, produced by queens attract ever-more workers, until the person is smothered (**2**).

Finally, to remove the bees, the queens are taken off first to try to lure the workers away of their own accord (**3**). Those that remain are helped along by the bearder jumping to dislodge them, while any stragglers are softly brushed away by helpers.

Bee-bearders are by no means immune to stings, but over time it's possible to build up a pain tolerance.

3

Charles "Lamar" LaCaze (left) from Texas, USA, was attacked by a swarm of bees after accidentally disturbing a nest while mowing his lawn in 2010. At the hospital, doctors removed 1,200 stingers from his skin.

The all-time record for **most bee stings survived**, however, is 2,443. Johannes Relleke (ZWE) was the unlucky victim at the Kamativi tin mine in Wankie District, Zimbabwe (then Rhodesia), on 28 Jan 1962.

✚ MORE STUFF!

In the grand scheme of *stings*, the average honey bee's weapon isn't much to write home about. That is, at least according to the Schmidt Sting Pain Index. Since 1983, American entomologist Justin Schmidt – aka "King of the Sting" – has been developing a four-point scale that rates the severity of stingers and the duration of pain (see below). Each type of sting is also given a brief, colourful description.

According to Schmidt, the Level-4 sting of a bullet ant is likened to "walking over flaming charcoal with a three-inch nail embedded in your heel". By comparison, your average honey bee sting is rated at Level 2 on the index.

ASIAN GIANT HORNET 10 min	VELVET ANT 30 min	RED PAPER WASP 5-10 min	WARRIOR WASP 150 min	TARANTULA HAWK 5 min	BULLET ANT 300 min

LEVEL 3

LEVEL 4

7 SUPERHUMANS

GWR celebrates people who seem to have superhero-like abilities. Here, we select seven super-powered superhumans and ask: What makes them so special?

All our record-breakers are, by definition, the best in the world at something. They represent a combination of nature and nurture – some are taking advantage of the gifts (powers?) they were born with, while others built up their powers through hard work and endless practice. Most often, however, it's a combination of both these things that makes them superhuman.

They're perhaps not quite superheroes – it's hard to think of a world-threatening scenario that could be averted by having someone cram themselves into a tiny box, or smash a concrete block with their face – but they're impressive all the same.

2 ABOMINABLE SNOWMAN

Wim "The Iceman" Hof likes to keep cool, *really* cool; back in 2000, this Dutch daredevil set a record for the **longest full-body-contact ice endurance** – 30 min. That's a fancy way of saying that he sat in a bath of ice water for half an hour. He later extended this record to 1 hr 53 min, though finally lost the title to Chinese adventurer Jin Songhao in 2014. However, he still holds the record for **fastest barefoot half marathon on ice or snow**: 2 hr 16 min 34 sec.

Wim credits his cold endurance to a breathing technique, which seems to trick his body into burning stored fat, keeping his body temperature steady.

1 DAREDEVIL DANI

Daniella D'Ville (UK) holds several GWR titles thanks to a combination of strength and fearlessness. She has had concrete blocks smashed on her stomach – **fastest time to break 16 concrete blocks on the body** (30.40 sec) – and had apples chainsawed out of her mouth – **most apples held in the mouth and cut in half by chainsaw** (12).

3 FLEXI GIRL

On 15 Sep 2011, contortionist Skye Broberg (NZ) folded her whole body into a box that measured just 52 x 45 x 45 cm (20 x 17 x 17 in) in just 4.78 sec, setting a new record for **fastest time to cram into a box**.

It's not entirely clear how contortionists such as Skye manage these feats – some are helped by a genetic predisposition towards flexibility, but others achieve them through constant training. Contortionists often lose their ultra-flexibility if they miss just a day of training, and have to work for weeks to get it back.

Smaller than the checked bag allowance on an airline!

On the inside, he looked like this!

4 MR MANGETOUT

France's Monsieur Mangetout ("Mr Eat-all"), aka Michel Lotito, had unusual taste in food. Between 1966 and his death in 2007, he consumed a total of 18 bicycles, 15 shopping carts, numerous televisions (back when TVs were bigger) and an entire Cessna 150 light aircraft.

His odd meals, which secured him the Guinness World Records title for **strangest diet**, were the result of a disorder called pica. This takes the form of a strong appetite for things that aren't food. In later life, he made his quirk into a career, eating bizarre things on stage.

7 REAL-WORLD SPIDER-MAN

French rock-climber Alain Robert has scaled more than 120 tall buildings – the **most buildings climbed** – since making the switch from rock faces to skyscrapers in 1994. His famous climbs include a solo ascent of the 828-m (2,716-ft 6-in) Burj Khalifa (the **tallest building**) in 2011 and the Petronas Towers in 1997 (which was then the **tallest building**). Alain prefers to climb without safety harnesses or ropes (so-called "free climbing"), though he sometimes wears one (as in the picture below) when his sponsor insists on it.

5 NINJA SWORDSMAN

No one is faster with a samurai sword than Japanese martial artist Isao Machii. Fire an air rifle at Machii (not something you should do) and he can draw his sword and slice the pellet out of the air *before it hits him*!

In addition to his 2013 record for **fastest BB pellet cut by a sword** (158.29 km/h; 98.36 mph), he also broke the record for **fastest 1,000 martial arts sword cuts** (left) – after a 36-min 4-sec slicing session. This Japanese art form – known as *tameshigiri* – involves years of intense mental and physical training.

6 HUMAN ANVIL

American wrestler and strongman John Ferraro (aka Gino Martino) can take a lot of punishment. He holds records for **most nails hammered with the head in one minute** (13) and **most concrete blocks broken on the head with a bowling ball in three minutes** (45). He owes his unique human piledriver abilities to an unusually thick skull – MRI imaging has shown that it's more than twice as thick as a normal person's.

IT'S ALIVE!

157

FALCON WING

This is the Tesla Model X, an all-electric luxury SUV from the sister company of rocket pioneers SpaceX (see pp.10–11). Tesla's other luxury car, the Model S, has been used to break the records for **most countries visited by electric car on a single charge** (seven, Jul 2016) and **shortest charging time to cross the USA** (12 hr 48 min 19 sec, Apr 2015). Electric vehicles have long been billed as the cars of the future, but they have always tended to look disappointingly non-futuristic. The Model X, with its space-age interior and vertically opening "falcon wing" doors, changes this, allowing owners to ride in space-age comfort and arrive like James Bond movie villains.

AWESOME INVENTIONS

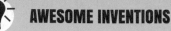

Fuel levels displayed in the HUD helmet

RISE OF THE JETPACKS

Geddit? "Rise"!

If Hollywood promises us anything, it's that we'll one day be trading in cars for jetpacks. When that day will arrive is up for debate, but a few intrepid aviators are leading the way...

It's hard to imagine personal, jet-powered aviation taking off any time soon. But the truth is that the forerunners of that technology already exist.

Take ex-Royal Marine Richard Browning (right). This British inventor has created the closest thing to Tony Stark's Iron Man suit ever seen to date.

His *Daedalus* suit comprises six micro gas turbines – basically mini aircraft engines (two on his back and two on each hand). They are mounted to a bespoke exoskeleton, also fitted with a heads-up display (HUD) helmet.

If you're wondering what it feels like to fly in the *Daedalus* rig, Browning describes it as like "riding a bike in three dimensions". We guess that's cool...?

Total thrust of 130 kgf (286 lbf) – or 1,274 N

Lightweight fireproof arr

TIL
TODAY I LEARNED

Browning is constantly enhancing his *Daedalus* suit, and plans to add new features such as auto-balancing, 3D-printed metal mounts and even LCD screens so it can be made invisible! Keep tabs on its development at Project Gravity's site: www.gravity.co.

Snakebite-resistant boots

NOT a jetpack!!!

1

2

Bzzzzz...

3

HUBLOT WATCHES

4

INSTANT EXPERT

INSIDE A JET ENGINE... The basic principle of a jet engine is simple. Air is drawn in and compressed to put it under great pressure. Fuel is then injected and ignited. The burning gases expand, blasting through the nozzle and exhaust, providing thrust. The gas also turns the turbines, which in turn help to spin the blades of the compressor.

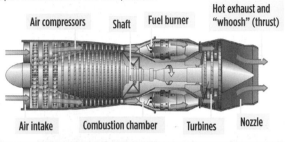

Air compressors · Shaft · Fuel burner · Hot exhaust and "whoosh" (thrust)

Air intake · Combustion chamber · Turbines · Nozzle

FOR THE RECORD

Rather than compressing air and setting fire to fuel, aquatic jetpacks and hydroflyers gain thrust by sucking up water under high pressure then redirecting it downwards.

The **longest journey by water jetpack** was 36.45 km (22.6 mi), achieved by Pollyanna Woodward (UK, below) in Malta on 8 Nov 2013. Pictured right is Franky Zapata (FRA), a former holder of the title for **most backflips with a hydroflyer in one minute**; he did 26 flips in 2014.

Water is forced out of the hydroflyer, pushing the rider as high as 50 ft (15.2 m) in the air!

Hose attaches to a jetski and acts as one big water pump; the power is set by the throttle

An engine pumped seawater into Pollyanna's back-mounted jetpack, which she then controlled with a trigger on the hand grips

Hands were always overrated anyway...

Kerosene was the fuel of choice as it doesn't tend to blow up!

Wheeeeeeee...

AWESOME INVENTIONS

EVOLUTION OF JET-POWERED FLIGHT

Made as a prototype flying platform for military recon, the Hiller VZ-1 Pawnee (**1**) launched in the 1950s. It used rotors rather than jets, though; it was essentially an upside down helicopter.

William Suitor, aka the "Rocketman", flew Bell Aerosystems' rocket belt (**2**). Its propulsion came from pressurized hydrogen peroxide, enabling high jumps or 20 sec of flight.

Leaping forward, Swiss pilot turned stuntman Yves "Jetman" Rossy has been setting records with his bespoke "jet wing" (**3**) since 2004. He was the **first person to fly horizontally**.

Probably the most classical design is the Martin Jetpack (**4**). Unveiled in 2008, it has a petrol engine and two ducted fans for propulsion.

Doing his best Green Goblin impression in 2016, Franky Zapata used a Flyboard Air (**5**) to complete the **farthest hoverboard flight**: 2.25 km (1.39 mi).

Richard Browning's Iron Man-esque suit (**6**) is driven by six kerosene thrusters. *Daedalus* offers 12 min of vertical flight, but Browning is working to extend this.

HOT SHOT

DO A BARREL ROLL!
Following the success of their 2015 loop-the-loop stunt (see pp.164–65), on 11 Jul 2017, car-maker Jaguar teamed up with stunt driver Terry Grant for another spectacular record attempt.

This time around, Terry set a record for the **farthest barrel roll in a car**, flipping over a brand-new Jaguar E-Pace compact SUV in mid-air while flying 15.3 m (50 ft 2.4 in). This multiple-exposure picture (four photos stitched together) shows the path of the twisting vehicle as it flew through the air.

This looks like a pile of dirt, but it's actually a precision-engineered steel ramp

LARGEST LOOP-THE-LOOP IN A CAR

We've all pinged a toy car around a loop-the-loop – launch it fast enough and it will get through just fine. But you can't do that with a real car – or can you...?

On 14 Sep 2015, professional stunt driver Terry Grant (UK) unveiled Jaguar's new sports SUV, the F-Pace. He did it in the most spectacular fashion, driving it down a track and through a 19.08-m-high (62-ft 7.1-in) loop-the-loop at the Frankfurt Motor Show.

This crazy-looking stunt broke the record for **largest loop-the-loop in a car** by more than a metre and made for a memorable centrepiece for Jaguar's 80th birthday celebrations. But what forces were at work to keep Terry's car from falling off the loop?

INSTANT EXPERT

G-FORCE... The feeling of weight caused by acceleration is known as g-force (or *g*).

Everything on our planet experiences a force owing to the pull of Earth's gravity, which has the effect of accelerating falling objects at a rate of 9.8 m/s² (Newton's First Law). This means that for every second an object falls, it adds another 9.8 m/s to its velocity. This acceleration is defined as one gravity – or 1 *g*.

Standing on Earth, we experience zero net force. Why? Because gravity is counteracted by the reaction force of the ground with our feet (Newton's Third Law) and the strength of our bodies to resist the pull.

Who knew standing still was so complicated!?

"Velocity" is a measure of speed in a particular direction, and a change in velocity is also experienced as acceleration. So, turning a corner at a constant speed is felt as g-force – as does accelerating or decelerating in a straight line (Newton's Second Law).

Any acceleration of a vehicle exerts force (see "Defying gravity..." opposite) on both the vehicle and its occupants in a similar manner; it's this force that keeps the car in the loop here, or a motorcycle and its rider on a wall of death (example below).

33.51 m/s²
(3.42 *g*)

17.88 m/s

9.8 m/s²
(1 *g*)

9.54 m

Speed (in metres per second)

Radius of the turn in metres

Resulting g-force (in metres per second square...

$$\frac{v^2}{r} = a$$

SO... $\dfrac{17.88 \times 17.88}{9.54} = 33.51$

23.6

Initial speed at start of loop: 85.3 km/h (53 mph; 23.69 m/s)	**Speed at the top of the loop:** 64 km/h (40 mph; 17.88 m/s)
Initial g-force: 6 *g* (58.8 m/s²)	**G-force at the top of the loop:** 3.42 *g* (33.51 m/s²)

$$F = ma = 1{,}775 \times 9.8 = 17{,}395 \, N$$

TIL
TODAY I LEARNED

Owing to their shape, Formula 1 cars generate a huge amount of aerodynamic downforce to maintain grip in corners. This downward pressure is so strong that the cars could, in theory, drive upside down without the need for a loop-the-loop.

58.3 m/s² (5.95 *g*)

OUCH!!

DEFYING GRAVITY... If you apply a force to an object, it moves in a straight line. This is the basis of Newton's Second Law of Motion (see p.199). But what's happening in the case of a loop-the-loop, when you're moving along a circular path?

The force pressing the car against the track is the same one that keeps water in a bucket when you spin it around your head. It's known as a "centripetal" force. If you swing the bucket around your head fast enough, the force this generates is greater than the forces pulling the water out. The net result is that the water stays in the bucket and you stay dry. Hopefully...

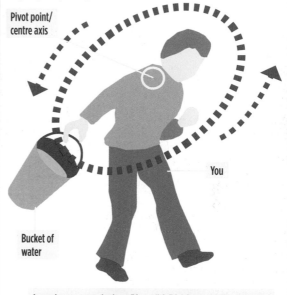

Pivot point/ centre axis

You

Bucket of water

Assuming your arm is about 50 cm (1 ft 7 in) long, you'll need to be spinning the bucket at around 2.3 m/s, or just over 7 ft/s (a bit less than one revolution a second) for the water to not fall out

WHY DO I FEEL SICK ON A ROLLER-COASTER?

THE BIG QUESTION **?**

Your inner ear is a set of fluid-filled tubes that act like a spirit level, sensing movement and orientation. Motion sickness happens when your brain is confused by the information it's getting from the inner ear.

When taking off in a plane, for example, your eyes are telling you that you're sitting still in a funny tube-shaped room, but your inner ear is saying that you're zooming into the sky.

Similarly, if you're wearing VR goggles, your eyes are saying that you're zooming through the sky, while the rest of your body is telling you that you're sitting on your sofa.

On a roller-coaster, your brain is simply being overwhelmed by the speed and intensity of the changes in direction and can't make sense of what's happening.

What's more, your internal organs are all being subjected to extreme forces, accelerating and decelerating at slightly different rates. This is what causes that "sinking feeling" in your stomach.

I DIDN'T KNOW THAT!

KITTY POTTY

I hate you so much

Some people devote their lives to inventing world-changing devices – such as nuclear fusion reactors or spaceships. Others decide to focus on the smaller problems, inventing marvels such as the steam-proof bathroom mirror, the electric guitar and, most recently, the training potty for cats. Australian couple Jo and Terry Lapidge were inspired to create the "Litter Kwitter" (right) by a scene in 2000 movie *Meet the Parents*. Apparently, the kit has an 80% success rate, though the makers say it would be higher if owners paid more attention to the instructions.

GAME MAN! Belgian engineering student Ilhan Ünal built this king-sized hand-held (arm-held?) for a local high school in 2016. It's more than six times the size of a regular Game Boy, but is fully capable of playing classic Nintendo titles, including *Pokémon Red/Blue* and *Tetris*. The **largest Game Boy**, it was designed around an old 19-in (48-cm) monitor, with all the components scaled to exactly match the proportions of the original gaming device.

The car of tomorrow?

People have wanted self-driving cars for as long as they've had cars. This marvellous thing is the Firebird II – a concept car built by General Motors in 1956. It had a gas turbine engine (like a helicopter) and was fitted with an "electronic guide" system, which allowed the car to drive itself by following wires embedded in special highways (these proved too expensive to be fitted on public roads).

These are actual turbine intakes, not just for the look

1.08 quadrillion tonnes of structural-grade steel would cost about $719,200,000,000,000,000 at 2017 prices. The world's economy is worth about $75,590,000,000,000 annually.

Q A HOW MUCH WOULD THE *DEATH STAR* COST?

It's hard to put a figure on the cost of the technology in Star Wars' planet-destroying space station (the first one), but we can give an estimate for the materials. If the *Death Star* had a density of steelwork similar to that of a modern warship, it would require 1.08 quadrillion tonnes of steel to build. The raw materials alone would cost about 10,000 times more than Earth's entire gross domestic product. The Galactic Empire supposedly ruled over thousands of worlds, but that's still a *lot* of money.

GIANT EARS! Before radar made it possible to detect incoming aircraft by bouncing microwaves off them, the only way to detect distant planes was by listening. Human hearing is good, but it's not *that* good, and even expert listeners couldn't hear enemy planes in time for their warnings to be useful.

The solution was simple: giant ear trumpets. These things looked ridiculous, but they did work, sort of... Listeners could detect planes as far as 24 mi (38.6 km) away. This was effective in the 1920s, but by the 1930s, fighter aircraft could cover that distance in a few minutes, making the trumpets a bit useless.

Three thumbs!

We can all agree that thumbs are great, yes? They may not be quite as elegant as our regular fingers, but without them we'd be rubbish at picking things up, holding pens or texting. In 2017, British artist and dedicated thumb fan Dani Clode designed what she calls a third thumb. This is a prosthetic digit that you attach to the opposite side of your hand to your real thumb. It has two small motors that give it degrees of freedom (open/close and pivot up/down) and it is controlled using a small motion sensor clipped to your big toe. We'll give this invention a big thumbs-up!

SCIENCE-FICTION DEATH CANNON

The US military, which is always on the lookout for exciting new ways of blowing things up, has a new toy: railguns. These weapons, which are still in the testing stage, work by accelerating blocks of tungsten to speeds of 7,350 km/h (4,567 mph) using a long "rail" of electromagnets. At this speed, the passage of the projectile through the air causes the air to catch fire (right).

No explosives are required because the hypersonic, soda-can-sized projectiles hit with as much energy (20 megajoules) as a 1,837-kg (4,050-lb) pick-up truck travelling at 375 km/h (233 mph). That much energy, carried by something that small, is enough to smash pretty much anything into dust.

TOMATOBOT

Have you ever found yourself, midway through a long run, suddenly craving a soft, fresh tomato? No... we haven't either, but apparently Japanese ketchup company Kagome thinks this is something that happens to people. In 2015, they invented this tomato-delivery system to give runners a boost during their morning jog. We somehow doubt that we'll be seeing these at the next London Marathon, though.

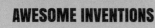
Ask a...
Mad Inventor

Backyard inventor Colin Furze from Lincolnshire, UK, is not your average engineer. He likes to take everyday objects and make them bigger, faster and... crazier. The plumber-turned-YouTube star reveals the secrets of extreme making.

Colin made his magnetic boots (above) using a microwave transformer with one of the coils taken out, a car battery and a shoe-shaped metal plate. Best ask your parents before you start ripping up your kitchen appliances and family car, though...

Would you describe yourself as a "mad inventor"?
I never know what to call myself. You can't really call yourself mad. That said, I always think an inventor makes things that solve problems – whereas my inventions mostly *cause* problems!

How did you go from mending leaky taps as a plumber to making jet-powered vehicles?
What started out as something I did after work and at weekends, has somehow turned into a job due to the madness of the internet. To put it simply, if you can build a following on the internet, then people will start giving you money no matter what you're doing... Good times!

Is being Q from the James Bond movies the ultimate end-goal for you?
Yeah, they missed a trick casting someone else in the new films as I was ready to step in. Q, Tony Stark or Wallace and Gromit are all good goals in my book.

How do you think YouTube has changed the way we engage with science?
It's changed everything. People can find out what they want and need to know straight away – and in far more entertaining ways. I never thought that I'd hear my videos were getting played in schools, but apparently kids find me more interesting than textbooks.

Which of your inventions are you most proud of?
They're each special in their own way, but as a good all-rounder, I'd pick my "magnetic boots" [inset left and right] as they were cheap to make and created out of bits and pieces that everyone can get hold of. The result was possibly a world first, as I couldn't

WHERE IT'S AT-ACT

If there were a record for **"coolest playhouse"**, Colin's AT-ACT would be a top contender! He told us: "The legs and belly are made from steel beams bolted and welded together with the body. The head and the outer 'skin' are all made from wood then painted to look a bit more battle-scarred. Inside are cool lights, carpet and, of course, lots of Star Wars-y gadgets."

Inspired by X-Men's Magneto!

find anyone else who had walked upside down before using magnetic shoes.

...and which would you rather never speak of again?

The "bin-stomper legs"... They kind of worked, but nearly set fire to the bin and also woke up the neighbours!

Do you have any battle scars?

I have little scars from many cuts and scrapes, but my worst injury was from a gas leak on a jet engine, which resulted in the workbench blowing up in my face and taking the skin off both arms! However, I caught it on camera from two angles so it wasn't all for nothing. What's more, the jet engine worked – even though it was made from a toilet-brush holder and a toilet-roll basket.

What has been the scariest invention to test?

Generally I'm not scared, but the night I first erected the 360-degree swing frame and saw how high it was [9.5 m; 31 ft] and then realized that I'd be twice as high was a nervous moment. But in the end, it was quite a pleasant experience.

Why do you think there has been such a big maker revolution in recent years?

Because never has information been so accessible or materials so easy to find. You can have everything

you need to build stuff arrive at your door after just a few finger taps and the instructions ready in your pocket.

What were the biggest challenges with building the fastest bumper car [see below right]?

Fitting a huge engine in a small space and still leaving room for yourself is always a task! To then hand over my work to someone else to drive felt very strange, but as it was The Stig, I made an exception.

You seem to like building deadly things like Wolverine's claws. Any other fantasy weapons planned – Wonder Woman's Lasso of Truth?

Yes, I love game and film gadgets and there are many more on the to-do list. So who knows, you may see Wonder Woman's lasso... Not sure I'd suit the costume, though.

FLUSHED WITH SUCCESS

Undoubtedly one of Colin's most bizarre inventions to date – albeit rather fitting for a former plumber – is his high-octane lavatory, built in 2013. Colin spent a month – and quite a lot of his own cash – constructing the **fastest toilet**, which can reach up to 53.2 mph (85.6 km/h). The base of the vehicle is a stripped-down mobility scooter with a four-speed electronic gear system built into the handlebars.

Special clip to hold your reading material of choice

Toilet paper, in case you get caught short...

Powered by a 40-cc motorbike engine

Emergency manual gear/brake disguised as a toilet brush

What projects are you working on right now?

Recently I've been making a book with projects for kids to try and build their skills, and also working on a YouTube Kids/Red show.

Any top tips for young inventors out there?

Just give it a go! Even if it doesn't work, just starting something will lead to learning more and getting better.

Test: We have a lawnmower engine, a surfboard, a coolbox and five fidget spinners – what can we make?

A rideable, water-going, fidget-spinning machine... with cold drinks.

FOR THE RECORD

Colin's latest record involved fitting out a classic 1960s bumper car with a 600-cc Honda motorbike engine. In the driver's seat was "The Stig" – a mystery professional driver who speed-tests cars on British TV series *Top Gear*. The **fastest bumper car** hit a top speed of 161.4 km/h (100.3 mph) at Bentwaters airfield in Suffolk, UK, on 23 Mar 2017.

AWESOME INVENTIONS

3D PRINTING

In the future, when we need a "thing" – whether it's a hammer, a T-shirt or a cake – we'll be able to just download the plans and print it. At least that's what 3D-printing enthusiasts believe. What is the new technology and what can it do?

On 12 Apr 2016, a restaurant opened in Venlo, Netherlands, where every dish, from the starter to the dessert, was 3D-printed. This eatery, which later went on a world tour, was the **first pop-up restaurant to serve 3D-printed food**.

The restaurant was the work of Dutch 3D printer makers byFlow. Back in 2015, they designed a 3D printer that could work with lots of different materials, including clay, silicon and ceramics.

At some point during the printer's development, its designers realized that it could also be made to print items such as chocolate, hummus, ground beef and pizza dough. This quickly became the main focus of the project, possibly because the testing was more enjoyable!

byFlow have also created a version that allows people to draw cake decorations at an in-store kiosk and have them auto-iced on to a cake while they wait. If nothing else, the future will be delicious...

3D-printed   Not 3D-printed

Obviously not all the food served could be 3D-printed; we're still a long way from being able to make tomatoes in a printer. The 3D printer works best when printing with sauce or batter.

1

2

3

pi-top

FOR THE RECORD

In Sep 2016, a group of engineers at General Electric's additive manufacturing facility used a 3D printer that can print metal parts to build the **first 3D-printed jet engine**. This tiny turbine is about 1 ft (30 cm) long and runs at 33,000 revolutions per minute (the speed at which its blades spin). It was built as a demonstration of the 3D-printing techniques that many manufacturers are now incorporating into their commercial designs. Learn more about jet power on p.161.

INSTANT EXPERT

3D PRINTING... The term "3D printing" covers a variety of different processes, working with everything from pancake batter to aluminium. They all operate on a principle called "additive manufacturing" in which a 3D object is built up from numerous thin 2D layers. The printer functions by making hundreds of wafer-thin cross-sections and gluing them together as it goes.

To 3D-print something, you first need to make a 3D model of it on a computer. This file is then divided into slices by a special programme and fed to the printer as instructions on where to move the print nozzle. As a general rule, if you can make a 3D model of it, you can 3D-print it – even another 3D printer! The 3D printer below, called the RepRap Snappy, is the **most 3D-printed 3D printer**, and can be used to make copies of itself.

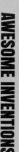

CAN GUNS BE 3D-PRINTED?

THE BIG QUESTION

As often happens with new technology, sadly it didn't take long for 3D printing to be used for nefarious purposes. Various plastic 3D-printed guns have been made, and the best known of these was The Liberator (above), plans of which were released online in 2013. The Liberator and its successors do work, technically speaking – they go bang, and a bullet comes out of the end – but they're hopelessly inaccurate, with a range of just a few metres. Most only hold one bullet, and all have a tendency to explode. For now, a 3D-printed gun is still less effective than hitting someone with the printer itself!

FIRST 3D-PRINTED...

1 **Car:** Unveiled in Sep 2014, the Strati is a car with a 3D-printed body and chassis (structural frame).
2 **Aircraft:** Airbus made this 4-m-long (13-ft) unmanned plane (called *THOR*) for 2016's Berlin Air Show; everything other than the electrical systems was 3D-printed.
3 **Laptop chassis:** Launched in 2014, the "pi-top" combines a 3D-printed case with a Raspberry Pi computer and a 13.3-in (33.7-cm) screen.
4 **Dress:** This dress, made by US design house Nervous System in Sep 2014, was created using triangular pieces joined by flexible sections.
5 **Motorcycle:** A total of 76 of this bike's 100 components were 3D-printed by TE Connectivity (CHE/USA) in May 2015. It's a replica of a Harley-Davidson.
6 **Bionic ear:** Researchers at Princeton University, USA, made this bionic ear in 2013. The organ was formed by 3D-printing a hydrogel lattice then growing connective tissue around it and contains a radio antenna.

AWESOME INVENTIONS

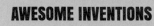

ELECTRIC SUPERCARS

After years of golf carts and false starts, we have now entered the age of the electric supercar. In the USA, a team of engineers are going one further and attempting a land-speed record.

On 22 Jun 2016, the AMZ Racing team used their custom-built racing car, *Grimsel*, to break the record for **fastest 0–100 km/h acceleration in an electric car**. *Grimsel*, which was designed for the Formula Student racing league, accelerated to 100 km/h (62.1 mph) in just 1.513 sec. This means that the driver was subjected to around 1.8 *g* of acceleration – nearly twice the force of gravity. AMZ Racing is run by a group of students from Swiss universities ETH Zürich and Hochschule Luzern.

On 21 Sep 2016, after two years of bad weather and other annoying problems, the *Venturi Buckeye Bullet 3* was finally able to set a new record for **fastest electric car (non-FIA)***, beating the old record of 307.6 mph (495 km/h) set by its predecessor – the *Buckeye Bullet 2.5* – in Aug 2010.

This super-streamlined land-speed-record car managed an average speed of 341.4 mph (549.4 km/h) over two passes at the Bonneville Salt Flats in the US state of Utah. For context, that's about 100 mph (160 km/h) faster than the fastest road-legal supercars, and comparable with the speed of a World War II fighter plane.

The team believe they can still go faster, however. The car – designed by students from the Ohio State University's Center for Automotive Research in partnership with French electric car maker Venturi Automobiles – was designed for a top speed of around 400 mph (643 km/h). With upgrades, they hope to one day beat the fastest wheel-driven (not jet-engined) land-speed-record cars.

🤓 INSTANT EXPERT

ELECTRIC MOTORS... Electric engines are much more simple than petrol-powered ones. Their only moving part is an axle with an electromagnet on it, which is located between two opposing (north and south) fixed magnets. When you add an electric current, the poles of the electromagnet are pulled towards the opposing poles of the fixed magnets (because that's what magnets like to do), which spins the axle. It would stop there, but the electromagnet is wired in a way that causes the direction of the current to flip when the axle turns, causing the magnet's poles to flip as well, keeping it spinning.

Fixed magnet | S S | − + | N N | Fixed wires from power supply

Electromagnet | Axle

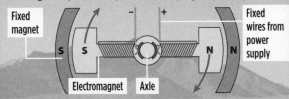

TIL
TODAY I LEARNED

The fastest car crash survived was by land-speed racer Art Arfons on 17 Nov 1966. One of the wheels on his jet-powered car failed at around 610 mph (981 km/h), sending it tumbling across the Bonneville Salt Flats. He somehow walked away with only cuts and bruises.

*The Fédération Internationale de l'Automobile (FIA) is the global body that presides over motor-racing and land-speed records. Despite many of the feats they monitor being over in seconds, it can take the FIA months, or even years, to verify whether a new land-speed mark has been set. This is why we have two Guinness World Records categories for speed milestones: one approved by the FIA and one that isn't.

Early electric cars were easily a match for the petrol-powered vehicles of the time. The first three official land-speed records were set by electric cars, peaking with a 105.8-km/h (65.7-mph) run by *La Jamais Contente* in 1899.

Electric cars were held back by a lack of suitable batteries. Compared with later petrol-powered cars, electric cars were slow and had too limited a range to be useful. It was not until the development of better battery technology that high-performance electric cars such as the Tesla Model S became possible.

1888: Flocken 7

1899: *La Jamais Contente*

1959: Henney Kilowatt

2012: Tesla Model S

Only about 60 of these were ever sold

👤 VENTURI BUCKEYE BULLET 3

Land-speed-record cars such as the *Venturi Buckeye Bullet 3* are some of the weirdest and most specialized vehicles on the planet. They're designed to do one thing: go really, staggeringly fast. They don't carry shopping or race other cars. They can't even turn corners!

The *Buckeye Bullet*'s phenomenal power comes from a pair of 1,100-kW (1,475-hp) electric motors, each about the size of a large washing machine drum. There's one attached to each axle, driving a pair of wheels through a two-speed gearbox. This four-wheel-drive arrangement allows the car to accelerate quickly on the slippery salt flats.

The batteries are the heaviest part of the vehicle, making up some 45% of its weight. The two battery banks (one per engine) contain 2,000 lithium-ion cells, providing more than 2 MW of power.

Rear battery pack

Rear motor assembly

Braking parachutes

Carbon-fibre cockpit

Front battery pack

Battery control module

Aircraft-style disc brakes

Two-speed gearbox

Venturi 1,500-hp motor

Engine power controllers

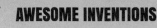
TESTING TO DESTRUCTION

If you want to be absolutely sure that something is safe, you have to test it to its limits. Ultimately there's no better way to understand how much strain something can cope with than to keep adding more until it breaks.

This amazing place is NASA's Reverberant Acoustic Test Facility (RATF), the **loudest room on Earth**. It was designed to put space-bound objects through the deafening noise of a rocket launch without the need for rockets.

Those things on the wall are speaker horns, each driven by high-pressure nitrogen gas. There are 36 of them and they create a wall of sound that goes from 25 Hz to 10,000 Hz – that's from a deep, Earth-shaking rumble to a high-pitched screech.

Combined, the speakers generate a sustained noise level of 163 dB, which is enough to deafen a person in a few seconds. This almighty roar quickly reveals any loose connections in satellites that might have been shaken apart in a real rocket launch. Just be sure to be *outside* the room during the test.

I should probably run away

This speaker generates a 25-Hz tone, which is low enough to make you feel sick

While the RATF is dangerously, possibly even fatally, loud, the anechoic chamber (right) is really creepy. You can apparently hear your blood moving and your nerves zinging away. Some people have reported hearing voices and other weird things.

⊛ FOR THE RECORD

At the opposite end of the spectrum from the RATF is Microsoft's anechoic chamber in Redmond, Washington, USA – the **quietest place on Earth**. Inside the insulated room, which is covered in soft baffles that absorb sound, the ambient noise level is -20.35 dB. Zero on the decibel scale is the quietest sound a person can hear, so anything quieter than that shows up as a minus number.

Head-shaped microphone

It's for testing how loud new gadgets are

Computer being tested

INSTANT EXPERT

Fully articulated neck that whips around in crashes

The flexible plastic "bib" is folded over the shoulders during tests and covered by a vest

Anatomically correct ribs

Pelvis moulded into a permanent sitting position

ANATOMY OF A CRASH-TEST DUMMY...

These plastic daredevils are used in thousands of tests every year, sustaining injuries that would probably kill a real person several times over. They're made from metal and moulded plastic filled with accelerometers (devices that measure acceleration), motion sensors and load sensors that calculate impact force, so that investigators can understand how a real person would have fared.

All leg joints are fitted with load sensors to measure damage

RUSTY HAIGHT

American crash investigator William Russell "Rusty" Haight has personally crashed more than 1,000 cars, the **most car crashes by an individual**. This isn't because he's a terrible driver: it's all part of his job. Rusty is what is known as a "crash reconstructionist", meaning that he deliberately smashes cars to exactly recreate the circumstances of real-world crashes.

He is typically hired by police investigators or insurance companies who are trying to figure out who was at fault for a particular crash. He prefers to drive the cars himself – while wearing crash-test-dummy-style accelerometers – because it allows him to replicate the collision in question.

He has crashed cars at speeds of up to 54 mph (86 km/h) and has had around 100 airbags deploy in his face. Despite all the dangers, the worst injury he has ever sustained is a small cut from an airbag. He generally walks away with just some bruising and a stiff neck.

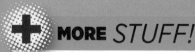

MORE STUFF!

- One of the strangest pieces of testing equipment used to check the safety of aircraft is the "chicken gun". As the name suggests, this is a gun that blasts aircraft with (dead) chickens to mimic airborne bird strikes.
- On 1 Dec 1984, NASA and the FAA (Federal Aviation Administration) carried out a test called the Controlled Impact Demonstration. This involved taking a recently retired Boeing 720 airliner, fitting it with remote-control systems and filling the cabin with crash-test dummies. The aircraft was then crashed into a fake airport in the desert, for science! Post-crash analysis showed that only about 25% of the plastic passengers would have escaped the raging inferno.

Mmm... Stylish

Also, flames are not good

The wing isn't supposed to do this; this is bad

Before the invention of the crash-test dummy, people had to use real corpses in tests. It worked, but it made a horrible mess.

LONGEST FULL-BODY BURN

On 23 Nov 2013, Austrian stuntman Josef Tödtling voluntarily spent 5 min 41 sec on fire. How does someone survive being on fire for this long?

Picture the scene – you're standing in a beautiful Alpine meadow in Austria; birds are singing and the wind is blowing through the trees. You stop to pause and admire the view when suddenly a man runs past, on fire, trailing thick black smoke behind him. Er... what?

That man is Austrian stuntman Josef Tödtling – holder of the Guinness World Records title for **longest full-body burn (without oxygen)**. He can endure being on fire for long enough that you could cook a steak on him (if you don't mind it very rare, tasting of lamp oil and smelling slightly of burnt hair).

Although they look crazy, these stunts are the result of months of planning. You can't just buy some fire-resistant clothes and light yourself up (please, please don't do that!). There's a whole technique to breathing and moving while on fire that takes years of training to get right...

👤 JOSEF TÖDTLING

Professional stuntman Josef Tödtling has appeared in some 49 movies, working as a stunt double or stunt co-ordinator. He decided to get into movies after stints as a chimney sweep, soldier, cabaret performer and pilot. In addition to his endurance record, he also holds the Guinness World Records titles for **farthest distance pulled by a horse (on fire)** and **farthest distance pulled by a vehicle (on fire)**, with 500 m (1,640 ft) and 582 m (1,909 ft), respectively.

Josef is on fire, not the horse.

To protect himself from the flames, Josef wore several layers of fire-resistant clothing. The first layer was a set of insulating undergarments (pictured) that had been soaked in heat-resistant gel (the goo in the tub). He then followed this up with another smearing of gel (particularly on his head and neck). Finally, he put on a set of fire-resistant overalls that could be coated with burning fuel without catching fire themselves.

WHAT IS FIRE?

The unhelpful technical answer is that fire is a "self-sustaining exothermic chemical reaction", but if you knew what those words meant you wouldn't be asking this question!

The simple version is this: fire is what happens when a substance (the fuel) is heated to a point (called the ignition temperature) where its molecules are energized enough to react with the oxygen in the air.

This reaction, once it gets going, creates more energy than it uses (this is the "exothermic" part). This then escapes in the form of heat and light. Flames are hot gases escaping from the fuel and reacting with oxygen in the air.

The interesting thing about fire is that once the reaction has started, it creates enough heat to start the reaction elsewhere (this is the self-sustaining part).

FUEL

OXYGEN

CHAIN REACTION

HEAT

How it starts...
When you strike a match, the heat from the friction of the match head rubbing against the striking surface exceeds the ignition temperature of the chemicals on the match. These chemicals then start to burn. Holding this hot flame – matches burn at around 600°C (1,112°F) – to a piece of paper heats the paper past its ignition temperature, causing it to burn as well... and before you know it, your house is on fire (don't do this!).

PROFESSOR ORBAX

Guinness World Records' resident mad scientist, Burnaby Q Orbax, knows more than most about the dangers of fire. In 2003, while performing a stunt involving smashing a flaming cinderblock with his head (for science!), he accidentally set his whole head aflame. Although he was only on fire for about 10 sec, and by burn-injury standards he got off pretty lightly, the result was still weeks of excruciating pain, a long stay in hospital and the permanent loss of all the hair on his head above his moustache.

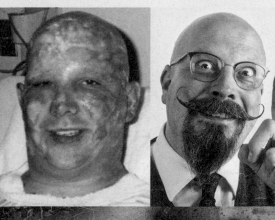

INSTANT EXPERT

FLAME TEMPERATURES... Not all flames are created equal. The lamp oil (kerosene) that Josef Tödtling used in his record attempt burns at around 230°C (446°F) if burned in the open air. If it is pushed into a confined space along with lots of oxygen (as happens in a jet engine), it burns at as much as 1,400°C (2,552°F).

30,000°C (54,032°F)
The air around a lightning strike (the hottest place on Earth)

5,505°C (9,941°F)
Surface of the Sun

3,315°C (5,999°F)
Space Shuttle main engine

1,950°C (3,542°F)
Gas stove

1,700°C (3,092°F)
Jet engine afterburner

1,400°C (2,552°F)
Candle flame

700–1,250°C (1,292–2,282°F)
Lava

600–800°C (1,112–1,472°F)
Match flame

FLYING BUTT

It's a bird! It's a plane! No, it's a... giant flying butt?! This vessel is the 92-m-long (302-ft) *Airlander 10*, the **longest aircraft** currently flying and perhaps the future of air travel.

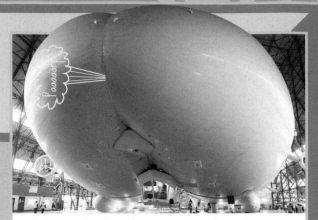

The *Airlander*'s butt-shaped body behaves like the wing of a conventional aircraft, generating lift as it moves forward.

On 17 Aug 2016, the prototype *Airlander 10* took off from outside the century-old airship hangars at Cardington airfield in Bedfordshire, UK. Slightly silly appearance aside, it was a graceful flight, reaching speeds of 90 mph (144 km/h).

The *Airlander* is what's called a "hybrid airship", a unique design developed by British firm Hybrid Air Vehicles. It uses a mixture of lighter-than-air gas (like an airship or hot-air balloon) and aerodynamic lift (like a plane).

This design allows it to use less fuel than a conventional aircraft, while remaining fairly small and manoeuvrable. It can stay in the air for up to five days and lift cargo weighing as much as 10 tonnes (22,000 lb).

The gas-filled body of the aircraft has stiff ribs in a few places to help it stay in shape; this makes it a semi-rigid airship – half blimp, half Zeppelin

Tailfins

Hybrid Air Vehicle (HAV) skin, composed of military-grade bullet-proof material

Rear propulsion ducts

INSTANT EXPERT

WHAT'S THAT AIRCRAFT...? If it has wings, it's a plane (or perhaps a bird, they're generally pretty easy to tell apart). If it has no wings but a huge spinning rotor on the top, it's a helicopter.

If it's a big balloon filled with hot air, it's a hot-air balloon (obvious, really). Finally, if it's a gas-filled cylindrical thing with a cockpit on the bottom, engines on the sides and fins at the back, it's an airship. These come in three flavours: rigid (like the *Hindenburg*, the **largest airship ever**), semi-rigid (like the *Airlander 10*) and non-rigid (called "blimps").

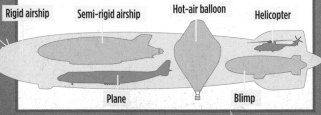

All to scale (the *Hindenburg* was massive)

Rigid airship   Semi-rigid airship   Hot-air balloon   Helicopter

Plane   Blimp

Not for people who are afraid of heights!

The *Airlander 10* has floor-to-ceiling windows in its two-person cockpit, providing excellent views of the ground below.

178

The word "blimp" was coined during World War I, and reputedly comes from the noise old blimps made when you flicked the gas bag with your finger

USS Macron

New York (1933)

WHY NO AIRSHIPS?

THE BIG QUESTION

?

Airships look like a nice way to travel – slow and stately like an ocean liner, except in the sky – so why don't we use them more often? One reason is that technological developments in other forms of aircraft resulted in faster travel times. There are also issues with the gases used. Two lighter-than-air gases are suitable for use in airships – helium, which is safe but very, very expensive, and hydrogen, which is cheap but explosive.

MORE *STUFF!*

- At the time of its maiden voyage in 1923, the airship USS *Shenandoah* had to use the majority of the world's helium reserves to fill its gas bags.
- In Oct 2015, an unmanned US Army blimp broke free from its moorings and drifted away, dragging a 6,000-ft-long (1,828-m) steel cable behind it. It travelled about 120 mi (193 km), with its trailing cable snapping power lines and generally causing chaos, before it was brought down by a policeman with a shotgun near Muncy in Pennsylvania.
- The *Airlander 10*'s second test flight ended with a crunch when it tipped nose-first into the ground, smashing the cockpit. It was rebuilt with a pair of inflatable cushions (pictured below) to prevent this happening again.

Oops!

AIRLANDER

Engines are located on mounts that pivot to manoeuvre the airship

Hull filled with a mix of helium and air, just above atmospheric pressure

AIRLANDER

Strakes – inflatable ridges that provide aerodynamic stability

Cockpit (not visible)

AWESOME INVENTIONS

⭐ FOR THE RECORD

Weighing 285 tonnes (314 US tons) empty, the Antonov An-225 "Mriya" is the **heaviest aircraft ever**. Its 88.4-m (290-ft) wing-span also makes it the **largest aircraft flying** (as of Jul 2017).

The An-225 is a jumbo-sized version of the already gigantic An-124 cargo plane. It was built in the late 1980s to carry the

Soviet Union's answer to the Space Shuttle (the *Buran*). After that programme's cancellation in 1993, the An-225 found a new purpose as a carrier of unbelievably heavy things, including locomotives, 189-tonne (417,000-lb) powerplant generators and 63-tonne (139,000-lb) main battle tanks (four at a time!).

Longer than a blue whale!

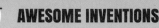

7 CRAZY CONTRAPTIONS

Doesn't have a fidget spinner though...

Here, in no particular order, we present our selection of the world's most over-engineered inventions – gargantuan gadgets built so needlessly complicated just for the fun of it. Are they practical? Heck no! Are they awesome? Of course!

While many people seem to think that the "maker" revolution is a recent development, the truth is that we humans have been making things since... well, ever.

Unearthed in Kenya, the **oldest stone tools** have been dated to 3.3 million years old. The **first use of wheels** is documented from ancient Mesopotamia, some 5,500 years ago, while the **oldest analogue computer** was made in ancient Greece circa two millennia before the first Mac.

But Guinness World Records isn't just about celebrating sensible and practical inventions that changed the world. Sometimes, we like to turn the spotlight on the marvellous minds behind a few of the world's wackier creations...

1 A CUT ABOVE THE REST

This record will give you a buzz! It's the **largest chainsaw** – a school-bus-sized monstrosity that would probably shred a school bus to metallic ribbons in seconds. Made by Moran Iron Works of Michigan, USA, it's known as *Big Gus* and measures 6.98 m (22 ft 11 in) long.

It's powered by a V8 engine but rarely gets revved up to the max – its owner, Jim "Hoolie" DeCaire, is terrified that the chain will fly off into the traffic of the nearby Highway 41.

2 COMING THROUGH!

Sometimes a bell just doesn't cut it when trying to make yourself heard in the urban jungle. British inventor Yannick Read doesn't have that problem. In collaboration with the Environmental Transport Association (UK), he used an old freight train horn and a scuba-diving tank to make the **loudest bicycle horn**: *The Hornster*. It registered 136.2 dB(A) from 2.5 m (8 ft 2 in) away. For context, a 150-dB noise can rupture your eardrum...

See more noisy stuff on pp.126-27

3 A TOOL TALE

Packing in 87 tools with 141 different functions, the Swiss Army Giant Knife 2007 – manufactured by Wenger SA (CHE) – has the **most tools on a penknife**. As well as classic attachments such as a corkscrew and tweezers, the superlative Swiss Army knife also boasts a laser pointer, can opener and flashlight. It does require rather big pockets, though…

4 NO ONE-FLUSH WONDER…

Some people get their best ideas when answering the call of nature… So who knows what crazy contraptions might be conceived while using the Neorest – the **toilet with the most functions**? Made by Japanese washroom specialist TOTO, this model has 10 features beyond the basic flush, including an auto-lifting lid, heated seat and built-in air freshener!

5 F1 PRAM

Colin Furze from the UK has made a career out of strapping engines and jets to slow-moving things such as bumper cars, mobility scooters and, um, toilets. In 2012, he hit 53.46 mph (86.04 km/h) while riding a supercharged stroller – the **fastest pram** (right).

You can see more of Colin's amazing work, and learn a bit more about the man behind the mad inventions, on pp.168–69.

6 LOOKING SHARP

Peter Svensson's (SWE) pencil sharpener is the epitome of over-engineering. Made in 1999, the souped-up stationery is driven by a V12 engine borrowed from a tank! Rated at 670 hp – about the same as a McLaren F1 LM sports car – it's the **most powerful pencil sharpener**. Although the engine works at about 2,500 rpm, the machine is designed so that the sharpener operates at nearly normal speed, so it won't shatter your pencils – or your arm!

7 SUPER-SIREN

Sirens are supposed to be loud, right? But perhaps the 1952 Chrysler air raid alarm – the **loudest siren** ever made – slightly overdid it…

At a distance of 100 ft (30 m), it still registered 138 dB – the same as a jet plane taking off. The only drawback was that anyone standing within 200 ft (60 m) could be deafened.

In total, the siren was about 12 ft (3.7 m) long, weighed 3 US tons (2.7 tonnes) and included six horns. It could be heard up to 25 mi (40 km) away!

I just said it was a false alarm…

Ask a... Maker

Apparently it's pronounced "Yetch"...

Sweden-born Simone Giertz is most famous for building robots that are a bit, well... rubbish. Whether it's an alarm clock that slaps you awake or a breakfast bot that can't feed you cereal, this online star is winning at failing.

Did you ever imagine that this would be how you make a living?
I built a lot things as a kid, but mostly out of wood.

Simone makes all of her robots and puts them to the test in her own workshop, where she also displays some of her most iconic builds (see above). She told us: "I live in a tiny house in San Francisco, but have somehow managed to fit a pretty well-stocked workbench in there."

I think I imagined becoming an inventor in the same way I might imagine finding prehistoric treasure in a sandbox... a nice thought, but a venture that probably wouldn't survive growing up.

Who inspires you from the world of making? Anyone you go to for tips/advice?
My mentor Adam Savage [see opposite] is a marvel of making stuff for the heck of making stuff. I like that.

You're most famous for making robots that are... rubbish. What drew you to go down that path?
Limited skills and a teaspoon of flukes!

What's the best worst robot that you've ever made?
I like the popcorn helmet [pictured above]. Most of my projects make me feel really stupid when I wear them,

but the popcorn helmet makes me feel like a million bucks.

Where do you get ideas for your creations?
Everyday problems. I'm always looking for creative ways to solve things I'm struggling with, like brushing my teeth and wiping my butt. Or... err... Maybe not so much things I'm struggling with, more things I'm bored with.

How long does it take to go from concept to completion?
It really depends, but usually it's around a month from the initial idea to finished project. The videos generally take 2–3 days for filming and editing.

Is there any robot/device you've tried to make but haven't been able to complete as yet?
I always have a few projects in the pipeline. Some ideas I've abandoned along the way, but I wouldn't declare them as fully dead just yet. They're like zombies that I haven't decapitated. Still watching, still waiting.

Simone's favourite se of overalls to wear when she's making

1

Who doesn't like an early-morning high five to the face?!

2

If you were stranded on a desert island and only had one tool, what would it be?
Something non-electric obviously... Probably a machete. For both utility and "badassery".

What's it like to be an official member of the Tested team?
I'm a huge *MythBusters* fan. I grew up watching that show, and managed to come on as a volunteer the first time I lived in San Francisco. So getting to work with Adam and some of the *MythBusters* crew is a constant "Is this really happening or am I going crazy?" kind of thing for me. And being a part of Tested is great. My work life would be very, very lonely if it weren't for the people there.

What's the weirdest comment you've ever had posted on one of your videos?
People wanting to marry one of my clones always makes me pause for thought. Like, would I be invited to the wedding?

How far do you think robots will have developed by 2117? Will they be making funny videos showing humans doing things badly?
No, but I hope that we humans will be making funny videos of how badly we did things back in 2017.

What's on the horizon? Any new ventures?
YES! Still legally very secret, unfortunately. But there will be stuff.

Can you imagine all your robots being featured in a travelling exhibition some day?
That would be fun! I've exhibited some of my robots around the world, but bringing all of them would be the perfect amount of creative headache.

In 2016, Simone became one of the regular hosts on Tested.com, a hugely popular making website and YouTube channel (see p.209). This means that she now gets to work closely with one of her idols – former MythBuster Adam Savage (above). The first project that they collaborated on was the "Popcorn Feeding Helmet" (opposite).

People should see it because I'll give them the best high five of their lives.

Have you made any progress on your dream to go to space?
Well, I did develop my own space programme. I don't know if I made much progress, but at least I got to spend 48 hours locked in my bathroom as isolation training.

Any advice for someone new to making/building robots?
Find an idea you really like. Solve one problem at a time. Profit.

What's the secret to creating a GIF that will go viral?
Have *way* too much free time.

SIMONE'S MAKES

1 The "Wake Up Machine" comprises an alarm clock and a revolving hand that slaps the user until they're awake. It's one of her most popular videos.
2 The "Lipstick Robot" is just like having your very own personal make-up artist – a very bad one.
3 Too busy to prepare food in the mornings? Then let the "Breakfast Machine" take care of business. Just expect to still be hungry afterwards...
4 The thing that Simone is most proud of making that isn't rubbish is a side table/lamp that looks like a thread spool.
   "My friend Marcos and I made it from 32 layers of individually cut pieces of plywood and designed a needle out of solid aluminium."

3

4

ENERGY OF THE FUTURE?

This is the view from inside the Alcator C-Mod, a nuclear fusion reactor at the Massachusetts Institute of Technology in the USA. Nuclear fusion (the same process that powers the Sun) could be used to generate an almost-limitless supply of cheap energy if the reactors could be made to work. The problem is that keeping them going for as little as one second is amazingly difficult.

The difficulties are caused by the heat of fusion reactions (more than 35,000,000°C/63,000,000°F). No solid material can withstand those temperatures, so researchers have designed devices such as tokamaks (the Alcator C-Mod is one of these) and stellarators, which contain the fusion plasma using magnetic fields. In Sep 2016, the Alcator C-Mod set a new record for the **highest plasma pressure in a fusion reactor**, running at 2.05 atmospheres for two entire seconds! (It doesn't sound like much, but it's an important step forward.)

MAD SCIENCE

8 WEIRD EXPERIMENTS

Science is all about answering the big questions. Oh, and the strange questions. Sometimes the process of finding even sensible answers means doing some *very* weird science.

We live in a complicated world, and it's often hard to figure out what causes what. Baked beans seem to make you fart, for example, but perhaps it's not the beans' fault; perhaps it's the sauce, or the process of canning them. Maybe you're just stinky and can't stop farting regardless of what you eat. A good experiment is a test that isolates one factor to see what effect it has.

Some effects are harder to measure than others, however, and require some extremely odd experiments to figure out.

Weird science can also happen when people apply the tools of science in surprising places, answering questions that no one realized needed answering. They might seem strange, but generally even the weirdest experiments teach us something about the world...

1 THE TICKLE TEST

Why do we laugh when tickled? Is it because tickling just does that, or is it because we learned to associate tickling and laughter as children? In 1933, psychologist Clarence Leuba devised a strange experiment to answer this question. He made his wife promise to never laugh or smile when tickling their newborn son, and committed to a routine of humourless, straight-faced tickling.

The experiment went well until, one day, the child's mother laughed while bouncing the child on her knee. Clarence suspected this may have tainted the results, as the child started laughing when tickled not long after, at seven months of age.

To be sure, he repeated the experiment (without any mistakes) with his next child two years later. It led to the same results. His conclusion: laughing when tickled is natural and innate.

He also covered his face with a sheet of cardboard, which seems like overkill

2 A SLEEPLESS WEEK

Ever had one of those nights when you don't get a moment of sleep? Well, in Jan 1959, American radio DJ Peter Tripp (above) had more than a week of them!

He'd decided to perform a wake-a-thon, broadcasting from a glass-walled studio in Times Square, New York, USA, for 200 hours straight.

This feat of endurance took a heavy toll on Tripp; after a few days he was hallucinating, with imaginary mice and kittens scampering around his studio and deathly apparitions lurking outside. The effects lasted for several months after he eventually went to sleep, causing wild mood swings and paranoia.

3 EERIE MICE

This peculiar beast is the Vacanti mouse (named after its creator, Charles Vacanti). In case you're wondering what you're looking at, it's a naturally bald mouse with the cartilage form of a human ear growing under the skin on its back (of course!).

The mouse was created as part of a study looking for ways to regrow damaged organs. It had an ear-shaped biodegradable lattice implanted under its skin, which was then covered by its own cartilage tissue. The ear wasn't functional, though.

I said, "The ear wasn't function– Oh never mind...

4 SLOW SCIENCE

Pitch is weird stuff. It's a liquid so thick that at room temperature you can shatter it with a hammer. In 1927, researchers in Queensland, Australia, set out to prove that it's definitely still a liquid, even when it's rock-hard. They heated some and poured it into a sealed funnel. Once the pitch had settled, they removed the seal and let it flow out.

To give you an idea of how slowly pitch flows, the experiment was still going in 2017 – making it the **longest-running laboratory experiment**. So far, only nine drops have come out!

5 LONGEST LIE-IN EVER

In 1986, 11 Russian men were offered the chance to spend a year in bed doing nothing, for science. The downside was that they had to *literally* spend the whole year in bed – eating meals, going to the toilet, the whole deal. The experiment was designed so that researchers could learn more about how people might respond to a long-term stay in space.

As it turned out, the physical ill-effects were less of a problem than the mental strain of being cooped up for a year. One group fell out so badly that they had to be moved to different rooms.

6 SPIDER-GOAT

What's a spider-goat, you say? We're glad you asked. Canada-based Nexia Biotechnologies have spliced together genes from goats and spiders to produce a pair of spider-goats, called Peter and Webster. Sadly, to the untrained eye, Peter and Webster look just like ordinary goats.

The hope is that in the future the spider genes they carry will be passed down to create goats that can produce large amounts of spider silk, one of the strongest, most flexible materials on the planet. That, or a race of eight-legged, bearded monstrosities.

MAD SCIENCE

7 SEE MOM, I WAS RIGHT!

Way back in the 1940s, Donald Unger's mother warned him that cracking his knuckles would give him arthritis. He thought she was wrong, but he had no proof, so he devised a test – he would crack only the knuckles of his left hand for the rest of his life.

In 1998, Unger, now a 72-year-old doctor, published his results – he had no arthritis in either hand and therefore his mother was wrong. He argued that this called into question other statements made by parents, including "spinach is nice" and "you need to go to bed early".

8 SUPER-GROSS

What's the worst thing you've ever drunk? Have you tried vomit? American researcher Stubbins Ffirth did. In 1804, he drank the vomit of people who had yellow fever to prove the disease was not infectious.

He'd already tested his theory by rubbing the stuff into cuts on his arms and in his eyes. When even drinking it didn't make him ill, he covered himself in the blood, saliva and urine of infected patients. He still didn't get sick!

Yellow-fever vomit (not really, it's worse – it's a kiwi & walnut smoothie)

Carrot (why is there *always* carrot?!)

Sweetcorn

HOTTEST CHILLI

Handle with care!

What makes the spiciest pepper in the world so very spicy? And what is spice anyway? Let's cut open the world's hottest chilli pepper and find out...

The **hottest chilli** is one of the most fiercely contested Guinness World Records titles. Record-breaking chillies go far beyond anything you've ever tasted, and often have a heat rating that's closer to riot-control spray than regular chillies.

The current king of the chillies is the Carolina Reaper, developed in 2011 by chilli connoisseur "Smokin'" Ed Currie in Fort Mill, South Carolina, USA. In tests conducted in 2013, scientists found the Carolina Reaper had an average heat rating of 1,569,300 Scoville heat units (see below) – that's more than 400 times more powerful than a Jalapeño pepper.

Amazingly, despite Carolina Reapers being strong enough to make an ordinary person vomit, seasoned chilli-eaters can speed-eat these monsters. The record for **fastest time to eat three Carolina Reaper chillies** is held by US dentist Jason McNabb, who wolfed them down in just 10.95 sec on 18 Sep 2014.

Chillies owe their success to a high concentration of a compound called capsaicin (pronounced cap-SAY-sin). As you'll see opposite, this is what causes the burning sensation associated with spicy food.

MYTHCONCEPTION

So, it turns out that the bit of red in your food wasn't bell pepper. Your mouth is on fire and you want it to stop. What do you do? The first instinct is to drink water. This is a bad idea – water (or fizzy drinks, or juice) only spreads the capsaicin around, making it burn more. You might try running around with your mouth open, like a whale, but this also won't help (and it will just make you look silly). What you should do is drink a glass of milk. Milk contains a protein called casein, which bonds with the tail of the capsaicin molecule and neutralizes it.

WATER COOLS YOU DOWN AFTER EATING CHILLIES

FALSE

THE SCOVILLE SCALE

The heat of chilli peppers is measured using a system known as the Scoville Scale, which was developed by American chemist Wilbur Scoville in 1912. It's based on a surprisingly simple test, called the Scoville Organoleptic Test, which works using people's sense of taste rather than chemical analysis.

The chilli to be tested is dissolved in alcohol, then added in small amounts to glasses of sugar water and given to test subjects. The quantity of dissolved chilli is decreased until the test subjects can't taste it any more. The rating comes from the ratio of dissolved chilli and water that can still be detected.

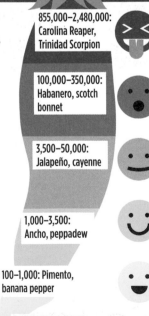

855,000–2,480,000: Carolina Reaper, Trinidad Scorpion

100,000–350,000: Habanero, scotch bonnet

3,500–50,000: Jalapeño, cayenne

1,000–3,500: Ancho, peppadew

100–1,000: Pimento, banana pepper

0: Bell pepper, toast

Jason also formerly held the record for **most Bhut Jolokia chillies eaten in two minutes**: 66 g (2.33 oz). With a Scoville score of 1,001,304, the Bhut Jolokia was once the world's **hottest chilli**.

CHILLIES AS WEAPONS

As anyone who has rubbed their eyes after chopping peppers knows, capsaicin is capable of causing incredible pain and can effectively blind you for short periods of time.

This is annoying when you're trying to cook, but it makes chillies an effective weapon.

The Aztecs and Mayans (left) were the first to figure this out. They would burn mounds of dried chillies upwind of enemy armies, covering their foes with clouds of capsaicin-infused smoke. Today, police forces around the world use pepper spray – a capsaicin-based compound – for riot control (right). Pepper spray has a Scoville rating of up to 5,000,000 heat units, meaning it's about twice as powerful as a Carolina Reaper.

INSTANT EXPERT

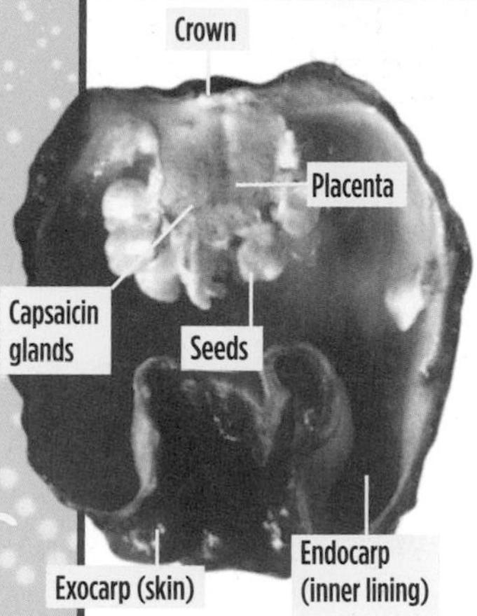

Crown

Placenta

Capsaicin glands

Seeds

Exocarp (skin)

Endocarp (inner lining)

CHILLI ANATOMY... It's often said that the hottest part of the chilli is the seeds. This is not quite true. The seeds don't contain much capsaicin at all – the real tongue-burning horror is found in the placental tissue (the white stuff) that connects the seeds to the crown. There are tiny capsaicin glands inside this tissue that flood the pepper with capsaicin as it grows. It spreads throughout the fruit, but as the closest part to the glands, the placental tissue gets an extra-large dose.

WHY DOES CAPSAICIN BURN?

THE BIG QUESTION

?

Capsaicin creates a painful burning sensation by binding to a protein called TrpV1, which is found in the walls of mammal nerve cells. TrpV1 is a temperature sensor that creates the sensation of burning pain when it gets too hot (it's how you know when you're burning yourself on something). Capsaicin essentially short-circuits TrpV1, causing it to activate the cell and send out pain neurotransmitters when there is no heat.

Peppers evolved this weapon because it helps spread their seeds farther. Birds aren't affected by the TrpV1 trick, and so will happily eat even the spiciest peppers, spreading their seeds, undamaged and unchewed, farther than mammals would.

TO BRAIN

NERVE CELL 2

Activation of next cell

Capsaicin molecule

Neurotransmitters

TrpV1 pain receptor

NERVE CELL 1

MENTOS AND SODA MAYHEM!

On 15 Nov 2014, some 4,500 poncho-wearing experimenters set off Mentos and soda fountains at an open-air festival in León, Mexico. Around 150 people were disqualified for doing it wrong or at the wrong time, bringing the final tally down to 4,334 – the **most Mentos and soda fountains set off simultaneously.** The event was organized by Perfetti Van Melle and Chupa Chups Industrial Mexicana (both MEX). For more fun (and mess) with Mentos and soda, turn to pp.98–101 for our Mentos and soda rocket-car experiment.

Ask a...
Pyrotechnician

Fireworks aficionado Mike Tockstein uses an explosive mix of chemistry and creativity to dazzle thousands of spectators every year. He explains the science behind the *ooh*s and *ahh*s.

How did you get into your job?
I've loved fireworks ever since I was a kid – so much so that I amassed a huge collection of pyrotechnic-related books prior to being old enough to start training.

In my day, there wasn't a clear-cut way into the industry. It was one of those situations where you had to know someone who was licensed and willing to train you as their apprentice. This was the main reason I started my company, Pyro Innovations: to make it much easier for those with the same passion to get started.

After apprenticing for two years, I received my licence two weeks after I legally could [you have to be 21 in the USA].

Do you ever make your own fireworks from scratch?
I'm not personally involved with manufacturing, but I can tell you what goes into it. Prior to fireworks being assembled, the internal components must be made. The effects that you see illuminating the sky are called "stars". Stars are different chemical compositions combined with a binder and then moistened, so that they can be rolled into small balls. The stars are then coated with a "primer" – typically just black powder – so that they are highly flammable.

Once the stars are ready, they're placed inside both halves of the cardboard shell casing, which will already have a time fuse glued in. Tissue paper is then added to form a cup of sorts to hold the burst charge in the centre. The shell is covered in many layers of brown craft paper, pasted on one strip at a time. When this dries, it's very solid, giving the shell structural integrity, which allows the casing to build up enough pressure before exploding. The final step is to add the black-powder lift charge outside of the shell.

What firework was your favourite as a kid?
I can't say I had a favourite. I'd look up to the sky, fascinated with everything I saw, wondering how it all worked. As an adult, I can now appreciate what actually goes into making those effects.

Shell

Electric igniter fuse

Mortar tube

INSTANT EXPERT

SHELL STRUCTURE... Inside, a firework is laid out in layers so that ignition is staggered. After the fuse is lit, black powder combusts to propel the firework high into the sky. A slower-burning fuse then detonates a bursting charge (more black powder), which ignites the chemical bundles, aka "stars", that give us the bursts of light and colour.

Time-delay fuse

Gobstopper-sized "stars" (the colourful bit)

Cardboard shell

Bursting charge (multi-stage fireworks have several of these, divided by discs of cardboard called "breaks")

Main fuse

Fast-acting side fuse

Lifting charge

Fireworks are a thing of beauty, but they don't start that way... Above is one of Mike's electric-fired "mortar racks" loaded with shells prior to a display. Electric firing enables fireworks to be set off remotely in rapid succession – a far safer and more efficient method than lighting by hand!

My favourite effect is known as "ghosting" – and takes a tremendous amount of skill and time to make. These shells break open, and the stars you see in the sky fade and illuminate in sequence across and through the sphere.

What's the most powerful firework you've set off?

The size of the fireworks we work with are limited by the amount of clearance between us and the audience, so in a densely populated city it's rare to work with shells much bigger than 5 in [12.7 cm] in diameter. The largest I've personally handled is a 16-in [40.6-cm] aerial display shell.

Talk us through what happens after a firework is lit.

Your basic aerial display firework is loaded into what we call a mortar or fireworks gun.

A quickmatch fuse is lit, which then burns down into a pouch of black powder underneath the shell, known as the "lift charge". The lift charge fires the shell out of the mortar, at the same time igniting the "time fuse". Think of the time fuse as a cardboard straw packed with a slow-burning composition. The bigger the shell, the longer the time fuse burns, so that the shell can reach the ideal height before functioning.

When the time fuse reaches its end, it spits fire into the centre of the shell, which contains the "burst charge". The burst charge consists of rice hulls coated with a chemical composition, similar to black powder, but engineered to: a) burn hot and produce a lot of gas in a very short period of time, b) ignite all of the stars, and c) create a rapid overpressure that breaks open the shell at high velocity, producing the visual effects you see in the sky.

Why do some fireworks make weird noises?

There are special compositions, known as "whistle mix", that when compressed into a resonant tube will produce loud, whistle-like sounds. The chemistry of whistle mix allows it to burn in a high-frequency manner. When this pulsating combustion is confined within a tube that's open at one end, it creates an acoustic resonance.

Which of your displays are you most proud of?

One that comes to mind was the 125th anniversary of the Statue of Liberty, where we had two barges full of aerial fireworks positioned off-shore, in addition to low-level pyro positions around the edges of Liberty Island. In addition to it being a spectacular display, it was really neat to be part of such a historic event.

What should people study for a career in pyrotechnics?

There's no one course of study perfect for a career in pyrotechnics, but a background in science or engineering is certainly beneficial. All of our pyrotechnicians are required to go through our online training programme, which is free and accessible to anyone, prior to beginning hands-on training in the field. This online training is focused on the exact type of work they will be doing.

COLOUR CHEMISTRY

1 Blue: copper chloride
2 Orange: calcium salts
3 Yellow: sodium salts
4 Red: strontium/lithium
5 Green: barium chloride

MAD SCIENCE

FOR THE RECORD

Made by Alps Fireworks Industry Co., Ltd (JPN), the **largest aerial firework shell** tipped the scales at 464.8 kg (1,024 lb 11 oz). It was launched at the 13th Kōnosu fireworks festival in Kōnosu, Saitama, Japan, on 11 Oct 2014. On exploding (below), the firework spanned 748 m (2,454 ft) across the sky – about the same as two Empire State Buildings end to end!

Mortar rack

STINKY & GROSS

What's the worst smell to ever enter your nostrils? The worst taste in your mouth? Unless you're very unlucky, they're nothing compared to these record-breakers.

Smell is an odd sense. It works by analysing the chemicals in the air, turning, say, a few molecules of 3-methyl-1-butanethiol (the main cause of a skunk's potent stench) into an overwhelming urge to cover your nose and run away screaming. This also means that when you smell a fart, you are inhaling particles that were recently inside someone's butt.

Taste works in a similar way, though you do at least have the luxury of deciding what you taste. Unless you go around licking things at random (we advise not doing this), you probably only ever taste food.

More than any other senses, taste and smell have the power to utterly gross us out, to make us want to run away and never go near something again.

FOR THE RECORD

The **smelliest substance** is US Government Standard Bathroom Malodor. It's a noxious clear liquid made from all the chemicals that make poop smell so bad, mixed together in their most concentrated form.

Its smell is detectable in concentrations as low as one part malodor to 999,999 parts water. That's like a teaspoonful in an Olympic–sized swimming pool.

The malodor is the pinnacle of man-made stench technology, but the natural world isn't far behind. To the right are a selection of the nastiest natural stinks.

US Government Standard Bathroom Malodor's horrific busted-toilet reek is used to test the effectiveness of air fresheners

The **smelliest mammal** is the striped skunk, whose stink juice contains compounds so gross that the human nose can detect it more than 1 mi (1.6 km) away carried in the wind

FOR THE RECORD

The games for the Nintendo Switch come loaded on tiny, edible-looking memory cards. To deter kids from putting them in their mouths, Nintendo coated them with denatonium benzoate, a "bittering agent" that's perfectly safe but absolutely disgusting – it's the **bitterest substance**. The chemical (molecule pictured below) was effective in stopping small children from eating the cartridges, but it only seems to have encouraged adults (who should know better) to lick them for fun.

WHY DOES TOOTHPASTE MAKE EVERYTHING TASTE BAD?

THE BIG QUESTION

One of the ingredients in toothpaste is a substance called sodium lauryl sulphate (SLS). This is what's called a surfactant – it breaks up the surface tension of liquids, which makes it possible to get grease off stuff. It's not poisonous, but it does have an odd side effect if you put it in your mouth. The SLS breaks up fats called phospholipids, which usually block a few of your bitter-sensing tastebuds, making everything taste more bitter. The molecules also block the tastebuds that sense sweetness. The result? Nasty orange juice.

The **smelliest bird** is the hoatzin; this bizarre evolutionary throwback to the age of the dinosaurs smells like rotting hay because of its strange digestive system

PAM DALTON

American psychologist Pam Dalton is the world's foremost expert on horrible smells. In the early 2000s, her unique expertise brought her to the attention of the US military. They had a job for her: develop the worst smell imaginable.

The army wanted a smell so disgusting that no one could stay put once it was released, something that could break up riots and clear bunkers in minutes. They wanted the non-lethal nuclear weapons of the stink-bomb world.

Dalton's research led her on a tour of the world's most horrible smells – she visited sewers, left meat out for weeks, even burned sacks of human hair – but in the end nothing she found was worse than the existing champion stink, US Bathroom Malodor (see left).

Flies lay their eggs in the cheese

Maggots! Bleeurgh!

Banned on French public transport

This harmless-looking cheese is Vieux Boulogne, the **smelliest cheese** – its stench can clear a train carriage from a range of up to 50 m (164 ft)

The Venezuelan skunk frog oozes many of the same chemicals as its furry namesake, earning it the title of **smelliest frog**

Casu marzu is not that stinky, but it's definitely gross. The maggots add flavour, but they also cause internal bleeding and vomiting, earning it the title of **deadliest cheese**

INSTANT EXPERT

FOUL SMELLS AND HORRIBLE TASTES...

Our dislike of certain smells and tastes is an evolved trait that keeps us safe. The things that we perceive as disgusting are ones that are associated with things that are dangerous to our health.

Handling poop, for example, is an excellent way to get very sick, very fast – so our sense of smell is set up to make us want to get as far away from it as possible. The same is true for the sulphurous (eggy) smell associated with rotting things.

With taste, our aversion to certain flavours – particularly strongly bitter ones – exists because those are flavours associated with mould and decay.

This same self-preservation instinct is why we're grossed out by things that look dead or rotten, like the lemons below, which you're probably trying not to look at right now...

TIL
TODAY I LEARNED

In 2013, American scientist Christina Agapakis used bacteria taken from people's feet to make cheese. The human-foot cheese apparently smelled like feet, which isn't hugely surprising as our skin bacteria are pretty similar to the ones that make cheese.

I DIDN'T KNOW THAT!

Think "hockey on horseback"

CLONIES! In Dec 2016, champion polo player Adolfo Cambiaso won a match at the Argentine Open tournament riding six horses (ponies in polo speak) that were all the same horse.

The ponies were all cloned by an American company called Crestview Genetics from a single polo pony called La Dolfina Cuartetera. They were given the charming names Cuartetera 01, 02, 03, 04, 05 and, you guessed it, 06. There's big money in clonies too, and not just from their winnings: the clones sell at auction for as much as $800,000 (£617,000)!

FIG.1 FIG.2 FIG.3 FIG.4 FIG.5 FIG.6

Not at the same time

WEIRD INVENTIONS

If you invent something, you need to apply for a document called a patent to officially confirm it was your idea first. People have patented all sorts of odd things over the years, including automatic kitty-petting devices, high-fiving robots and the revolutionary invention pictured above. It's patented as a "Method of concealing partial baldness" and the illustrations are from the application itself. Yes, it's a patent for a comb-over – a sneaky way to hide a balding scalp!

Run! Don't let it ketchup with us!

Groan—

Atomic vegetables

It's a well-known fact that exposure to strong radiation gives things mutant superpowers (or irreversible DNA damage... one of the two). In the 1950s, scientists tried to harness this DNA-rejigging effect to create new crops. They built "atomic gardens", with rows of plants growing around a block of radioactive cobalt-60, and waited for something to happen. Ultimately not much did – they made some sausage-sized peanuts and a few odd tomatoes, but most mutations were useless. Superheroes would be much more dull in real life, it seems.

Q A WHY DO BOOKSHOPS MAKE ME POOP?

We have no idea, quite frankly, but you're not alone. The volume of apparently unconnected reports from around the world suggest that this odd problem is real for some people.

It was first publicly discussed in Japan, where it's known as the Mariko Aoki phenomenon (after the woman who first mentioned it in a letter to a magazine in 1985). Explanations include an association between books and poop formed by reading on the toilet, or some unknown laxative chemical in printing fumes, or something about the posture adopted while looking at bookshelves.

WINNIE THE POO by Lou Reid

PRINGLE RINGLE! Pringles potato chips are a very strange shape, properly known as a "hyperbolic paraboloid". They curve in two different directions at once, which makes them surprisingly strong (which is why the company chose it). Its strength, when combined with its rough, friction-tastic surface, make it an excellent, if unconventional, building block. In Oct 2016, a post by writer Jane Espenson kicked off a craze for building what were dubbed "Pringle ringles", and even the ever-patient Harlso the Balancing Hound got in on the action.

$$z/c = y^2/b^2 - x^2/a^2$$
Obviously...

KNITTING THE IMPOSSIBLE

Shapes that are hyperbolic paraboloids – check out the Pringles (left) – are considered "non-Euclidean". This means that they don't conform to the rules of geometry set out by the Ancient Greek mathematician Euclid. (This is the geometry you learn at school. Yawn!) Non-Euclidean shapes have often proven difficult to visualise – however, as one creative mathematician discovered, they can be knitted! The surreal thing of beauty above is the **largest non-Euclidean crochet**. It's 70 cm (2 ft 3 in) long and was crocheted by Latvia's Daina Taimina to help teach her students the concept of hyperbolic geometry.

THAT LIGHT SWITCH IS STARING AT ME!

Our brains are wired up to look for patterns. It's this pattern recognition that allows us to, for example, pick out a specific face in a crowd or understand what someone is saying in a noisy room. It's hard to turn this off, though, which means that we also tend to see patterns in random noise. This is a phenomenon called "pareidolia" (pronounced parry-DOH-lee-a) and it explains why we hear words in backwards music or see faces in objects – such as this intercom, stepladder and garbage can.

PAPER TOWERS! Fold a piece of paper in half and you double its thickness, making it two layers of paper instead of one. Fold it in half again and it doubles once more, becoming four. Do it again, eight; and again, 16. In theory (assuming an infinitely large and strong piece of paper), if you fold paper 42 times, the stack would reach from Earth to the Moon.

In reality, with each fold the material gets harder to fold again, and more material is used to form the fold itself. Even with all the brute force you can bring to bear, you're unlikely to get past seven or eight folds before the paper tears. The record for the **most folds in a piece of paper** is 12, set by Britney Gallivan in 2002 as part of a high-school science project. She used a huge roll of $85 deluxe toilet paper!

103 folds = thickness of the observable universe = 93 billion light years!

MAIRIE DE PARIS
NE DÉPOSEZ RIEN SUR LA VOIE PUBLIQUE
TRIEZ VOS DÉCHETS
UTILISEZ LE BAC APPROPRIE

Talking of comb-overs and unruly hair, does this remind you of anyone?!

Unruly hair
The search for interesting problems sometimes leads mathematicians off on some pretty strange tangents. In the late 19th century, for example, mathematician Henri Poincaré started to ponder this important question: can you comb a hairy sphere flat? Many generations of mathematicians have since looked at this question and agree the answer is no – it doesn't matter how neat you are, there will always be a tuft somewhere. On the other hand, you *can* comb a hairy doughnut flat (we don't know why you'd want to touch one). These models have actually proven very useful when figuring out large-scale weather patterns.

No tuft

Tuft

MOST SLAM DUNKS IN ONE MINUTE

Some people dunk basketballs as easily as you dunk doughnuts in coffee. But what's their secret? Can you use science to give you the edge on the court? Of course you can! Here's how...

The Harlem Globetrotters travel the world playing – and usually winning – exhibition games. With their mix of skill, flair and (very) high jinx, this team of 2-m-tall (6-ft 7-in) exhibitionists typically leave their opponents looking lazy and flat-footed.

The Globetrotters are more than just players, though. They've also harnessed science to notch up a string of GWR titles – with unprecedented hook shots, three-pointers and even shots while blindfolded or sitting on the floor. On 7 Nov 2016, for example, Globetrotter forward Zeus McClurkin strode out on to the court at the AT&T Center in San Antonio, Texas, USA. His target? The **most slam dunks in one minute by an individual**. With the energy of a Greek god, Zeus clocked up an amazing 16 dunks, beating his own record from the previous year.

So, what's the secret to a successful slam? Here we take you step by step through the science behind the ultimate gravity-defying dunk.

2

Next, you need to convert your horizontal velocity into vertical velocity (i.e., jump). To change your forward momentum – and overcome the effect of gravity – you apply a downward force with your foot, pushing you upwards (see Newton's Third Law, below right)

c.510 Newtons upward force to overcome pull of gravity

Gravity = 9.8 m/s²

★ FOR THE RECORD

The Globetrotters have mastered the art of basketball record-breaking, as these recent achievements show:

- **Farthest shot under one leg**: 15.98 m (52 ft 5.1 in) – twice as long as a classic London bus – by Thunder Law.
- **Longest shot blindfolded**: 22.5 m (73 ft 10 in) – longer than a bowling lane – by Ant Atkinson.
- **Most three-pointers in one minute (single ball)**: 10 by Ant Atkinson, equalled by Cheese Chisholm.
- **Most bounced three-pointers in one minute**: 5 by Zeus McClurkin (left).
- **Farthest blindfolded hook shot**: 17.74 m (58 ft 2.4 in) – as long as six cars – by Big Easy Lofton.
- **Farthest shot made sitting down**: 17.91 m (58 ft 9.1 in) by Thunder Law.

Weight: 127 kg (280 lb)
Height: 1.8 m (6 ft)

1

Let's say you're a 1.8-m-tall (6-ft) player weighing about 127 kg (280 lb). Okay, you're a little short for the NBA, but that's fine for this demonstration! For the ultimate dunk, you want to be approaching your take-off at about 4 m/s (that's nearly 9 mph).

$$W = mg\Delta h$$

work = weight × gravity × change in height
= 127 kg × 9.81 m/s² × 0.61 m
= 464.83 joules
= energy needed to overcome gravity

Top of hoop:
10 ft (305 cm)

SLAAAAAAM!

3

It's "hang time" now – you'll spend less than a second in the air (it's almost impossible for a human to spend longer than this airborne, no matter how hard they push off the ground – see "Mythconception", right). You'll be following a "parabolic" flight path: this is the curve that all projectiles take as a result of the effect of gravity. When you're at the top ("apex") of the parabola, slam the ball through the hoop. SLAM!

4

As you reach the rim, your velocity will be about 6 m/s (13.4 mph) – that's about the same as a charging bull. All that's left is for gravity to take its effect and bring you back down to Earth.

Parabolic curve

MYTHCONCEPTION

MICHAEL JORDAN COULD HANG IN THE AIR *WAAAAY* LONGER THAN ANYONE ELSE

Basketball legend Michael Jordan was known as "His Airness" because he seemed to fly above the court and stay airborne for ages. Of course, Jordan's "hang time" was as limited by the same laws of science that we all face – as we know from Sir Isaac Newton (see below), gravity pulls everyone down with the same force. However, his longest hang time, about 0.92 sec, is impressively longer than the average human leap (0.53 sec). But *surely* he was hanging longer? Nope, it just *looked* like he was flying – the position of his legs and his shifting centre of gravity gave the impression of a super-long hang, but it was just an optical illusion!

TRUE-ISH

INSTANT EXPERT

NEWTON'S LAWS...
Famous apple-watcher Sir Isaac Newton (UK, 1643–1727) never played basketball (it wouldn't be invented by James Naismith until 164 years after the great scientist died). But if he did, he would've been able to demonstrate on the court that his three Laws of Motion are constantly at work in the sport.

1
An object stays at rest or in motion unless an outside force acts on it. The ball is motionless until a player picks it up and shoots/passes it. A moving ball will keep moving until a force (e.g., gravity or friction) acts on it.

2
Acceleration (change in velocity) is the result of a force applied to a mass. The strength (force) of a player's throw determines how fast – and how far – the ball will travel. The greater the force applied, the more energy the ball will have.

3
For every action, there is an equal and opposite reaction. When dribbled, a ball exerts force on the ground, but the floor also exerts force back. The resulting energy is stored as the ball makes contact and is released as it bounces.

BACK FROM THE DEAD

Scientists have made amazing advances in the field of genetic tinkering recently – could it be time to make *Jurassic* (well, *Pleistocene*, technically) *Park* a reality?

What's the world's biggest moth? A mam-moth!

There's not a lot to look at on the Taymyr Peninsula in Russia. It's a treeless expanse of Arctic tundra, covered in snow for most of the year and muddy grass during the few weeks of summer. Perhaps this is why nine-year-old Simion Jarkov's eyes were drawn to the two yellowed tusks sticking out of a distant riverbank when he was travelling with his family in 1997.

Those tusks belonged to a mammoth that had died some 20,000 years ago, sinking into the mud before being frozen solid, perfectly intact.

Getting it out

Simion's family told the director of the Taymyr Nature Reserve, but little else could be done – the mammoth was, after all, buried under several metres of rock-hard permafrost and hundreds of kilometres from the nearest town.

In 1999, the discovery was brought to the attention of French mammoth hunter

Bernard Buigues. He arranged for a team to go to the site with lifting gear and cut the giant creature out of the ground.

The mammoth (by now called "Jarkov") was too fragile to expose to the elements, so the team left it inside a truck-sized brick of permafrost. This 23-tonne (50,700-lb) block of mud and mammoth (pictured below) was then slung under a massive Mi-26 helicopter (the **largest helicopter in production**) and flown 300 km (186 mi) to a lab in the town of Khatanga.

Finds like this are a fairly regular occurrence in Russia's frozen north, and they raise the tantalizing possibility that we might be able to bring mammoths back to life. They've not been dead that long – not when compared with dinosaurs, anyway – and they've been in the freezer the whole time.

Scientists studying the Jarkov mammoth have worked out that it was about 47 years old (fairly elderly for a mammoth) when it died, and probably looked something like this modern reconstruction. It most likely wandered into a swamp and got stuck, dying of exhaustion as it tried to pull itself out.

Despite being 20,000 years old, the Jarkov mammoth is remarkably well preserved. Investigators even found its thick, bristly hair (left) was still there. This particular mammoth probably can't be cloned, though; thousands of years of thawing and freezing have broken up its DNA strands into unusable fragments.

These ropes go up to the massive helicopter

MORE *STUFF!*

- In 1951, The Explorers Club of New York, USA, held a dinner party at which mammoth meat was listed on the menu. When a sample was tested recently, however, this meat (below left) was found to be *just* sea turtle.
- People really have eaten prehistoric beasts, though – or at least bits of them. One researcher described mammoth as tasting like the "worst freezer-burned meat you've ever eaten in your life".

Grand Ballroom, The Roosevelt Hotel,
New York, Saturday Evening, January 13, 1951.

The EXPLORERS CLUB
47th ANNUAL DINNER

MAD SCIENCE

INSTANT EXPERT

RESURRECTING THE MAMMOTH... Cloning a mammoth, *Jurassic Park*-style, might be possible, although it would be very, very difficult. You'd need to get an unbroken DNA sequence from a frozen mammoth and implant it in an elephant embryo. Even if it lived, however, the clone would be a genetic dead-end unless you could find other bits of mammoth DNA (which isn't very likely).

The other method would be to take the closest living relative of the mammoth (the Asian elephant, above) and replace the sections of DNA in which it differs from mammoths (there aren't very many) with mammoth DNA. This would give you an elephant-mammoth hybrid (mammophant? elemoth?).

LYUBA

One day around 40,000 years ago – probably in late winter or early spring – a herd of woolly mammoths was crossing a frozen lake in what is now Siberia, Russia. During the crossing, one of the herd's youngest members, a one-month-old calf, fell through a weak spot in the ice and drowned in the thick mud underneath.

Thousands of years later, in May 2006, the preserved remains of this little mammoth – which was named Lyuba – were found by reindeer herder Yuri Khudi and his sons (including Ivan, pictured right). Lyuba's skin and internal organs were in perfect condition, some fur was still present, and her eyes and trunk were intact. This makes Lyuba the **most complete woolly mammoth** found to date. She's now housed at the Shemanovsky Museum and Exhibition Centre in Salekhard, Russia.

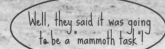

Well, they said it was going to be a 'mammoth task'!

Ask a... ///
Science Teacher

"Science Bob" (aka Bob Pflugfelder) is probably the most famous science teacher in the USA, although nowadays he does most of his lessons on TV or online rather than in a classroom. He's made it his mission to get people as excited and inspired about science as he is.

SCIENCE BOB

How does it feel to be one of the biggest names in science?
Being able to inspire people and get them excited about science is an amazing privilege. When a culture is scientifically literate, they have the power to problem-solve and move civilization forward. Besides, science can be an awful lot of fun! I do get stopped a lot to answer questions. The public is so curious about the world, and almost everyone I meet has something they wonder about in the world of science.

Who was your best science teacher at school?
I had a ninth-grade biology teacher who really enjoyed teaching science. She would bring knowledge and humour to her classes, and she connected her lessons with our own world experiences – that made a big difference.

What's the main quality that every good science teacher should have?
When I hear people talking about their favourite teachers, the word "passion" comes up more than any other. Teachers who are passionate about what they teach and are able to share that enthusiasm with students will almost always be effective and memorable.

How did you go from classroom to TV?
Back when YouTube was still new, there was a push for me to get some videos of my demonstrations. So, I rented a studio in Boston and shot a few experiments. One of them got seen by a producer at *Jimmy Kimmel Live!* Before I knew it, I was off to Hollywood to be on the show, and the rest is history.

Science Bob in his lab coat is now a familiar sight on US primetime TV. Credits include *Jimmy Kimmel Live!* (above), *Live! with Kelly*, *The Dr. Oz Show* and *Good Morning America*.

INSTANT EXPERT

One of Science Bob's favourite home experiments is "elephant's toothpaste" – an explosion of foam generated by mixing together a few everyday household products.

The ingredients list (**1**) comprises a large (clean) soda bottle, water, yeast, food colouring, washing liquid and half a cup of hydrogen peroxide (a chemical found in hair dye). It's best to get an adult to help you with this.

Ingredients are divided into two lots for mixing. The hydrogen peroxide, food dye and tablespoon of liquid soap all go into the bottle, where they can be given a good shake. Meanwhile, a tablespoon of dry yeast is added to three tablespoons of warm water in a cup (**2**).

With the bottle sitting in a tray or on a surface that's easily wiped down, pour in the yeasty water. Then stand back and watch the foamy fountain erupt (**3**)!

Check out many more cool experiments at **sciencebob.com**.

The yeast causes the hydrogen peroxide to rapidly break down into oxygen and water. The oxygen bubbles mix with the soap to form foam

1

2
YEAST
WARM WATER

3

Tell us about a science project you worked on when you were younger...
I built a small robot on wheels when I was about 10 years old. The eyes would light up and the arms moved by a system of levers activated by the robot's long antennas. When the antennas touched each other, a buzzer would sound. His name was Karl. I rolled that robot around the neighbourhood all the time.

Which is your favourite experiment that kids can try out at home?
I'm a big fan of the "elephant's toothpaste" experiment [see opposite] and the home-made lava lamp. Who could resist fountains of foam or blobs of colour dancing in a bottle?

How do you envisage the science lessons and classrooms of the future?
With our world being more connected, science now happens in real time. When the *Curiosity* mission to Mars got underway, the public followed along live as it was built, launched and successfully placed on the Red Planet. Sensors, computer coding and technology in the classroom are more commonplace, and the maker movement is bringing the process of prototyping and innovation to more students than ever – it's an exciting time for science education!

Can you talk us through your "Random Acts of Science" philosophy?
Science is everywhere, and it's easy to experiment and explore science at home or in the classroom. "Random Acts of Science" reminds us to take time to learn something new by *doing*. I encourage fans to try an experiment from my website and then put their own twist to it – make it better or different... In other words, *experiment*!

Do you think the big push towards STEM subjects [Science, Technology, Engineering and Mathematics] is seeing positive results?
Oh yes. Many schools are modifying their science curriculums using project-based learning. Traditional experiments are being replaced with open-ended challenges that demonstrate the scientific process, the art of failure, and how to approach innovation and prototyping.

If you were to make any scientific discovery in the past or future, what would you like it to be?
I would like to invent a wireless electricity system to power all our devices. I don't think we'll be plugging things into walls in 50 years.

FOR THE RECORD

Science Bob was one of 30 high-school teachers who took part in an extreme demonstration of Newton's Laws of Motion in 2010. The educators were flown up in a reduced-gravity aircraft by the Northrop Grumman Foundation and Zero Gravity Corporation (both USA). During a series of steep dives and inclines, the passengers experienced short periods of simulated weightlessness (left). They also shared the cabin with 2,016 floating balls – the **most ping-pong balls released in zero-g**.

More commonly known as "vomit comets", these aircraft are also used by astronauts as a way to experience zero-g conditions

203

GRAPHENE:
WONDER MATERIAL

Graphene is the future: it's strong, light and conducts electricity better than any metal. At just a single atom thick, what are the potential applications of the **thinnest man-made material**?

Without knowing it, we've all created graphene-like structures when drawing with pencil on paper!

We tend to think of the process of invention as working like this: person discovers a thing, the thing is amazing, everyone uses the thing and the world changes. In practice, however, the process is much slower and more complicated.

A new discovery is rarely ready to be mass-produced straight away. And even if it was, people wouldn't know what to do with it anyway. New technology requires new ways of doing things, and this takes a while to work out. It took 30 years, for example, before businesses adapted to this new-fangled "electricity" stuff.

Graphene, which was discovered about 14 years ago, is currently in that "new-thing" limbo – it's cool, but it's expensive, hard to make and still has a lot of unsolved issues.

As the items on these pages show, however, it may finally be finding uses in the real world.

SUPER HELMETS

This motorbike helmet was made by Italian automotive parts maker Momo in Nov 2016. It has a graphene coating on its outer shell. The hard coating protects the plastic core from scratches and heat damage that could weaken the helmet. Future designs are expected to incorporate graphene into the plastic shell itself, allowing for a lighter and stronger helmet.

Graphene stays strong at high temperatures, so this helmet would keep you safe even if you crashed a motorbike while on fire. Well, your head would stay the right shape, anyway.

FLEXIBLE SCREENS

Bendy screens have been around for a few years now, but they're very fragile and not practical for everyday use. The model pictured above (made by LG in 2016), for example, had problems with repeated bending breaking connections between the coloured LEDs and power supply. Graphene circuits, like the one pictured below, are much more flexible and stronger than conventional copper, allowing the construction of flexible screens that can actually withstand being bent.

NANOTUBE COMPOSITES

Graphene sheets can be rolled up and joined back on to themselves to make microscopic hollow threads known as "nanotubes".

Nanotubes are fantastically strong for their size, but a microscopically small fibre isn't much use on its own. To make them into something useful, you need to weave them together and seal them inside resin or plastic.

This has been done, sort of, but only on a very small scale. Nanotube-reinforced resins have been used to make things like drone propellers (above) and components for state-of-the-art fighter jets.

BENDY CIRCUITS

A continuous sheet of graphene conducts electricity better than copper, meaning that circuits can be made smaller and lighter. This property, when combined with its flexibility, makes it ideal for tiny, bendy electronic components such as this fingernail-sized wi-fi antenna.

These tiny devices could be woven into fabrics to make durable "smart clothing" (whatever *that* is!), assembled into floppy smartphones, or implanted under the skin as tracking devices for our future robot overlords.

WHAT IS GRAPHENE?

THE BIG QUESTION ?

To understand what graphene is, we need to dive into sub-atomic physics for a moment (sorry!).

All atoms, including the carbon atoms that graphene is made from, consist of a central nucleus and surrounding rings, or shells, of electrons.

Carbon atoms have four gaps in their outer shell, which make them unstable. When they're thrown together, the atoms share electrons in an effort to fill out this shell, bonding themselves to each other in the process.

Carbon atoms can join together in several different ways, some stronger than others. This is why diamonds and pencil lead (graphite) are so dissimilar, despite both being made of carbon.

In graphene, the carbon atoms are joined together to form a two-dimensional sheet, with each atom joined to three others. All these bonds make graphene incredibly strong and flexible.

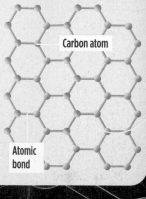

A GRAPHENE SHEET

Carbon atom

Atomic bond

It doesn't really look anything like this, but this is easier. The sub-atomic world is weirder than you can imagine.

MAD SCIENCE

BIONICS

One field that looks set to be revolutionized by graphene technology is bionics. Graphene's flexibility, high conductivity and chemical stability make it an excellent candidate for implanted biomedical sensors. Skin-mounted sensors (such as the ones pictured below) have already been made, but the real promise lies in internal implants.

There's currently no sensor with a high enough density of connections to accurately map brain signals. Graphene could fill that gap, making mind-controlled prosthetics possible, or allowing for electronic "bridges" that could reconnect the brain and body after a spinal injury.

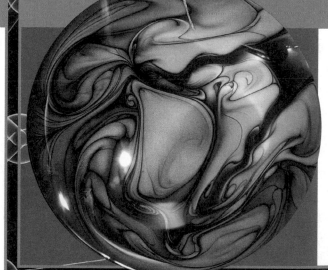

INKS

Flakes of graphene can be mixed with a liquid solvent to make graphene ink. In addition to being satisfyingly black (it's, like, *really* black), this ink is a good electrical conductor, making it possible to quickly and easily print electrical circuits on to anything from paper to human skin (electrified tattoos, anyone?). Printable circuits are already a thing, but they use silver, which is not as good at conducting electricity and, of course, a lot more expensive.

This isn't graphene, it's just a shiny plastic hand

THE PHYSICS OF

Fe 26 Iron 55.847
Li 3 Lithium 6.941
Ne 10 Neon 20.1797
S 16 Sulfur 32.066

What can cats tell us about the laws of the universe?
Everything, if you can spot the tell-tale signs!
Here we present the *claws* of physics,
as explained by our feline friends.

FIRST LAW OF THERMODYNAMICS

Energy cannot be created or destroyed. So might as well just have a nap.

Thermodynamics is the branch of science dealing with energy and heat. Its First Law asserts that energy can neither be created nor destroyed. It's about the conservation of energy, which is perfect when it comes to cats, as they're more than happy to conserve their energy. All this talk of physics is exhausting, so perhaps before going any further we should take a little nap.

NEWTON'S FURRED LAW

For every action, there is an equal and opposite reaction

GRAVITY
Falling cats accelerate towards Earth at 9.8 m/s²... and will always land on their feet

ANTI-GRAVITY
Buttered toast always lands butter-side down. So, what would happen if you strapped toast to your cat?!

Spins indefinitely without hitting the ground

Newton's ~~Furred~~ Third Law states that if you push an object, the object pushes back equally hard in the opposite direction. Or in felinese, if one cat takes a swipe at another cat, the other cat will swipe back just as viciously. It only ends when the cats get bored... or if they hear the refrigerator door opening, or catch a whiff of that can of tuna you've just opened.

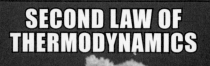

SECOND LAW OF THERMODYNAMICS

Heat flows from a warmer body to a colder body. Except in the case of cats, when all available heat flows to the cat

The Second Law of Thermodynamics states that "heat flows naturally from an object at a higher temperature to an object at a lower temperature". Energetic hot particles bump into slower cold particles and make them move faster. This continues to happen until all the particles are moving at the same speed. Or until a cat comes along and claims all of the heat for itself.

HEISENBERG'S UNCERTAINTY PRINCIPLE

The more you think you know your cat, the less you actually know

Quantum theory tells us that you can never really understand anything with any certainty. This goes especially for cats, who will always do the thing you least expect. Unless they *know* that you know this, in which case they'll do something else, just to wind you up.

ARCHIMEDES' PRINCIPLE
The volume of displaced fluid is equivalent to the volume of a cat fully immersed in a fluid

If you could ever convince your cat to have a bath, then you would see Archimedes' principle in action. If the bath was full to the top, the amount of water that would flow out would be equal to the volume of the cat you drop in. Yeah, good luck with that – it's more likely to be a blood bath...!

STRING THEORY
The universe is made from at least 10 dimensions of vibrating strings

Oops, I destroyed your universe, puny human

String theory is a ridiculously complicated idea that says everything in the universe is made from string. Or spaghetti. Or something. If this is the case, the universe must be kept away from cats at all cost. Seriously. A cat will treat the cosmos as a play thing and shred us all to confetti in seconds.

"Liquid" is defined by the Oxford English Dictionary as "a substance that flows freely but is of constant volume". This means that liquids conform to the shape of any container... just like a cat does. (For more cats in containers, go to p.132.)

Liquids take the shape of the container while maintaining a constant volume. Therefore, cats are liquid.

MAD SCIENCE

8 SCIENCE YOUTUBERS

Thanks to the internet, getting your fix of science knowledge is no longer relegated to dusty libraries and funny-smelling school labs. Here's our pick of some of the coolest channels on YouTube celebrating science, technology and making.

TIL
TODAY I LEARNED

Vsauce is so popular that it has spawned two spin-off channels. Vsauce2, led by Kevin Lieber (above left), focuses on cool tech, odd human habits and hypothetical science, while Vsauce3, hosted by Jake Roper (above right), covers the science of movies and gaming.

In total, the three main Vsauce channels have racked up almost 20 million subscribers!

1 VSAUCE

Subscribers: 12,403,956
Vsauce is the **most subscribed science channel on YouTube**. Set up by Michael Stevens (USA, above middle) in 2010, it covers all the bases, including physics, maths, space and humans. In 2017, Stevens teamed up with Adam Savage (see #7) on the *Brain Candy Live!* tour – billed as a "play date with Walt Disney, Willy Wonka and Albert Einstein".

2 CRAZYRUSSIANHACKER

Subscribers: 10,067,535
CrazyRussianHacker – hosted by Ukraine-born Taras Kulakov – is all about survival tips, cool science experiments and everyday life hacks. Taras is here to tell us why we're all failing at basic tasks like peeling a banana (do it from the base, duh). He even has a whole section dedicated to dry ice, because, you know, frozen CO_2 is awesome, right?

3 MANUAL DO MUNDO

Subscribers: 8,844,053
Hailing from Brazil, Iberê Thenório is the face of Manual do Mundo ("World Handbook"). Content ranges from home experiments and recipes to handicrafts and pranks. Iberê has also starred in a fictional Netflix series about a director trying to make a show about experiments. You'll have to brush up on your Portuguese before you watch it, though...

4 ASAPSCIENCE

Subscribers: 6,902,850
Nature, tech, health and food are just a few of the topics covered on AsapScience. The channel is run by Canadian duo Gregory Brown and Mitchell Moffit, who have also created some catchy songs to make things like the periodic table a bit less scary. Their most popular post to date is a scientific take on the "What colour is this dress?" meme.

The dress was blue and black, but some saw it as white and gold.

Depending on how the brain interpreted the ambient lighting

Take that, elements!

MINUTE PHYSICS

ADAM SAVAGE'S **TESTED**

BRUSSPUP
illusions and science

> Optical illusions aren't a new phenomenon. In 350 BCE, Aristotle noted that switching his gaze from rocks after looking at a waterfall resulted in seeing the rocks moving upwards. We now refer to this as "motion after-effect".

WHAT'S (IN)SIDE?

There's even a What's Inside? video looking at what's inside a YouTube Gold Play Button (awarded to channels that surpass 1 million subs). How meta...

5 ▶ WHAT'S INSIDE?

Subscribers: 4,918,375
Ever wondered what's going on in an Etch A Sketch, a wasp's nest or a smartphone? Father and son Daniel and Lincoln Markham from Utah, USA, have been asking and answering questions like this hundreds of times on their channel, What's Inside?. It all began as Lincoln's school science project investigating the properties of sports balls.

6 ▶ MINUTEPHYSICS

Subscribers: 3,962,525
For anyone lacking the time – or patience – to read long-winded books about science's hardest-to-grasp concepts, let us introduce you to "minutephysics". Whether you're trying to wrap your head around gravity, dark matter or wave/particle duality (or other such fun things), Henry Reich's (USA) brief illustrated vids are the ultimate quick guides.

7 ▶ TESTED

Subscribers: 2,925,309
Hosted by *MythBusters* star Adam Savage (USA), Tested is the home of making on YouTube. Whether you're interested in creating a Chewbacca outfit, a spacesuit or a ping-pong machine gun, this channel has you covered. It also has a number of guest presenters, such as "not-so-great" robot builder Simone Giertz (inset; see pp.182–83).

8 ▶ BRUSSPUP

Subscribers: 2,540,086
If you want to mess with your mind, check out "brusspup". The main focus of this YouTube channel is optical illusions and it's guaranteed to have you scratching your head. There's also a section on mind-boggling science tricks that you can try at home using household objects like candles, balloons and duct tape (yep, duct tape).

Subscriber counts correct as of 5 Sep 2017

INDEX

Aaaaarrgh, what IS it? 22, 78, 124, 139, 142

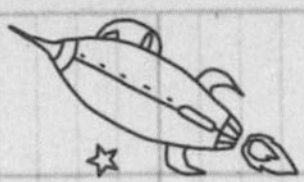

Burn, baby, burn 18, 175, 176

Don't try this at hom 31, 154, 15

210

INDEX

INDEX

I want one! 46, 62, 158, 160, 168, 171

PICTURE CREDITS

Cover ESA, NASA, Shutterstock, SPL, Richard Bradbury/GWR, Paul Michael Hughes/GWR; **Back Cover** Al Diaz/GWR, Horniman Museum, Paul Michael Hughes/GWR; **1** Alamy, Shutterstock, Paul Michael Hughes/GWR; **2** Karla Gowlett; **3** Getty, Alamy; **4** NASA, Shutterstock, Alba Giertz, Richard Bradbury/GWR; **5** Paul Michael Hughes/GWR, Alamy, Daniel Simon, Ryan Schude/GWR, AFP; **7** Paul Michael Hughes/GWR, Alamy, Shutterstock; **8** NASA, **10** SpaceX, YouTube; **11** Shutterstock, USAF; **12** NASA, **14** Virgin Galactic; **16** Shutterstock, NASA, Boeing, Shutterstock; **17** Shutterstock, James St John, NASA; **18** Shutterstock, Alamy; **19** Shutterstock, Getty, Science Photo Library, CSA; **20** Getty, Paul Michael Hughes/GWR; **21** Alamy; **22** ESA, Getty, NASA; **23** Shutterstock, NASA; **24** NASA; **25** NASA; **26** USAF, NASA; **27** Smithsonian, ESO; **28** NASA, ESA; **29** Shutterstock; **30** Dreamstime, Getty; **31** Shutterstock; **32** NASA, ESO; **33** Alamy; **34** Olivier Grunewald; **36** Shutterstock, iStock, Alamy, Getty; **37** Alamy, Shutterstock; **40** Shutterstock, Superstock, Nature PL, Alamy, Nature PL; **41** Alamy, Getty; **42** NASA, Shutterstock, Josh Landis/NSF; **43** Alamy, NASA, Climate Central; **44** NASA; **45** NOAA, Alamy; **46** Shutterstock, Alamy, Reuters; **47** Shutterstock, NASA, Alamy; **48** Caters; **50** Shutterstock, Alamy; **51** Ryan Schude/GWR, Body Worlds; **52** Famous Redwoods, National Geographic; **53** Shutterstock, iStock, Maltings Partnership; **54** Reuters, iStock, NOAA, Øyvind Hagen, Shutterstock; **55** Shutterstock; **56** Getty, Shutterstock; **57** NOAA, Shutterstock; **58** Shutterstock, Barry Rice/Center for Plant Diversity, Alamy; **59** Science Photo Library, Heinz Schneider/Unibas, Alamy, Shutterstock; **60** Alamy, Shutterstock, Nigel Andrews; **61** Alaska State Fair, Shutterstock; **62** Getty; **66** Shutterstock, Nicola Pitaro; **67** Alamy, Shutterstock; **68** Alamy, Getty, Science Photo Library; **69** Getty, Alamy, Shutterstock; **70** Alamy; **71** Alamy; **72** Twitter, Boston Dynamics; **73** Shutterstock, iStock; **75** Shutterstock, Alamy, Eijaro Miyako, Shutterstock; **76** Shutterstock, Reuters, Moby Games; **77** Reuters, AP; **78** Richard Bradbury/GWR; **80** Daniel Simon; **81** Shutterstock; **84** Getty, NASA; **85** NASA; **86** Mark Dadswell/GWR, Rubelelo; **87** Alamy, Shutterstock, Dominick Reuter/MIT News; **88** Paul Michael Hughes/GWR; **90** Paul Michael Hughes/GWR; **91** Shutterstock; **92** Paul Michael Hughes/GWR, Shutterstock; **93** Shutterstock; **94** Paul Michael Hughes/GWR; **96** Paul Michael Hughes/GWR; **98** Paul Michael Hughes/GWR; **100** Paul Michael Hughes/GWR; **102** Shutterstock; **103** Alamy, Paul Michael Hughes/GWR; **104** Paul Michael Hughes/GWR; **106** Paul Michael Hughes/GWR; **108** Paul Michael Hughes/GWR; **109** Alamy, Shutterstock; **110** Paul Michael Hughes/GWR; **112** Paul Michael Hughes/GWR, Shutterstock; **114** Paul Michael Hughes/GWR, Shutterstock; **115** Paul Michael Hughes/GWR; **118** Paul Michael Hughes/GWR; **119** Shutterstock, Alamy; **120** Paul Michael Hughes/GWR; **121** Sam Christmas/GWR; **122** Paul Michael Hughes/GWR; **124** Science Photo Library; **126** Ranald Mackechnie/GWR, Shutterstock, iStock, Alamy; **127** Science Photo Library, Alamy; **128** Shutterstock, Alamy; **129** Alamy; **130** Getty, Dreamstime, Shutterstock; **131** Shutterstock, Museum of NZ, MBARI; **132** Shutterstock, National Museum of Natural History, Alamy; **133** Alamy, Shutterstock, Heinrich Frank, Caters; **134** Kevin Scott Ramos/GWR, Science Photo Library; **135** Science Photo Library, Ranald Mackechnie/GWR, Alamy; **136** Natural History Museum, London; **137** Alamy; **138** Viralhog; **139** Per-Ola Norman; **140** Shutterstock; **141** James Ellerker/GWR, Alamy, SPL; **142** Alamy, Shutterstock, Science Photo Library; **143** The Lancet, Getty; **144** Shutterstock, RC McKellar/Royal Saskatchewan Museum, Lida Xing; **145** Shutterstock; **146** Alamy, iStock; **147** iStock, Shutterstock, Alamy; **148** Al Diaz/GWR, Shutterstock; **149** Ann Porteus; **150** Shutterstock, Alamy, Ryan Schude/GWR, Drew Gardner/GWR, John Wright/GWR, Kevin Scott Ramos/GWR, Paul Michael Hughes/GWR; **151** Shutterstock, Jay Williams/GWR, Alamy; **152** Alamy; **153** Alamy, Horniman Museum; **154** Compound Chem, Getty; **155** Shutterstock, Science Photo Library, AP; **156** John Wright/GWR, Paul Michael Hughes/GWR; **157** Ranald Mackechnie/GWR, Shinsuke Kamioka/GWR, Caters, Shutterstock; **158** Shutterstock; **160** Red Bull, Getty, Lightworkx Photography; **161** Jeff Dahl, Ranald Mackechnie/GWR, Alamy; **162** Nick Dimbleby; **164** Alamy, Richard Bradbury/GWR; **165** Clipart Panda, Getty; **166** Ranald Mackechnie/GWR, Shutterstock, Alamy; **167** Alamy, AFP; **168** Shutterstock; **169** Shutterstock, Rod Fountain; **170** Frederik Buyckx, Dreamstime; **171** Steve Marsel; **174** NASA, Getty; **175** NHTSA, Richard Bradbury/GWR, NASA; **176** Richard Bradbury/GWR, Shutterstock; **177** Shutterstock, Paul Michael Hughes/GWR, NASA; **178** Alamy; **179** US Navy, Shutterstock, Alamy; **180** Ranald Mackechnie/GWR, Paul Michael Hughes/GWR; **181** Getty, Ranald Mackechnie/GWR; **182** Alba Giertz; **186** Getty, Shutterstock; **187** University of Queensland, Shutterstock, NASA; **188** Science Photo Library, Alamy, Dreamstime; **189** Alamy, Ryan Schude/GWR; **192** Lorenzo Vinluan; **193** Shutterstock; **194** Shutterstock, Fotolia; **195** Alamy, Getty, SPL, Fotolia; **196** Shutterstock, NottsExMiner; **197** Instagram, Shutterstock; **198** Getty; **199** Shutterstock; **200** Shutterstock, Francis Latreille; **201** Shutterstock, Science Photo Library; **202** Steve Boxall; **204** Shutterstock; **205** Ramon Josa; **206** Shutterstock; **207** Shutterstock; **208** Shutterstock, YouTube.

ACKNOWLEDGEMENTS

Arizona State University/World Meteorological Organization; Gareth Butterworth; Center for Automotive Research, Ohio State University; Randall Ceveny; Christine Choi (Virgin Galactic); Great Pumpkin Commonwealth; Colleen Herr; Ed Hollingum; Dora Howard (slimeologist); Ryan Johnson; Aisling Lewis (Natural History Museum); Jonathan McDowell (Harvard-Smithsonian Center for Astrophysics); Greg Munson (BattleBots); NASA; Natural History Museum; Orbax & Pepper; Science Bob Pflugfelder; Clara Piccirillo; Cam Alfred Schwarz; Kristy Wheless (NOAA). And special thanks to Eve Attwood.

COUNTRY CODES

Code	Country
ABW	Aruba
AFG	Afghanistan
AGO	Angola
AIA	Anguilla
ALB	Albania
AND	Andorra
ANT	Netherlands Antilles
ARG	Argentina
ARM	Armenia
ASM	American Samoa
ATA	Antarctica
ATF	French Southern Territories
ATG	Antigua and Barbuda
AUS	Australia
AUT	Austria
AZE	Azerbaijan
BDI	Burundi
BEL	Belgium
BEN	Benin
BFA	Burkina Faso
BGD	Bangladesh
BGR	Bulgaria
BHR	Bahrain
BHS	The Bahamas
BIH	Bosnia and Herzegovina
BLR	Belarus
BLZ	Belize
BMU	Bermuda
BOL	Bolivia
BRA	Brazil
BRB	Barbados
BRN	Brunei Darussalam
BTN	Bhutan
BVT	Bouvet Island
BWA	Botswana
CAF	Central African Republic
CAN	Canada
CCK	Cocos (Keeling) Islands
CHE	Switzerland
CHL	Chile
CHN	China
CIV	Côte d'Ivoire
CMR	Cameroon
COD	Congo, DR of the
COG	Congo
COK	Cook Islands
COL	Colombia
COM	Comoros
CPV	Cape Verde
CRI	Costa Rica
CUB	Cuba
CXR	Christmas Island
CYM	Cayman Islands
CYP	Cyprus
CZE	Czech Republic
DEU	Germany
DJI	Djibouti
DMA	Dominica
DNK	Denmark
DOM	Dominican Republic
DZA	Algeria
ECU	Ecuador
EGY	Egypt
ERI	Eritrea
ESH	Western Sahara
ESP	Spain
EST	Estonia
ETH	Ethiopia
FIN	Finland
FJI	Fiji
FLK	Falkland Islands (Malvinas)
FRA	France
FRG	West Germany
FRO	Faroe Islands
FSM	Micronesia, Federated States of
FXX	France, Metropolitan
GAB	Gabon
GEO	Georgia
GHA	Ghana
GIB	Gibraltar
GIN	Guinea
GLP	Guadeloupe
GMB	Gambia
GNB	Guinea-Bissau
GNQ	Equatorial Guinea
GRC	Greece
GRD	Grenada
GRL	Greenland
GTM	Guatemala
GUF	French Guiana
GUM	Guam
GUY	Guyana
HKG	Hong Kong
HMD	Heard and McDonald Islands
HND	Honduras
HRV	Croatia (Hrvatska)
HTI	Haiti
HUN	Hungary
IDN	Indonesia
IND	India
IOT	British Indian Ocean Territory
IRL	Ireland
IRN	Iran
IRQ	Iraq
ISL	Iceland
ISR	Israel
ITA	Italy
JAM	Jamaica
JOR	Jordan
JPN	Japan
KAZ	Kazakhstan
KEN	Kenya
KGZ	Kyrgyzstan
KHM	Cambodia
KIR	Kiribati
KNA	Saint Kitts and Nevis
KOR	Korea, Republic of
KWT	Kuwait
LAO	Laos
LBN	Lebanon
LBR	Liberia
LBY	Libyan Arab Jamahiriya
LCA	Saint Lucia
LIE	Liechtenstein
LKA	Sri Lanka
LSO	Lesotho
LTU	Lithuania
LUX	Luxembourg
LVA	Latvia
MAC	Macau
MAR	Morocco
MCO	Monaco
MDA	Moldova
MDG	Madagascar
MDV	Maldives
MEX	Mexico
MHL	Marshall Is.
MKD	Macedonia
MLI	Mali
MLT	Malta
MMR	Myanmar (Burma)
MNE	Montenegro
MNG	Mongolia
MNP	Northern Mariana Islands
MOZ	Mozambique
MRT	Mauritania
MSR	Montserrat
MTQ	Martinique
MUS	Mauritius
MWI	Malawi
MYS	Malaysia
MYT	Mayotte
NAM	Namibia
NCL	New Caledonia
NER	Niger
NFK	Norfolk Island
NGA	Nigeria
NIC	Nicaragua
NIU	Niue
NLD	Netherlands
NOR	Norway
NPL	Nepal
NRU	Nauru
NZ	New Zealand
OMN	Oman
PAK	Pakistan
PAN	Panama
PCN	Pitcairn Islands
PER	Peru
PHL	Philippines
PLW	Palau
PNG	Papua New Guinea
POL	Poland
PRI	Puerto Rico
PRK	Korea, DPRO
PRT	Portugal
PRY	Paraguay
PYF	French Polynesia
QAT	Qatar
REU	Réunion
ROM	Romania
RUS	Russian Federation
RWA	Rwanda
SAU	Saudi Arabia
SDN	Sudan
SEN	Senegal
SGP	Singapore
SGS	South Georgia and South SS
SHN	Saint Helena
SJM	Svalbard and Jan Mayen Islands
SLB	Solomon Islands
SLE	Sierra Leone
SLV	El Salvador
SMR	San Marino
SOM	Somalia
SPM	Saint Pierre and Miquelon
SRB	Serbia
SSD	South Sudan
STP	São Tomé and Príncipe
SUR	Suriname
SVK	Slovakia
SVN	Slovenia
SWE	Sweden
SWZ	Swaziland
SYC	Seychelles
SYR	Syrian Arab Republic
TCA	Turks and Caicos Islands
TCD	Chad
TGO	Togo
THA	Thailand
TJK	Tajikistan
TKL	Tokelau
TKM	Turkmenistan
TMP	East Timor
TON	Tonga
TPE	Chinese Taipei
TTO	Trinidad and Tobago
TUN	Tunisia
TUR	Turkey
TUV	Tuvalu
TZA	Tanzania
UAE	United Arab Emirates
UGA	Uganda
UK	United Kingdom
UKR	Ukraine
UMI	US Minor Islands
URY	Uruguay
USA	United States of America
UZB	Uzbekistan
VAT	Holy See (Vatican City)
VCT	Saint Vincent and the Grenadines
VEN	Venezuela
VGB	Virgin Islands (British)
VIR	Virgin Islands (US)
VNM	Vietnam
VUT	Vanuatu
WLF	Wallis and Futuna Islands
WSM	Samoa
YEM	Yemen
ZAF	South Africa
ZMB	Zambia
ZWE	Zimbabwe

FOR MORE STUFF VISIT:

GUINNESSWORLDRECORDS.COM/SCIENCE

Behind-the-scenes footage

Step-by-step instructions

LO

PHOTOS

VIDEOS

QUIZZES

PUZZLES

Static Balloons

Super Slime

Fruit Batteries (continued)

PLUS: All the rules and guidelines you need to attempt our science-experiment records!

And even more... stu